# THE BIG STICK

### A MAN'S GUIDE TO (ALMOST) EVERYTHING

### COLLECTED & APPLIED WISDOM FROM THE TEACHINGS OF DR. ROBERT GLOVER

BY TONY ENDELMAN

### WITH CONTRIBUTIONS FROM DR. ROBERT GLOVER

# INTELLECTUAL PROPERTY

# PROFESSIONAL DISCLAIMER

Although you may find the information, principles, applications, and assignments in this book to be useful, they are presented with the understanding that the author is not engaged in providing specific medical, psychological, emotional, or sexual advice. Nor is anything in this book intended to be a diagnosis, prescription, recommendation, or cure for any specific kind of medical, psychological, emotional, or sexual problem.

Each person has unique needs, and this book cannot take these individual differences into account. Each person should engage in a program of treatment, prevention, cure, and/or general health only in consultation with licensed, qualified physicians, therapists, and/or other competent professionals.

If you get something out of reading this book please consider leaving a review on Amazon. Positive reviews are the lifeblood of book sales. Your heartfelt review will help others discover the life-changing information contained in this book.

Thank you
Tony & Robert

FOR MORE INFORMATION AND
SUPPLEMENTAL DOWNLOADS, VISIT:
**WWW.BIGSTICKBOOK.COM**

TO JOIN A COMMUNITY OF MEN PRACTICING THE PRINCIPLES
PRESENTED IN THIS BOOK,
WE INVITE YOU TO VISIT: **INTEGRATIONNATION.NET**

FIND DR. GLOVER AT **DRGLOVER.COM**

FIND TONY ENDELMAN AT **TONYENDELMAN.COM**

# TABLE OF CONTENTS

*For every man who seeks a better way.*

The stories in this book are true.
The people described are real.
Certain names and details have been changed to
preserve confidentiality.

# FOREWORD
## by Dr. Robert Glover

In 1988 my life was a mess.

I had just gotten divorced and left my career as a minister. I was anxious, stressed, depressed, and dealing with a ton of fear, shame, and neurotic guilt. I was unemployed. I desperately missed my two-year-old son. I was paralyzed with financial uncertainty.

While trying to get my life back on track, I searched for a counseling gig in local counseling centers. When nothing panned out, I decided that since I was making no money doing nothing, I might as well start my own therapy practice and make no money doing that. So, I subleased some office space from another therapist a couple of nights a week; and to help pay the bills, I took on a part-time job delivering and installing murphy beds for a company called Create Space.

In hindsight, this was one of the most transformative periods of my life.

I learned so much in that minimum-wage job – how to manage my time, how to focus, how to be a self-starter, how to follow through, how to work with tools, how to measure twice, cut once, how it isn't done until it's done right, and how to take pride in a job well done.

I also found a mentor.

Mr. Nelson, the owner of the company, took a liking to me. He knew I was over-educated and under-paid for the position, and that I wouldn't be around very long. In fact, he often encouraged my future exit from his company. He knew that I was building a private therapy practice and he was supportive of it. He gave me a lot of much-needed business experience and advice. He used to tell me regularly that I needed to write a book. (Thank you, Mr. Nelson.)

What stands out the most from my time at Create Space working for Mr. Nelson was a seemingly insignificant "trip to the woodshed." One morning, when I was about to head out from the main showroom to the shop, Mr. Nelson came up beside me and said, "let's walk." While walking to the shop, he said that he needed me to be more accurate on the mileage statements I submitted for reimbursement. The odometer on my old truck didn't work; so, I usually just guessed at the mileage. (This was long before Google Maps.)

I told Mr. Nelson about my odometer and promised to get it fixed.

"Perfect," he said. "That's all I need.".

"That's it?" I asked.

"That's all," he replied. "Just take care of it."

I told him that was the most pleasant trip to the woodshed that I had ever experienced.

Mr. Nelson took out the proverbial big stick and used it exactly as it needed to be used – no more, no less. It was effective, powerful, and memorable. I realized for the first time the importance of having a mentor and the power of loving, effective discipline.

We men need mentors – wise, experienced, masculine role models. We need tribe and initiation. We need instruction, support, encouragement, and accountability from other initiated men. Sometimes, a kind word or a solid hug is all that is needed. Sometimes, it's a trip to the woodshed and a measured whack upside the head.

Over the last 35 years, so much has changed in my life – both personally and professionally. I built a successful private practice and finally wrote that book Mr. Nelson kept urging me to write (*No More Mr. Nice Guy*). I then evolved from having a local private practice to gaining a worldwide presence with online courses, workshops, and seminars. I got married and divorced again, spent several years as a single man, moved to Mexico, and got married once more.

For the last 25 years, I have worked almost exclusively with men. I love the work that I do. It is my passion and purpose. I love that so many men desire to do better. I love their readiness to challenge themselves and be challenged.

With men, I can be clear and direct. I don't have to hold back. I can say just what needs to be said – and they like it. They crave it.

Men love clear, firm instruction. They like knowing what works and what doesn't. They actually appreciate a loving whack upside the head to get their attention - like the one Mr. Nelson gave me 35 years ago.

I've given countless men what I believe is clear, clean, to-the-point direction. I think men feel my love when I bring out the proverbial big stick and hit them upside the head with it. And I bring it out because I do love them. If I don't, who will?

Bringing out the big stick gets their attention, wakes them up, sets them straight, and sets them on a better path.

Which brings me to this book.

I currently have three books in publication and a half-dozen more in process. But my body of work entails so much more than the books I have published. It includes over 200 podcasts, several online courses, online forums, blogs, interviews, recorded workshops and Q&A calls – literally thousands of hours (and pages) of content.

For a while, I was looking for a way to pull all of my work together in one place - in a comprehensible manner - while weaving in some biographical context. I shared this idea with one of my good friends and certified No More Mr. Nice Guy coaches, Tony Endelman. Tony and I frequently discuss our endeavors - creative or otherwise. Tony is a powerful and impressive writer with a truly unique style. And he has a hustler's attitude around taking on big tasks. When I shared my idea with Tony, he shared that - coincidentally - he had already been pondering something similar.

Initially, neither of us had any idea what this project might look like. I simply cut Tony loose and gave him full access to everything that I have created over the last 40 years. I honestly wasn't sure why anyone would want to do such a deep dive and take on such a massive project. Tony, however, was not only up to the challenge, he was eager to conquer it.

Our working title for this project was just "The Big Book." But as Tony dove into all of my material and reflected on his own experiences, he began referring to the project as *The Big Stick*. I never realized how many men use the phrase to describe my work. And I never realized just how much I say it myself. That is until Tony pointed it out to me. He was right. I constantly say, "I'm going to take out the big stick." And like I mentioned, I think men appreciate what it implies.

To be honest, Tony has accomplished something I wasn't sure was possible – and he pulled it off beautifully. Here, in one place, is the depth and breadth of what I teach. Well researched and thoroughly documented, *The Big Stick* presents my message with Tony's bravado. I think it's a perfect combination.

It is my hope that this book opens up even more doors for the reader – points men in the direction of even more resources for becoming their best selves and living their best lives.

And we're not done.

*The Big Stick* inspired an even bigger project.

As this book draws close to publication, something new is about to be born.

Shortly after this book becomes available, so will an all-new online community for men. Along with Tony and a handful of my other certified coaches, I have been building Integrated Nation (integrationnation.net), which I hope to make the most extensive platform for community, coaching, and content ever presented for men.

I intend for Integration Nation to be my legacy. If *The Big Stick* gets your attention, Integration Nation will give you everything you need to start putting what you read into practice.

Tony and I both look forward to hearing from and supporting you. Please feel free to drop either of us a friendly note. And please do check out all of the resources we offer to help you on your journey towards becoming an Integrated Man.

Dr. Robert Glover
Puerto Vallarta, Mexico
5 April, 2023

robert@drglover.com
www.drglover.com

# INTRODUCTION

Dr. Robert Glover changed my life.

This is not hyperbole. Nor is it some grand attempt to butter up the man. It's just a fact. Dr. Robert Glover changed my life.

To be fair, though, if I am to give this kind of credit to Dr. Glover, then I should also acknowledge Tracy, the woman who unknowingly led me to him.

I'd recently moved from my hometown of Omaha to New Orleans after falling in love with the city while visiting some months before. New Orleans, as you may know, is a powerful hypnotic that can leave you joyfully stupefied well after you're gone. I was taken by the colorful, shotgun-style houses, the rolling streetcars, the decorated oak trees, the rich culinary traditions, the ever-present sound of brass music, the second line parades, the festivals, the 24-hour-a-day parties, and the collective, let-the-good-times-roll approach to life. New Orleans spoke to me, and it did so at precisely the right time.

I was living in a loft apartment in downtown Omaha and had been for nearly a decade, the last few years of which were particularly depressing. My father's sudden death left me questioning the purpose of life. I detested my low-paying, nine-to-five job. I published a humor book that didn't sell. I started a marketing company that failed. I ruined a number of friendships and had far less sex than I care to admit. I grew bitter and resentful. I became reclusive. Often, I was crippled by the morbidity of my own thoughts. If someone had come by my apartment to check on me, there's a good chance they'd have found me sprawled out in the bathtub, man-crying and smoking cigarettes.

I just didn't get it. I watched others form relationships, blossom in their careers, achieve their goals, and find happiness, while the Universe seemed to get a kick out of leaving me with my dick in the dirt. Good things never came my way.

The self-help books on my nightstand told me to **take action** because **action breeds motivation** and **action is the key to success** and **action cures everything!** Except none of them specified which action to take. I didn't know what the fuck I was supposed to do. But I did know that I desperately needed change.

I stumbled across one model of Neuro-Linguistic Programming (NLP) suggesting that there are six levels of human change. The first, easiest, and outermost of these levels is your environment. Of course, this brought to mind a familiar old chestnut: *Wherever you go, there you are.* I knew that outer change wouldn't magically lead to inner change. But from what I gathered, if I were wholeheartedly committed to deep, personal transformation, outer change would make for a pretty decent start. Which is why on my 32nd birthday, with the help of my friend Brian, I put the bulk of my possessions in a moving truck and headed south for the Big Easy.

I arrived with some semblance of a plan - a kind of mental checklist to guide me on my path towards change. I'd already managed to secure an apartment and a job; so, my checklist began with more formidable undertakings like overcoming my social anxiety and my debilitating insecurities around dating, relationships, and sex. Nothing if not a hedonistic playground, New Orleans seemed like the perfect place for such endeavors.

I challenged myself to approach women, the mere thought of which used to paralyze me with dread. I smiled at passersby. I frequented festivals and signed up for social events. I danced in parades. I dropped in on drag shows and brushed up on my knowledge of burlesque. I spent time in speakeasies, strip joints, and swingers' clubs. I did drugs. Went to play parties. Bellied up to bars in the wee hours of the night. I painted the town with chummy locals and reveling tourists and immersed myself in a culture that can easily confound the minds of the uninitiated. After six months in New Orleans, I'd made more friends, been on more dates, and had more sex than I did in as many years in Omaha.

I had a newfound sense of confidence. Each time I put myself in an unfamiliar situation, I came out better for it. I was enjoying myself again. I was exploring my sexuality, acting on whim, embracing my inner weirdo. I was starting to let go of the limiting beliefs that had kept me captive for so long. Changing my environment was proving to be the psychological jolt that I needed. *Maybe I'm not such a schlub after all*, I thought.

Then, I met Tracy.

Tracy is a caramel-colored, Creole goddess with a smile that can level you. Her eyes are big and brown with flecks of green, accentuated by long, fluttering lashes. Though not markedly tall, her legs slink on forever. She is some otherworldly combination of exotic sexpot and unassuming girl next door - the kind of woman who, upon first meeting, makes you wonder how a creature so magnificent came to exist. When she agreed to go out with me, I just assumed there was a sudden glitch in the matrix.

Our first date began with an early dinner at a small Caribbean bistro in New Orleans' Uptown neighborhood. Tracy told me about her growing psychotherapy practice, her continuing education, and her community volunteer work. She animatedly showed me pictures of her two young sons. She spoke fondly of her closest girlfriends. She gleefully praised her mother, an award-winning teacher and something of a trailblazer for women of color. I shared what I thought were the most interesting bits of myself while trying to maintain a slight air of mystery. We raised a glass to our mutual love of the blues and philosophy and stand-up comedy. I made her laugh. I listened. I teased her. We flirted. And just when the bill arrived, I posed an ever-important question: "Should we go see some music?"

Tracy and I had the quintessential New Orleans night - a sultry, boozy romp through the city that culminated with us kissing passionately in the backseat of her car. When we finally parted ways, I was certain I'd met the woman of my daydreams. Tracy was everything I wanted in a partner. A wiser, more self-assured man would have been intrigued by the prospect and then gone about his life with a healthy indifference. But not me. I was soon beleaguered by one all-consuming, pulsating thought:

*Don't fuck this up.*

Over the next few months, Tracy and I got together at least once a week, and each date was more enchanting than the last. Curiously, though, they all ended the same way – with us fondling each other in the car instead of the bedroom. Tracy liked to kiss me up and down my neck, nibble on my ear, and then whisper that she'd been dying to get naked with me. But whenever I invited her inside, she politely declined. And whenever I suggested her place, she firmly reminded me of her no-men-in-the-house policy. As much as I wanted things to progress, I never asked questions, terrified that I might scare her off. I'd already envisioned the rest of my life with Tracy. The thought of losing her was just too much to bear.

Tracy and I continued to see each other; though, not nearly as much as I wanted. We exchanged emails in the afternoon and spoke on the phone at night, excitedly brainstorming things we could do together. Some mornings, we met for coffee and then made out in her car before she went to work. But months went by without us having a proper date. She occasionally called to apologize, explaining that life as a busy, single mom makes it difficult to nurture a relationship. She promised to make it up to me; swore to create more time. She never did.

As the weeks passed, I grew more and more uneasy. Tracy's actions almost never matched her words. She seemed unwilling to integrate me into her life. She'd pull me in with compliments and then push me away with insults. She accused me of things I never did. She could be needlessly scornful and cold. But I didn't care. I was enamored. And desperate to make it work.

My life always felt like some sort of disassembled puzzle, the pieces chaotically strewn about in every direction. I believed I needed a woman like Tracy to bring the pieces together.

I began to hear from Tracy less frequently. Whenever I reached out, her responses were terse at best. Most of the time, I got radio silence, which left me pacing about the room in a sweaty panic. Tracy permeated every corner of my psyche; she was all I could think about from morning until night. She'd strapped me into an emotional rollercoaster, and I became addicted to the ride.

I sent her emails, letting her know I'd been thinking of her. I apologized incessantly, though I was never sure why. I asked about her kids. I offered to take her places, buy her things, and do her favors. I begged her to call me so we could talk. But Tracy never called. She did, however, send me a text message, assassinating my character and requesting that I never contact her again under any circumstances.

Tracy's message was so viciously unkind that it rattled me to my core. It was downright humiliating. It robbed me of my spirit, deflated my confidence, left me doubting my own worth. I lost my appetite. I couldn't focus. I stayed inside, balled up in the dark, convinced that nothing good could come from exposing myself to the world.

Then, I took to the internet.

Clearly, there was something wrong with Tracy. There had to be. And I needed to know what it was. I became a sleuth, spending hours upon hours reading articles and doggedly mining for clues: *Is she a narcissist? A sociopath? A garden-variety nut? Do I know anyone who knows her? What would her ex say about her? Are psychotherapists more psycho than therapist?*

I wanted closure, an explanation, anything that could help me make sense of my experience with Tracy. But my search for answers felt like an exercise in futility. And I began to wonder if maybe I was asking the wrong questions.

Tracy wasn't the first woman to unremorsefully toss me from her life. I'd had several other turbulent, short-lived affairs that came to an eerily similar conclusion. Dismissing the women as batshit crazy did seem to lessen the sting. But crazy or not, I got involved with these women, tried pathetically hard to gain their devotion, and then turned them off to the point that they didn't just back away, they went running for the hills. I resolved to never do this again.

Instead of pointlessly continuing to analyze Tracy's behavior, I needed to examine my own: *Why does this keep happening? Why do I constantly fall for the same type of woman? Why do I think a woman will complete me? Why do I love women who don't love me back? Why am I so goddamn needy? Why don't I walk away when I know I should? Why am I so heartbroken over a woman who wasn't even nice to me, especially when I was so nice to her?*

These seemed like the right questions – or at least better questions – and I scraped the crevices of my brain for answers.

Then, I took to the internet again.

I further immersed myself in research, reading countless studies on human behavior and relationship patterns. I signed up for seminars, listened to podcasts, and purchased courses. I watched videos, scrolled through forums, and downloaded ebooks. I locked myself in a room and devoured information without a goddamn clue as to what I was looking for, let alone what might actually help me. But I did notice something interesting…

Nearly every men's self-improvement blogger, every motivational podcaster, every content-creating counselor, every relationship coach, every self-proclaimed dating guru and attraction expert, every mildly off-putting pickup artist, every puffed-up, alpha male influencer, and every seemingly average mope just hanging around the "manosphere" all made mention of one single book as the ultimate mind-blowing, game-changing, world-rocking, life-altering manifesto on becoming a better, more attractive, more successful, more authentic, more resilient, and more confident man.

The book was *No More Mr. Nice Guy* by Dr. Robert Glover.

I immediately took comfort in knowing Dr. Glover is just that – a doctor. According to his biography, Dr. Glover received his Ph.D when he was 29, and had decades of experience as a marriage and family therapist. He also seemed to have a glowing passion specifically for helping men. Still, given the title, I was expecting *No More Mr. Nice Guy* to be a vague and pretentious set of instructions for becoming a raging prick. But that's not what I found when I started reading.

In the first few chapters, Dr. Glover writes candidly about his own personal and professional failures. He recalls his frustration with always trying to do everything right - particularly around women - and never getting back what he thought he deserved.

"I was the typical 'sensitive new age guy'-- and proud of it," he shares. "I believed I was one of the nicest guys you would ever meet. Yet I wasn't happy."

*Well, shit. This sounds familiar.*

Dr. Glover goes on to define what he calls *the Nice Guy Syndrome*, an anxiety and shame-based disorder characterized by a myriad of problematic behaviors like caretaking, people-pleasing, giving to get, repressing emotions, avoiding conflict, and constantly seeking the approval of others. He shares that after recognizing these behaviors in himself, he began to recognize them in a startling number of his male patients.

"It dawned on me that the script guiding my own life was not an isolated incident," writes Dr. Glover, "but the product of a social dynamic that affected countless adult males."

The opposite of a Nice Guy, I soon learned, isn't a raging prick, but rather an *Integrated Man* - a man who acts with integrity and accepts himself just as he is. In fact, the term 'Nice Guy' is a misnomer, as Dr. Glover points out, because Nice Guys aren't actually nice; they are fundamentally dishonest, controlling, and immature. The book then lays out a series of compelling and all-too-relatable case studies, each of which describes the plight of a perpetually frustrated Nice Guy who walked into Dr. Glover's office, desperate to understand why being nice didn't seem to be working out so well.

The more I read, the more transfixed I became. Had Dr. Glover never explained the genesis of his discoveries, I might have wondered if he'd been secretly following me around, taking meticulous notes on every aspect of my life. I blew through the book in one sitting, gleaning valuable insights from each page. By the time I reached the end, I felt like my whole world had just been turned upside down; so much so that I immediately went back to the beginning and started reading the book again.

*No More Mr. Nice Guy* was an eye-opening and exasperating look in the mirror. It put a name to the beliefs and behaviors that seemed to govern my existence. And clearly, the Nice Guy Syndrome was affecting far more than my romantic relationships. It was why I'd been failing to live up to my potential. It was why I'd been bouncing around from one soul-crushing job to another, plodding through the mire of mediocrity and longing for something more. It was why I never stood up for myself, or took chances, or asked for what I wanted. It was almost certainly why I was so afraid of change for so long.

Sure, moving from Omaha to New Orleans was an undeniably positive step towards change. But I'd committed to deep, personal transformation. After reading *No More Mr. Nice Guy* – and given my experience with Tracy – I knew that I still had a hell of a lot of work to do. And if there's one thing that Dr. Glover makes abundantly clear, it's that you can't do this kind of work alone. Which is why on my 33rd birthday, I paid for the only remaining spot in Dr. Glover's forthcoming men's workshop and booked a flight to Seattle.

Some weeks later, I arrived in Seattle with a churning stomach and a racing mind. I preferred to keep my feelings to myself, to sort things out on my own. Not to mention that I'd spent my entire life seeking the attention, affection, and approval of women. Spending three days revealing myself to a group of men didn't quite match my idea of fun. Then again, I wasn't going for fun. I was going because I was told this would be a uniquely transformative experience.

The workshop took place in a spacious office with floor-to-ceiling windows overlooking Lake Union. There were 12 of us, men from all over the world - as nearby as Spokane and as far away as Mumbai. We gathered for the first time on Friday evening and spent a few hours just getting to know each other. Admittedly, I found relief in learning that most of these men were worse off than I was. Some were in the throes of bitter and expensive divorce proceedings. Others had ongoing issues with alcohol. More than a few were seriously addicted to porn and masturbation. My troubles seemed trivial - almost absurd - in comparison.

Over the next two days, Dr. Glover guided us in conversation, often forcing us to confront our deepest insecurities. Each of us took the opportunity to share secrets, tell stories, and gather feedback. I told the group about my father's unexpected passing, my supremely unfulfilling career, and my heartbreaking experience with Tracy. We challenged each other, encouraged each other, enlightened each other. We learned. We laughed. We had breakthroughs. Occasionally, some of us cried. Dr. Glover created a safe space in which we could all be vulnerable, and it didn't take long to discover its remarkable healing power.

At the end of each day, I walked back to my hotel feeling lighter, more inspired, a little better about my place in the Universe. By the time I left Seattle, I had far more hope than heartache, recognizing that becoming an Integrated Man is a journey best conquered with small, incremental changes. And yet, I couldn't shake the thought that big changes were on the horizon.

When I got back to New Orleans, I immediately began applying some of what I'd learned at the workshop. I started a gratitude journal. I used breathing techniques to help soothe my anxiety. I practiced observing my thoughts instead of believing them. I got serious about meditation. I set big goals. I started saying 'No.' I also decided to take a break from dating and focus on building what Dr. Glover likes to call a "Great Cake of a Life."

I began to explore Dr. Glover's other work, particularly the courses that were part of his online university. I stayed active in the No More Mr. Nice Guy community and reached out to some of the men I'd met in Seattle. I started writing again, this time in the form of deeply personal essays with sprinklings of actionable advice. I posted my essays on a blog, which quickly garnered a following and led to other writing opportunities. I made a conscious effort to stay in touch with Dr. Glover, keeping him informed of my progress. I attended another one of his workshops. He invited me to assist him at another. And when people began asking how I'd helped myself, I uncovered a passion for helping them.

Over the next year or so, I rigorously studied a variety of psychological disciplines and earned a number of coaching certifications. I then became one of Dr. Glover's certified No More Mr. Nice Guy coaches. I expanded my blog into a more robust website, detailing my coaching services and allowing anyone to schedule a free introductory conversation with me. Because I had a day job, I could only take calls in the evenings and on the weekends, which was hardly the deterrent I expected it to be. Before long, I had a calendar full of appointments, most of which were scheduled by men who all made the very same admission: *Well, I discovered Dr. Glover's work and it was the Big Stick upside my head that I needed.*

As I write this, I am delighted to say that I have coached hundreds of men in both one-on-one and group settings, and I like to think that I've played an integral role in helping many of them radically improve their lives. I am equally delighted to call Dr. Glover both a mentor and a close friend. Dr. Glover is endlessly supportive. He offers direction when I'm stuck, encouragement when I'm down, and perspective when I need it the most. He's a sort of Zen-like uncle, regularly checking in to wish me well or impart me with wisdom. He is supremely generous with both his knowledge and his time.

Because of my work with Dr. Glover: I have learned to mitigate my depression and soothe my anxiety. I seldom let my mind get the best of me. I've learned not to take things personally. I set boundaries. I try to always act with integrity. I express myself. I have a healthier dating life and a more satisfying sex life. I'm a better ender. I ask for what I want. I make my needs a priority. I never let anyone treat me badly. Ever. I give without strings attached. I'm honest and transparent. I'm grateful. I can let go of attachment to outcome. I take more risks. And best of all, I believe in myself. Which is why on my

37th birthday, I quit my day job to pursue coaching, writing, and some of my other entrepreneurial ventures full-time.

Yes, it's true. Dr. Robert Glover changed my life. Though, he would probably tell you otherwise. He would probably tell you that I changed my own life and that he just gave me the tools to do so. And he would probably be right. He usually is. But I maintain my position. Dr. Robert Glover changed my life. I would be remiss if I didn't thank him.

Oh, and Tracy. I guess I should thank her, too.

# ABOUT THIS BOOK

In October of 2020, Dr. Glover and his wife, Lupita, boarded an airplane in Seattle, sat down in their first-class seats, and prepared for the four-and-a-half-hour flight back home to Puerto Vallarta, Mexico. Just as the plane was taking off, Lupita looked across the aisle to her right, only to see a woman deeply submerged in a book, occasionally picking up a pen to scribble down notes. The book was *No More Mr. Nice Guy*. The woman, it turned out, is a psychologist who had been given the book by a colleague to help her better understand some of her struggling male patients.

This was a satisfying experience for Dr. Glover – it was the first time he'd seen someone reading his book on an airplane. But it is also a testament to the kind of impact that *No More Mr. Nice Guy* has had – and continues to have – in the world of psychology and self-development. 20 years after its publication, the book is still being passed around by practitioners and recommended on reading lists as the definitive work on modern male behavior. It has been a beacon of hope for countless men who have struggled to find fulfillment in love, sex, and life. *No More Mr. Nice Guy*, in fact, may have very well put an end to the days when downtrodden men had nowhere to turn and suffered in silence as a result.

While Dr. Glover is best known for *No More Mr. Nice Guy*, his other work is no less enlightening. In 2012, Dr. Glover created Total Personal Integration (TPI) University with a mission to "better help men and women put their intention into action." TPI University is home to popular online classes including *Positive Emotional Tension, All the Way in: Relationship Essentials for Men, The Ruminating Brain*, and *Nice Guys Don't Finish Last, They Rot in Middle Management*. In 2019, Dr. Glover published his book *Dating Essentials for Men: The Only Dating Guide You Will Ever Need*, which gives men the tools to overcome self-limiting beliefs, develop better social skills, and interact more authentically with women. Then, in 2022, he released *Dating Essentials for Men: Frequently Asked Questions*, which contains his honest and uncensored answers to over 300 questions from men about dating, relationships, and sex. Loyal followers of Dr. Glover might also be familiar with his expansive library of podcast recordings, Q&A forums, articles, worksheets, and other resources for both men and women.

The book you are reading now pulls from all of it…and more.

This book took me many months to craft but, as you've learned, it has actually been decades in the making. It encapsulates well over 30 years of Dr. Glover's groundbreaking work as a marriage and family therapist, a dating and relationship coach, an educator, a public speaker, and a seminal figure in men's self-improvement. Dr. Glover gave me the "keys to the kingdom" – unprecedented access to his vault – so I could write this book. As for why I agreed to write it…well, you'll just have to figure that shit out on your own.

Throughout this book, I frequently paraphrase or directly quote Dr. Glover. I offer candid glimpses into Dr. Glover's life. I have also peppered the book with my own anecdotes and experiences. What I most want you to know, however, is that I am merely a conduit. Make no mistake: Every ounce of wisdom you'll find in this book comes from Dr. Glover, arguably one of the sharpest and most underappreciated psychological minds of his generation. Bandura may have given us self-efficacy and Erikson may have brought to light the identity crisis, but I'm willing to bet that Dr. Glover has directly impacted more lives with his work on the Nice Guy Syndrome, Positive Emotional Tension, and the Ruminating Brain.

This book is hefty. It is divided into nine major sections: **(I) The Nice Guy Syndrome, (II) Masculinity & Femininity, (III) Attraction, (IV) Con-**

scious Dating, (V) Sex & Sexuality, (VI) Relationships, (VII) Heartbreak, (VIII) Success, and (IX) Happiness & Well-Being. You might be tempted to cherry-pick, and you are welcome to do so. If you are in a relationship, for example, then you might think the dating section isn't for you. If you are thriving in your career, then you might assume the chapters on success are irrelevant. By all means, choose your own adventure. But I strongly encourage you to read the entire book – from start to finish - at least once. There is knowledge to be extracted from each page.

You will inevitably notice that some concepts appear more than once in the book. This is by design, not mistake. These concepts are particularly important, and they are applicable to multiple overarching subjects.

You will also notice that almost every chapter ends with recommendations for **Integrated Action** – a combination of journal exercises and action items designed to help you grow. If you intend to take these seriously - and I hope you do - you will need three things: (1) a journal or notebook, (2) a safe person (or safe people), and (3) an open mind. You can find additional information and free supplemental downloads at www.bigstickbook.com.

This book may trigger you. It may challenge your beliefs. Parts of it may even offend you. I've accepted this as a possibility. On the other hand, this book may completely and positively transform your world - if you want it to. This book may very well be the big stick upside your head that you need.

I have taken the best of what Dr. Glover has put forth over 30+ years, shaken it up, and included it all in the pages that follow, taking great care to organize it in what I believe is the most effective way. Should you take what you learn in this book and apply it, I believe that you'll experience greater fulfillment in every area of your life.

I am beyond grateful that Dr. Glover asked me to write this book. And maybe one day – 20 or so years from now – I'll see you reading it on an airplane, occasionally picking up a pen to scribble down notes.

# PART I:
# THE NICE GUY
# SYNDROME

*I'm tired of being a nice guy. I've been poor*
*all my life but don't know quite why.*
– Tupac Shakur

At some point during his second marriage, Dr. Glover began to wonder why it wasn't going very well. After all, he was a ridiculously nice guy. He did everything he could to satisfy his wife. He sacrificed his own needs to meet hers. He never rocked the boat. He kept the peace. He was always considerate. He expressed his love. He tried desperately to make his wife happy. Yet, she never was. She was frequently angry and critical. She was unappreciative. She was dismissive. And sex? Well, that was just out of the question. So, Dr. Glover did what many men do when they are helplessly confused and dejected: He tried harder, doubling down on the things that obviously weren't working.

> **We cannot solve our problems with the same thinking we**
> **used when we created them.**
> - Albert Einstein

Eventually, Dr. Glover's wife raised the stakes. She threatened to leave him, demanding that he get professional help. This only confused Dr. Glover - and understandably so. His wife was the one who seemed perpetually miserable. But having no other apparent options, Dr. Glover complied and went to therapy.

While working with his therapist to untangle the riddle around his marital discord, Dr. Glover noticed something in his own therapy practice: Nearly all his male patients seemed to be having the same befuddling experience in their relationships. They were airing the very same grievances. Session after session, Dr. Glover heard things like: *Why isn't she nice to me when I am so nice to her? It's never enough. I just want to be appreciated. Why doesn't she want to have sex anymore? And why is she so goddamn angry all the time?*

It didn't take long for Dr. Glover to realize that droves of other men were following a life script similar to his. Men like me and perhaps men like you. Men who can't stand upsetting anyone. Men who constantly seek approval from others, neglect their own needs, sacrifice their personal power, and suppress their masculinity. Men who are especially concerned with pleasing women. Men who rarely if ever stand up for themselves. Men who are frustrated and resentful, constantly struggling to experience the happiness they believe they deserve.

These men suffer from an anxiety and shame-based disorder that has become all too common. Yes, these men suffer from the **Nice Guy Syndrome**, and they have bought into a myth.

Nice Guys believe that if they are good and do everything right, they will be loved, their needs will be met, and they will live a smooth, problem-free life. When this strategy fails to produce positive results, Nice Guys just keep at it, employing the same ineffective tactics over and over…and over again. Einstein would call this fucking insanity.[1]

Until Dr. Glover published *No More Mr. Nice Guy* in 2003, nobody seemed to pay much attention to the plight of the Nice Guy - which is hard to believe given that the Nice Guy is everywhere.

As Dr. Glover points out:

- He is the husband who lets his wife run the show.
- He is the boyfriend who frustrates his girlfriend because he is so afraid of conflict that nothing ever gets resolved.
- He is the friend who will do anything for anyone, even though his own life is a mess.
- He is the boss who tells one person what they want to hear and then reverses course to please someone else.
- He is the employee who lets people walk all over him.
- He is the man whose life seems completely under control, until…oh fuck…one day he does something to destroy it all.[2]

For me – and for countless other men - reading *No More Mr. Nice Guy* led to one "Holy Shit" moment after another. Many men report that the book made them angry, as it forced them to confront the unfortunate reality of their lives. Others spring immediately into action with a kind of gleeful excitement, knowing they've found a viable solution to their problems.

While *No More Mr. Nice Guy* may be Dr. Glover's most recognized work, it is for a different reason that I chose to begin this book by discussing the Nice Guy Syndrome. It is because the Nice Guy Syndrome can – and *will* - permeate every part of your life, just as it did mine. It is like a slow-moving

---

1   Einstein famously said that "Insanity is doing the same thing over and over and expecting different results." The thing is, Einstein never said this. It's a commonly misattributed quote. For the purposes of this book, though, let's just pretend he really did say it.

2   Dr. Glover often uses these and similar examples of Nice Guys to describe how the Nice Guy is everywhere. You can find these examples on page 4 of *No More Mr. Nice Guy* and on www.drglover.com.

disease – a disease that takes root in childhood but doesn't reveal itself until years later, when it subtly begins to dismantle your relationships and sabotage your success, and then starts eating away at your mind, body, and spirit. It's best to get a grip on this thing as early as possible. But it's never too late.

The Nice Guy Syndrome also permeates every part of this book. It shows up everywhere and it shows up often. To understand the Nice Guy Syndrome is to understand why almost nothing seems to be going the way you'd planned.

In this section, I've included what I believe are the most important ideas from Dr. Glover's work on the Nice Guy Syndrome. You'll learn Dr. Glover's theories on how the Nice Guy evolved and why Nice Guys are more prevalent than ever. You'll learn the characteristics and behaviors commonly exhibited by Nice Guys of all shades, shapes, sizes, and backgrounds. You'll learn why Nice Guys are anything but nice. You'll also get a closer look at what I've identified as the more troublesome aspects of the Nice Guy Syndrome, based on both my own personal journey and my continued work as one of Dr. Glover's certified coaches. If you're a longtime sufferer of the Nice Guy Syndrome, you'll discover what it takes to start Breaking Free so you can live a more authentic and more fulfilling life.

For a much deeper dive into the Nice Guy Syndrome, you'll undoubtedly want to purchase, read (and probably re-read) *No More Mr. Nice Guy* - that is, if you haven't already. Between "Holy Shit" moments, you'll notice that the book includes dozens of what Dr. Glover calls **Breaking Free Activities** to help you on your journey towards recovery. Challenge yourself to do them and your world will begin to change.

# THE MAKING OF A NICE GUY

Everyone comes into this life as a dependent, needy little baby. And babies are annoying. This probably isn't news to you. But settle in; there's more to the story.

Because babies rely on others to meet their needs in timely and judicious ways, they have an overwhelming fear of abandonment. For babies, abandonment means death. And yet, every baby experiences some degree of abandonment:

He is hungry and nobody feeds him.

He cries and nobody holds him.

He is lonely and nobody pays attention to him.

Furthermore, babies are inherently narcissistic and grandiose. They believe that they are the cause of everything that happens to them – bad or good. As their little baby brains develop, babies think they are the center of the Universe.[3] (Yes, some very obnoxious adults still think this way.)[4]

The human brain is home to a collection of nuclei called the amygdala. Maybe you've heard of it. It's only about the size of your fingernail, but it plays a critical role in emotion and behavior. The amygdala is perhaps best known

---

3   Dr. Glover discusses the making of a Nice Guy in his virtual workshops. In his presentation, he explains how babies have an overwhelming fear of abandonment and believe they are the cause of everything that happens to them. Additionally, see Glover, Robert A. *No More Mr. Nice Guy* (Running Press, 2003) pp. 37-38

4   Here's looking at you, Kanye West.

for processing fear and controlling your fight-flight-freeze response. It also stores your internalized beliefs and memories. Theoretically, everything you experienced as a child is stored in your amygdala as emotional memory. You can't find words or pictures for these experiences, but the emotions are there.

The amygdala is your emotional operating system; it is hard-wired into every other part of your brain. Your current beliefs about yourself and the world are directly controlled and influenced by the amygdala. "This is true for every adult," explains Dr. Glover. "And every adult has created a persona based on their early life experiences. Nice Guys are no exception."

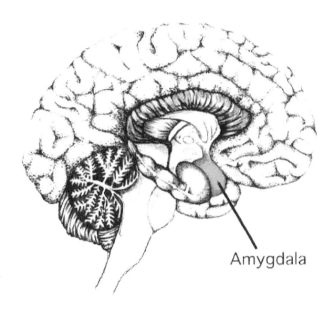

Amygdala

The Nice Guy inaccurately internalized his childhood abandonment experiences and developed the belief that he is bad, defective, and unlovable. In other words, **the Nice Guy believes he is not okay just as he is**. The Nice Guy's amygdala seems to contain a roadmap for life that reads: *I must become what I think others want me to be and I must hide anything that might cause others to reject me.*

This is the foundation for what is known as *toxic shame*, and it wreaks havoc on the lives of Nice Guys.[5]

# THE NICE GUY PARADIGM &
# THE TWO TYPES OF NICE GUYS

Because Nice Guys inaccurately internalize their childhood abandonment experiences, they develop survival mechanisms to help them do three things: (1) cope with the pain from these experiences, (2) prevent these kinds of experiences from happening again, and (3) hide their toxic shame from themselves and others. According to Dr. Glover, these survival mechanisms lead Nice Guys to live by the following paradigm: *If I can become what I think others want me to be and hide anything that might cause others to reject me, then I will be loved, my needs will be met, and I will have a smooth, problem-free life.*

Even though it is based on the faulty interpretation of childhood events, this paradigm controls everything Nice Guys do as adults.[6]

***

After years of working with Nice Guys, Dr. Glover began to see that their survival mechanisms generally manifest in one of two ways, creating two types of Nice Guys:

- **The I'm So Bad Nice Guy** believes he is a bad person, and he is convinced that everyone else believes this, too. He can give concrete examples of bad behavior that he exhibited in childhood, adolescence, and early adulthood. He is convinced that happiness lies in trying to hide how bad he is.
- **The I'm So Good Nice Guy** believes he is a truly good guy - one of the nicest guys you will ever meet. If he is conscious of his perceived flaws, he will work to correct them. As a child, he never caused any

---

5    Glover, Robert A. *No More Mr. Nice Guy* (Running Press, 2003) p.38
6    Glover, Robert A. *No More Mr. Nice Guy* (Running Press, 2003) pp. 46-47

problems. As a teenager, he did everything right. As an adult, he follows all the rules. He thinks that all the good things he does are what make him such an amazing person.

While the two types of Nice Guys may differ in the ways they try to deal with their toxic shame, they both operate from the same life paradigm. Both believe they are not okay just as they are. Dr. Glover only makes the distinction between the two types of Nice Guys to help each see their distortions more clearly. Neither is as bad or as good as they believe themselves to be. They are merely wounded souls, navigating the world with an inaccurate roadmap.[7]

# THE PARENT TRAP

As Dr. Glover points out, many Nice Guys recall growing up in perfect, all-American, *Leave it to Beaver* families.[8] Yet, these men still developed the Nice Guy paradigm, indicating that at some point in their early lives, their circumstances were less than ideal. This is because there are no perfect families. There are no perfect parents. And there are no perfect people.

Healthy parenting generally requires two mature adults who fulfill their own emotional needs. One parent helps check the imperfections of the other. They are attentive to their children. They protect their children. And they consistently meet their children's needs in timely and judicious ways.

When a child has healthy parents, he internalizes the beliefs that he is lovable, he is safe, his needs are important, and the world is like his family. But parents aren't always as healthy as they seem. Nice Guys who recall having a peachy upbringing often find that upon closer inspection, their family

---

7   Glover, Robert A. *No More Mr. Nice Guy* (Running Press 2003) pp. 47-48

8   Dr. Glover often makes this *Leave it to Beaver* analogy when discussing the origin of the Nice Guy. See Glover, Robert A. *No More Mr. Nice Guy* (Running Press, 2003) p.40. And for you youngsters out there, *Leave it to Beaver* is a classic American sitcom that aired from 1957 to 1963.

was less like the Cleavers and more like the Simpsons[9]. Suffice to say, no matter how wonderful your parents were, they very well could have sent you out into the world with an inaccurate roadmap.

Sadly, just as many Nice Guys report having childhoods that were far from the *Leave it to Beaver* experience. They had terribly unhealthy parents – Archie Bunker[10] dads and Peggy Bundy[11] moms - who provided a roadmap that wasn't just inaccurate, it was crumpled up and covered in cigarette burns. These parents were neither attentive nor protective. They failed to meet their children's needs in timely and judicious ways.

When a child has unhealthy parents, he internalizes the beliefs that he isn't lovable, he isn't safe, his needs aren't important, and the world is out to get him. Unhealthy parenting can manifest in numerous ways, from immaturity and unavailability to addiction and abuse. While unhealthy parenting is surely a matter of degree, it is safe to say that many boys grow up to become Nice Guys because they did not have mature parents. Maybe they had parents who were a little hard on the Beaver. Cue Eminem.[12]

# 20th CENTURY HISTORY 101

While parenting plays an integral role in the evolution of the Nice Guy, one can't ignore the profound impact of society at large. As Dr. Glover illustrates in the beginning of *No More Mr. Nice Guy*, several decades of dramatic social change and monumental shifts in the traditional family created an

---

9    DOH!

10   Archie Bunker, played by Carol O'Connor, is a famously gruff fictional character
     from the classic 1970s sitcom, *All in the Family*

11   Peggy Bundy, played by Katey Sagal, is the hilariously air-headed wife of Al Bundy
     from the American sitcom, *Married With Children*, which aired from 1987-1997.
     Man, I hope you already knew this.

12   During the final rap battle scene in the movie *8 Mile*, Eminem's opponent calls him
     "that dude from Leave it to Beaver." Eminem famously flips the script by saying
     "Ward, I think you were a little hard on the Beaver." Hilarity then ensues.

entire breed of Nice Guys - men who possess many if not all of the following characteristics:[13]

- **They are givers.** Nice Guys frequently say they are happiest when they are making others happy.
- **They fix and caretake.** If someone has a problem, Nice Guys will attempt to solve it, often without being asked.
- **They constantly seek validation from others.** Nice Guys say or do things to either gain approval or avoid disapproval.
- **They avoid conflict.** Nice Guys want their lives to be smooth and problem-free. They won't do anything that might upset anyone.
- **They hide their perceived flaws and mistakes.** Nice Guys believe that if they expose any shortcomings, others will get mad at them, shame them, or worse.
- **They try to do everything right.** Nice Guys believe this is the key to having a problem-free life: If they do everything "right," then nothing should go wrong.
- **They repress their feelings.** Nice Guys tend to analyze rather than feel. They go to great lengths to keep their feelings at bay.
- **They try to be different from their fathers.** Many Nice Guys report having unavailable, passive, absent, angry, alcoholic, or philandering fathers. These Nice Guys usually decide to be completely different from the men who raised them.
- **They relate more to women than men.** Due to their childhood conditioning, many Nice Guys have very few male friends. They seek the approval of women while convincing themselves they are different from other men.
- **They always put the needs of others before their own.** Nice Guys believe it is selfish to put their own needs first.

---

13   Glover, Robert A. *No More Mr. Nice Guy* (Running Press, 2003) pp. 22-23

- **They make their partner their emotional center.** Many Nice Guys put tremendous energy into their intimate relationships, believing that happiness lies in making their partner happy.

Men like this have probably always existed. Dr. Glover acknowledges that in recent history there hasn't been a notable shortage of simps, mamas' boys, and henpecked husbands. But after working with countless men, women, and couples, he came to realize that it is likely a series of social changes and events - beginning around the turn of the century and accelerating after World War II - that produced the extraordinary number of Nice Guys we see today. As Dr. Glover explains, these social changes and events include:

- The transition from an agrarian to an industrial economy
- The migration of families from rural areas to urban areas
- The growing absence of fathers from the home
- An increase in divorce, single parent homes, and female-headed homes
- An educational system dominated by women
- Women's liberation and the rise of feminism
- The Vietnam War
- The Sexual Revolution

It isn't difficult to see how these changes and events contributed to the Nice Guy phenomenon, particularly in the Baby Boom generation. Boys used to connect with their fathers by working alongside them on the farm, which provided an intimate model of masculinity. But after World War II, contact between fathers and sons significantly diminished as fathers left home to go work in offices and factories. According to the United States census, in 1910, over 30 percent of families lived on farms. By 1970, the number of families living on farms had dropped to less than five percent.

Fathers soon became unavailable to their sons in other ways. Many became addicted to work, television, alcohol, sex, and other vices, which likely contributed to a stark increase in divorce rates. Statistics show that the number of divorces tripled from 1940 to 1970. In 1940, just over five million households were headed by women. By the early 1970s, this figure jumped to over 13 million. Unfortunately, even the most wonderful, well-meaning mothers were not (and are still not) equipped to teach their sons how to be male.

Dr. Glover points out that boys were also raised by women in the educational system. Even today, men account for just one in four teachers nationwide. From daycare through elementary school, little boys in the post-war era were surrounded by women. If these boys were already disconnected from their fathers, the typical school system only exacerbated this issue.

In the 1960's, the Vietnam War further crystallized the disconnect between sons and fathers. Sons were protesting a seemingly pointless war, while a generation of veteran fathers could not understand the social rebellion of their sons. A growing anti-war movement spawned a new species of men focused solely on peace, love, and understanding. Cue Elvis Costello.[14]

At the same time, women's liberation was in its infancy. Women were beginning to work outside the home, while the advent of birth control led to a new kind of freedom. Many women could see a change in gender roles on the horizon and worked to prepare their daughters and sons for what was to come.

The subsequent radical feminist movement led to a variety of sweeping generalizations about men. Some feminists claimed that men were the cause of all the world's problems, while others asserted that men were just unnecessary pests. The majority of women during this time probably didn't share these radical views on men, but the feminist minority was vocal enough to convince many men that they were bad just because they were men.[15]

---

14 Perhaps the most obscure music reference in this book, Elvis Costello released a pretty awesome song in 1979 called "(What's so Funny 'Bout) Peace, Love, and Understanding."

15 Dr. Glover details how the Baby Boom generation, the rise of the sensitive guy, and dynamic social changes of the 20th century have created the "bumper crop of Nice Guys in our culture." See Glover, Robert A. *No More Mr. Nice Guy* (Running Press, 2003) pp. 49-56

Today, it is clear that the Nice Guy Syndrome didn't end with the Baby Boomers. Nice Guy conditioning seems more prevalent now than ever before. Masses of young men in their late teens, twenties, and thirties all exhibit the characteristics and behaviors that define the Nice Guy Syndrome. Nice Guy fathers raised Nice Guy sons who will create more little Nice Guys – and the process will very likely repeat itself again and again. When Dr. Glover published *No More Mr. Nice Guy* in 2003, he suspected that the third generation of Nice Guys was just beginning. As I write this, we both suspect that Nice Guys will be here for generations to come.

# WHAT'S WRONG WITH BEING A NICE GUY?

If I were to make a vague approximation, I'd say that half of those who pick up *No More Mr. Nice Guy* do so because the book was recommended to them - by a friend, a therapist, or one of their favorite motivational man-bloggers.[16] They crack open the book with tremendous curiosity and a kind of last-ditch desperation because they were told that the information inside would be life-changing.

The other half of those who pick up *No More Mr. Nice Guy* tend to do so ignorantly, without any real knowledge of what's enclosed, and respond to the book's title by asking: *What's wrong with being a Nice Guy?* It's an understandably common question, often trailed by its trusty companion: *So, I'm supposed to be an asshole?* The answer to this, of course, is: No.

Rest assured, there is nothing wrong with being nice to others. You would be wise to go through life as a decent human being. But there is a stark difference between being a nice person and being a *Nice Guy* as Dr. Glover defines it. In fact, the term Nice Guy is a misnomer because Nice Guys are anything but nice:[17]

---

16  Dr. Glover adds that men occasionally receive the book from a current or former romantic partner, or another woman in their life.

17  Glover, Robert A. *No More Mr. Nice Guy* (Running Press, 2003) pp. 23-26

- **Nice Guys are fundamentally dishonest.** They repress their feelings and say what they think other people want to hear.
- **Nice Guys are highly secretive.** They hide anything that might upset anyone. As Dr. Glover likes to say, Nice Guys live by the motto: *If at first you don't succeed, hide the evidence.*
- **Nice Guys are manipulative.** They tend to have difficulty making their own needs a priority and asking for what they want in clear and direct ways. So, they frequently resort to manipulation when trying to fulfill their needs.
- **Nice Guys are controlling.** Because they have an overwhelming desire to live smooth, problem-free lives, Nice Guys try to control the people around them.
- **Nice Guys give to get.** While they tend to be generous, Nice Guys rarely give without unspoken strings attached – particularly when they give to women. Nice Guys are perpetually frustrated and resentful because they give so much and seem to get so little in return.
- **Nice Guys are passive-aggressive.** They tend to express their frustration in indirect (and not-so-nice) ways.
- **Nice Guys are full of rage.** They might deny ever getting angry, but a lifetime of pent-up frustration and resentment creates a highly unstable pressure cooker. Nice Guys often erupt in anger at some of the most inappropriate times.
- **Nice Guys are addictive.** Because they keep so much bottled up inside, they often self-medicate to relieve stress. Addiction to porn and masturbation is not uncommon amongst Nice Guys.
- **Nice Guys rarely set boundaries.** They have a hard time saying No. They play the role of helpless victim and see others as the cause of all their problems.
- **Nice Guys isolate.** Even though they desire to be liked and loved, their behaviors make it damn near impossible for others to get close to them.

- **Nice Guys are attracted to people and situations that need fixing.** They spend a lot of time putting out fires and managing crises, likely due to their need for approval.

- **Nice Guys have problems with intimacy.** They are terrible listeners. Their fear of conflict keeps them from working all the way through a problem. And they tend to blame others for standing in the way of their happiness.

- **Nice Guys have issues with sex and sexuality.** Almost every Nice Guy is completely dissatisfied with his sex life. Many have a sexual dysfunction or some sort of sexual compulsion.

- **Nice Guys are rarely successful.** Most Nice Guys are talented and intelligent with a lot to offer the world. But they almost never live up to their potential.

Additionally, as Dr. Glover points out, Nice Guys are "notoriously slow learners and amazingly quick forgetters." This is especially true when their core beliefs and paradigms are challenged. Even though the Nice Guy paradigm is ineffective and leads Nice Guys to engage in various problematic behaviors, it is difficult for Nice Guys to consider doing something different. Is it time for you to start doing something different?

**INTEGRATED ACTION:**
- ✓ Take out your journal. If you don't have one yet, get one.
- ✓ Do you believe you're a Nice Guy? If so, which Nice Guy characteristics do you exhibit? Write your answers in your journal.
- ✓ Are you ready to do something different? Make the commitment now.

# MASKED MEN

"I'm a goddamn chameleon," shared Brian on our very first coaching call. Brian is a 45-year-old architect who lives in Tampa with his wife and two sons, and their golden retriever. He reached out to me with a sense of urgency.

"It's like I'm always putting on some sort of mask…depending on where I am and who's in the room. If I'm with a colleague who loves golf, let's say, I'll go to great lengths to make him think that I love golf, too. I'll actually research golfers and golf stats just to get him to like me. And that's just one silly example. I do this with everyone, all the time. It's ridiculous, and I'm beginning to see the dire consequences. I don't know what I like. I don't know what I want. I don't even know who I am anymore. I've lost any zest I had for life, and I'm scared of what might happen if I don't fix this."

To some, Brian's chameleon-like tendencies may seem strange - perhaps even pathological. But Brian is no different than I was when I began my own journey. Nor is he any different from the countless Nice Guys I've met along the way. Brian, in fact, has a trait that is ubiquitous among Nice Guys: He is guided by his unswerving and desperate need to gain the approval of others.

Because Nice Guys do not believe they are okay just as they are, they constantly seek external validation. They find a myriad of ways to convince others (and themselves) that they are lovable and desirable. They are certain that if others discover their perceived flaws and shortcomings, they will be shamed, abandoned, or worse. Nice Guys are masked men, and they are terrified of revealing their authentic selves.

"It's like the Nice Guy is constantly licking his finger and holding it up to see which way the wind is blowing," explains Dr. Glover. "He's trying to figure out: *Who can I be with this person? Who can I be in this situation?* A Nice Guy will often have a different persona at work, a different persona at home, a different persona with friends, a different persona at church, and it just continues to change. Nice Guys are always hiding or pleasing to gain approval. They're covering up their humanity. There's no sense of self; no core locus of control."[18]

Sadly, this incessant need for approval can lead Nice Guys into some very dark places, just as it did Brian. It is physically, emotionally, and spiritually draining. And it prevents Nice Guys from getting - and doing - what they really want. Dr. Glover asserts that when Nice Guys cover up their humanity, it makes them seem lifeless and uninteresting. I have found that it doesn't just make them *seem* lifeless and uninteresting; it also makes them *feel* lifeless and uninteresting. Not to mention that it keeps everyone at arm's length.

As Dr. Glover explains, "Nice Guys believe they'll gain the approval of others as long as they do everything right - as long as they hide their perceived flaws and come across as perfect. This is not a sustainable way to go about life. Plus, humans are not drawn to perfection. Humans are drawn to each other's rough edges."[19]

---

18  Locus of control is a psychological concept that refers to the degree to which an individual feels a sense of agency in regards to his or her life.

19  For more on how Nice Guys cover up their humanity, see Glover, Robert A. *No More Mr. Nice Guy* (Running Press, 2003) pp. 62-63

# THE ULTIMATE FORM OF APPROVAL

While Nice Guys seek approval from others in just about every situation, their need for approval is typically most pronounced in their relationships with women.

Nice Guys believe that the greatest confirmation of their worth is a woman's approval. Of course, Nice Guys also believe that if a woman is even the slightest bit moody, it is a sign of her firm **dis**approval.

Constantly seeking the approval of women has many negative consequences, one of which is that it requires Nice Guys to constantly monitor *the possibility of a woman's availability,* a term Dr. Glover uses to describe the subjective measure of a woman's sexual openness. Nice Guys see sex as the ultimate form of approval and believe that a woman must be in a perfect mood before she will even entertain the idea of having sex. Therefore, the Nice Guy tries exceptionally hard to avoid doing anything that might rub a woman the wrong way, particularly if he hopes to rub her the right way.

Furthermore, seeking the approval of women gives those women the power to both set the tone of a relationship and define a man's worth. Nice Guys frequently share that their own moods are tied to the moods of the women in their lives. Nice Guys also tend to believe that women are always right, no matter how illogical their estimations. If a woman calls a Nice Guy an asshole, he will likely agree with her just because she said so. A patient of Dr. Glover's once asked: *If a man is talking in the forest and no woman is there to hear him, is he still wrong?*

Of the many negative consequences that come from seeking the approval of women, perhaps the most disturbing is that it creates rage. Many Nice Guys claim to love and adore women when they are actually seething with resentment. This is because we often despise what we have made into our god (or goddess). When Nice Guys put women on a pedestal and try desperately to win their approval, the adoration quickly turns to rage when those women don't seem to approve. It is not unusual to hear a Nice Guy proclaim his love for a woman, only to deem her a colossal bitch just a few moments later.[20]

---

**INTEGRATED ACTION:**

✓ Are you a chameleon? How does this affect your life and relationships? Write your answers in your journal?

✓ Do you see a woman's approval as the ultimate confirmation of your worth? How does this manifest? How does it affect your relationships with women? Write your answers in your journal.

---

20  For more on how Nice Guys seek validation from women, see Glover, Robert A. *No More Mr. Nice Guy* (Running Press, 2003) pp. 60-62

# COVERT CONTRACTORS

Indeed, nearly everyone who reads *No More Mr. Nice Guy* claims that - from cover to cover - the book was truly eye-opening. It is quite telling, though, that most readers point to one specific concept from the book as being the biggest whack upside the head: **Covert Contracts**.[21]

As Dr. Glover describes, "Nice Guys have something of a dilemma: How can they keep their needs hidden while creating situations in which they might be able to get their needs met? To solve this dilemma, Nice Guys use *covert contracts* – unconscious, unspoken agreements with the people around them."

Nice Guys are guided by three general covert contracts:

- *If I am a good guy, then everyone will like me and love me (and the people I desire will desire me).*[22]
- *If I meet other people's needs without them having to ask, then they will meet my needs without me having to ask.*
- *If I do everything right, then I will have a smooth, problem-free life.*

"These covert contracts simply don't work," asserts Dr. Glover. "But Nice Guys are convinced that they should. And when a Nice Guy believes he has fulfilled his side of a contract, he becomes resentful when other people don't

---

21 For more on covert contracts, see Glover, Robert A. *No More Mr. Nice Guy* (Running Press, 2003) pp.81-82

22 Dr. Glover often adds, "and the women I want to have sex with will want to have sex with me."

fulfill their side of the contract. Of course, these other people don't even know they have entered into a contract because the contract is entirely unspoken."

For example, when Tracy (the woman I referenced in the introduction to this book) shared with me that her laptop died, I happily volunteered to take it to the Apple store for her. I met her at a coffee shop near her office so she could give me the laptop during her lunch break. I then drove 40 minutes to the mall, waited in a shockingly long line at the Apple store, and wandered around for more than two hours before a member of Apple's support team called to tell me that he'd fixed the problem.

For me, spending any amount of time in a suburban mall is a special kind of hell. But this time, I didn't care. I wanted Tracy to see what an amazing man I was. I wanted her to see what kind of partner I could be. And I wanted her to have sex with me. I wanted her to *want* to have sex with me. How could she not?

I'd worked it all out in my head. It was the perfect plan. I would drop off Tracy's fully repaired laptop later that evening, only for her to invite me inside, wrap herself around me, and give me the affection, attention, and appreciation I so desperately craved from her. Of course, none of this transpired. In reality, Tracy gave me little more than an unenthused Thank You. I drove home bitter, angry, and frustrated.

Covert contracts like the one I had with Tracy can be summed up in a more commonly known phrase: **_giving to get_**. While covert contracts seem to take their ugliest form in romantic relationships, they manifest in other areas too, like familial relationships and friendships, and in work and career.

As Dr. Glover explains, the Nice Guy's covert contract almost always manifests in this way:

1. I will [fill in the blank] for you so that
2. You will [fill in the blank] for me.
3. We will both act as if we have no awareness of this contract.

When you consider the Nice Guy paradigm, it becomes clear that Nice Guys simply have one big covert contract with life.

# CARETAKING

When Nice Guys aren't using covert contracts, they're usually caretaking.[23] Nice Guys believe that caretaking is fundamentally loving. Except that it's not. Caretaking is an immature and indirect attempt by Nice Guys to get their needs met. It consists of *focusing on another's problems or feelings to feel valuable or avoid dealing with one's own problems or feelings.*

---

## THE VICTIM TRIANGLE

Covert contracts and caretaking only lead to resentment. When this resentment builds long enough, it often spills out in some less than flattering ways, creating a cycle of craziness that Dr. Glover calls the *The Victim Triangle*.

The Victim Triangle consists of a predictable three-part sequence:

1. The Nice Guy gives to others hoping to get something in return.

2. When the Nice Guy doesn't get what he expected, he becomes bitter and frustrated. After all, the Nice Guy is keeping score. He isn't totally objective.

3. When the Nice Guy's frustration builds up long enough, it eventually comes out in the form of rage, pouting, tantrums, shaming, blaming, or abuse.

Once this cycle is complete, it usually begins all over again.

---

To be clear, *caretaking* is different from *caring*. Dr. Glover makes the distinction that those who *caretake* give to others what they need to give, come from a place of emptiness, and always have unspoken strings attached; while

---

23  For more on Nice Guys and caretaking, see Glover, Robert A. *No More Mr. Nice Guy* (Running Press, 2003) pp. 82-86

those who *care* give what the receiver needs, come from a place of abundance, and never have unspoken strings attached.

"Nice Guys caretake for a number of reasons." asserts Dr. Glover. "But none of them have anything to do with love."

**INTEGRATED ACTION:**
- ✓ Are you guided by covert contracts? How does using covert contracts affect your life? Write your answers in your journal.
- ✓ Write down one example of how you've used covert contracts within the last week. What could you have done instead?

# PROJECT MANAGERS

When Dr. Glover was still in private practice, Nice Guys would generally come to his office for one of two reasons: Occasionally, it was because they needed to deal with some kind of hidden behavior or addiction that blew up in their face and caused a shitstorm at home. But more often, it was because they were dissatisfied in their relationship. Their wife or girlfriend was depressed, angry, unavailable, unfaithful, no longer interested in sex, or all of the above.

"That was just the Nice Guys in relationships," shares Dr. Glover. "Plenty of single Nice Guys made appointments, too. They couldn't figure out why being nice wasn't getting them laid or getting them a girlfriend. Both the single guys and the men in relationships assumed they were being exactly what women claimed to want – a Nice Guy."

For Nice Guys, intimate relationships tend to be a source of great frustration and total fucking bewilderment. Many believe there must be some magically simple solution to their relationship problems. There's not. Relationships are complicated. But because Nice Guys have internalized toxic shame and flawed core beliefs, they struggle more than most at navigating relationships.

Real intimacy requires two people to make themselves totally vulnerable to one another. For Nice Guys, this is just about the most frightening goddamn thing in the world. Nice Guys - as you've learned - spend much of their lives trying to become what others want them to be while hiding their own perceived flaws. To experience real intimacy, a Nice Guy would need to open up and let someone truly get to know him. But Nice Guys believe that being known means being found out. So, intimacy represents everything Nice Guys fear most.

"When Nice Guys get into an intimate relationship, they must maintain a balancing act," asserts Dr. Glover. "They must balance their fear of vulnerability with their fear of isolation. Therefore, Nice Guys usually find partners who are severely wounded and share a similar fear of intimacy. Together, they co-create a highly dysfunctional relationship that simultaneously frustrates and protects them."

Yes, Nice Guys tend to pick some pretty unsuitable partners – women who have financial woes, women who are addicts, women who are supremely unhealthy, women who have mood disorders, or women who are just plain immature. But this is precisely why Nice Guys invite these women into their lives. These women are projects, much like my ex-girlfriend, Molly.

Molly is one of the most beautiful women I've ever seen. Her body is a work of art, perfectly toned and golden tan with a smattering of graceful tattoos and a tiny, steel rod through each nipple. She loves animals, so much so that watching her care for a newborn puppy can melt even the coldest of hearts. When she laughs, it's as if the world slows to a pause and all of its chaos seems inconsequential. She's a kind and loving soul. She would often surprise me with gifts – small tokens of her affection – like a batch of freshly baked muffins, or some peace lilies for my windowsill, or a bottle of my favorite cologne.

During the course of our relationship, Molly was fired from four different jobs, had her car repossessed, got arrested for shoplifting, dropped out of nursing school, and started stripping (again) to make extra cash. I watched her experiment with a variety of medications, which may or may not have caused her abrupt and violent mood swings. In a matter of seconds, she could go from gentle, doting girlfriend to vicious, fire-breathing devil-woman. She would give me the silent treatment for days on end. She was always late. She regularly lost her purse. And she drank like Bukowski during his Black Sparrow years.[24] But what the hell did I care? I was certain I could help her. Plus, the sex was amazing. And she bought me a really cool welcome mat.

Molly wasn't the first project I'd taken on. She was merely the latest in a string of women whose problems I tried to swoop in and fix. I was the proverbial white knight, emerging from the mist to rescue these women from their most pernicious demons. And in doing so, I could focus all of my attention on them instead of dealing with my own insecurities and toxic shame. This is a common pattern amongst Nice Guys. Unfortunately, as Dr. Glover affirms, "it almost guarantees that what is supposed to be a Nice Guy's most intimate relationship is actually his least intimate."[25]

# RECREATING CHILDHOOD RELATIONSHIP PATTERNS

It is human nature to prize what feels familiar. Subsequently, Nice Guys often cultivate adult relationships that mirror their earliest childhood relationships - specifically, the relationship they had with their parents. This is yet another way that Nice Guys co-create dysfunction. If a Nice Guy felt abandoned in childhood, for example, then he is likely to choose partners who are unavailable or unfaithful. Similarly, if a Nice Guy grew up with angry, demeaning or controlling parents, he is likely to choose partners with the same traits.[26]

---

24  Author, essayist, and poet Charles Bukowski flailed around in anonymity until he finally received an offer from John Martin of the small, independent publisher Black Sparrow Press. Bukowski was notoriously addicted to booze, drugs, and women. His live poetry readings were legendary, as he would often show up drunk and then fight with the crowd. Bukowski died in 1994 but his work lives on.

25  For more on how Nice Guys pick projects and co-create dysfunction,  see Glover, Robert A. *No More Mr. Nice Guy* (Running Press, 2003) p 136

26  For more on how Nice Guys recreate childhood relationship patterns, see Glover, Robert A. *No More Mr. Nice Guy* (Running Press, 2003) pp. 138-139

Dr. Glover often shares that his own life - especially his second marriage - is a case study in recreating childhood relationships patterns. While growing up, Dr. Glover never knew what mood his father might be in when he walked through the front door.

"More often than not, it wasn't good," he recalls. "I learned to come home prepared for the worst. I later recreated the same pattern in my marriage. I projected my father's unpredictable moods onto my wife and would frequently arrive home prepared for her to be angry. Even if she was in a good mood, my defensiveness often triggered some kind of confrontation between us. Thus, my wife came to look like my angry father and I perpetuated a familiar, though dysfunctional relationship dynamic."

**INTEGRATED ACTION:**

✓ Think about your most intimate relationships. Do you co-create dysfunction? Do you take on projects? Do you recreate childhood relationships patterns? How so? Write your answers in your journal.

# NURSERY DWELLERS

Men born right after World War II had the misfortune of growing up during a time when being male was viewed as some kind of character flaw. Because of the social changes that took place in the post-war era, they were forced to accept a female definition of what it means to be male. They internalized the belief that becoming what women wanted them to be was the only way to be loved, get their needs met, and live a smooth life. Sadly, though, this belief system isn't limited to men of the Baby Boom generation. As Dr. Glover asserts, "it's obvious that each successive generation of men is becoming more and more passive and more and more domesticated."

Nice Guys in particular aren't just passive and domesticated; they are completely disconnected from their own Masculine energy and from other men. They tend to have a strong Feminine side and a noticeable lack of male friends. They spend far too much time with women – usually women they're not sleeping with. They just love the warm, fuzzy feeling they get from being around and pleasing the opposite sex. They are, as Dr. Glover likes to say, "stuck in the nursery."

The nursery may be a perfectly appropriate place for little boys, but it is no place for grown-ass men. The confines of the nursery prevent men from stepping fully into their Masculinity and embracing their Masculine energy. There's nothing to challenge men in the nursery. This is a problem.

As Dr. Glover explains in *No More Mr. Nice Guy,* "Masculinity is the part of a man that allows him to survive as an individual, as part of a clan, and as part of a species. Without this masculine energy, we all would have died off eons ago. Masculine energy allows a man to create and produce. It empowers a man to provide for and protect those he loves. Masculine energy is defined by strength, courage, discipline, integrity, persistence, and passion."

Almost every Nice Guy who reaches out to me is stuck in the nursery. He is tethered to his wife or girlfriend, if he has one. If not, he is tethered to the couch, perpetually in the friend zone and jerking off to porn. He never challenges himself. He lacks purpose. And he has approximately zero male friends.

"One of the best ways a Nice Guy can challenge himself is by getting out of the goddamn nursery and hanging out with other men," insists Dr. Glover. "Go to the gym. Join a sports team. Whatever. Spend time with guys doing guy things. Other men will positively bless your life."

Sadly, I have found that Nice Guys like to make any number of lame excuses for why they don't hang out with other men:

*I'm not comfortable with other men.*

*I relate better to women.*

*My relationship makes it hard to spend time with other men.*

*I don't know what to talk about with other men.*

*Men are idiots.*

*Men are douchebags.*

*Men only care about sports, money, and smashing beer cans on their heads.*

For the record, I used to make the same excuses. They're all bullshit.

Many Nice Guys believe that they are – or that they need to be – fundamentally different from other men. Nice Guys who think this way likely tried to be different from their fathers in childhood. So, they create a similar dynamic with their male peers in adulthood. Unfortunately, when Nice Guys do this, they cut themselves off from the many benefits of male companionship and the remarkable power of having a Masculine community.[27]

"Usually, the real reason a man - especially a Nice Guy - doesn't have any male friends is because he's stuck in the nursery and he's afraid to leave," asserts Dr. Glover. "He feels safest around boobies. Or he feels safest in isolation – playing video games, binge-watching TV, scrolling through social media, and engaging in other completely pointless activities. A lot of men, especially Nice Guys, really need to get out of the nursery and start challenging themselves in the world of masculinity."

**INTEGRATED ACTION:**

✓ Are you stuck in the nursery? How do you stay disconnected from your own masculinity and from other men? How does this affect your life and relationships? Write your answers in your journal.

---

27  For more on how Nice Guys are disconnected from their masculinity and from other men, see Glover, Robert A. *No More Mr. Nice Guy* (Running Press, 2003) pp. 113-119

# TABLE DOGS

Barry, a successful, 51-year-old real estate investor, came to me with a bit of an issue. He'd been dating Kathy on and off for several years. Occasionally, they talked about getting married. Barry even bought Kathy a ring. A very big, very expensive ring. Barry didn't seem to care that Kathy was a conniving, gold-digging, emotionally volatile, cold-hearted witch who would make for a disastrously unhealthy life partner.

"I don't know what's wrong with me," shared Barry. "I can't get this woman out of my head. She's all I think about. When we're together, she treats me like shit. And I just go with it. When we're not together, I try the no-contact thing, and I can't do it. I just can't. I try, and I can't. She goes off and parties and sleeps with other guys, and then she rubs it in my face. Meanwhile, I'm not motivated to do anything. I can't focus on work. I'm not interested in dating other women. I don't spend time with my friends. I'm not present when I'm with my kids. I don't get any sleep. I just think about her. And every time she pops back into my life, I'm right there to welcome her back with open arms. Now, she's sending me messages about getting a house together. I'm seriously considering it because I think she'll change."

In *No More Mr. Nice Guy*, Dr. Glover illustrates that Nice Guys in relationships can typically be classified in one of two ways:

- The Nice Guy is emotionally unavailable to his primary partner yet plays the Nice Guy role outside of the relationship. This is what Dr. Glover calls an **Avoiding Nice Guy**.

- The Nice Guy becomes so involved in his intimate relationship that he neglects himself and his own interests. This is what Dr. Glover calls an **Enmeshing Nice Guy**.

I have no doubt met - and worked with - some Avoiding Nice Guys. An Avoiding Nice Guy seems to put everything else before his primary relationship. He is nice to everyone but his partner. He may volunteer to help others. He may spend weekends taking care of his mother. He may work multiple jobs. But he still uses covert contracts. He believes that his partner should be available to him even though he isn't available to her.[28]

In my experience, however, Avoiding Nice Guys seem to be relatively few and far between. Most of the men I work with are Enmeshing Nice Guys. And Barry is a classic example. (Barry's experience with Kathy is also a classic example of a *Trauma-Bonded Relationship*, discussed further in an upcoming section).

An Enmeshing Nice Guy - like Barry - makes his partner his emotional center. His entire world revolves around her. She is more important than his family, his friends, his career, his passions, and his hobbies. He will do whatever it takes to win her love. He will sacrifice his own needs. He will give her gifts, re-arrange his schedule, and attempt to fix all her problems. He will gladly tolerate her moodiness, her addictions, her sexual unavailability, and her disrespectful behavior. After all, he just loves her so much.

Dr. Glover has another name for Enmeshing Nice Guys: **Table Dogs**.

"Enmeshing Nice Guys are like little dogs who stand beneath the table waiting for a scrap to fall their way," describes Dr. Glover. "They hover around their partner just in case she happens to drop him a scrap of sexual interest, a scrap of her time, a scrap of a good mood, or a scrap of her attention. Even though they are settling for the leftovers that fall from the table, Enmeshing Nice Guys think they are getting something really good."

---

28  For more on Nice Guy patterns of enmeshment and avoidance, see Glover, Robert A. *No More Mr. Nice Guy* (Running Press, 2003) pp.137-138

One would think that an Enmeshing Nice Guy is ready and available for an intimate relationship; but this isn't so. Enmeshing behavior is a Nice Guy's way of hooking up an emotional hose to his partner. He uses the hose to fill the empty void inside himself. But this never yields the desired results. In fact, it is a tried-and-true recipe for frustration and heartbreak, and it frequently sends Nice Guys into a downward emotional spiral.

> **INTEGRATED ACTION:**
> ✓ Are you an Avoiding Nice Guy or an Enmeshing Nice Guy? How has your pattern of avoidance or enmeshment affected your life and your relationships? Are you a table dog? Write your answers in your journal.

# VAGIPHOBES

Well, this is where it gets awkward.

As Dr. Glover illustrates, if you take everything about Nice Guys – the toxic shame, the self-sacrifice, the approval-seeking behavior, the tendency to do the opposite of what works, the indirectness, the covert contracts, the relationship dysfunction, and the noticeable lack of Masculine energy – and you put all of it into one giant container, shake it up, and look inside, you'll have a pretty good idea of how Nice Guys do sex.[29]

Oh boy.

For Nice Guys, sex tends to magnify the hell out of their toxic shame, anxieties, fears, and insecurities. When Nice Guys seek help, it's often because they're looking to solve their problems around sex. Some of the most common problems are:

- They don't get enough sex.
- They constantly settle for less-than-satisfying sex.
- They have sexual dysfunction.
- They are sexually repressed.
- They engage in hidden, compulsive sexual behavior.

All of these problems can be linked directly back to shame and fear.[30] And almost every Nice Guy has some degree of shame and fear around being

---

29  Glover, Robert A. *No More Mr. Nice Guy* (Running Press, 2003) p. 154
30  Glover, Robert A. *No More Mr. Nice Guy* (Running Press, 2003) pp. 155-156

sexual. As Dr. Glover explains, if you were to look inside a Nice Guy's head and find the part of the unconscious mind that controls sex, this is what you are likely to find:

- Memories of childhood abandonment experiences
- Pain from not getting his needs met in healthy ways
- Residual effects from growing up with sexually wounded parents
- Sexual illusions and distortions from living in a fucked-up society
- Sexual guilt and shame from years of religious influence
- Trauma from sexual violation
- Memories of his early (highly secretive) sexual experiences
- Unrealistic images of sex from porn
- Memories of any sexual failures and rejection

It's no surprise then that Nice Guys haphazardly navigate sex. "When Nice Guys have sexual feelings or find themselves in sexual situations," explains Dr. Glover, "they must always wade through their unconscious muck."

Interestingly enough - and despite how much they seem to crave sexual intimacy - one of the primary ways Nice Guys navigate sex is by avoiding it altogether. To describe this behavior, Dr. Glover proudly coined the term *vagiphobia*.[31] As he describes, "Vagiphobia is merely a survival mechanism that protects Nice Guys from having to experience shame and fear. Of course, it also guarantees they won't have all that much sex."

> **vagiphobia** [va-ji-foh-bee-uh]
>
> *noun Psychiatry*
>
> a syndrome where the penis tries to stay out of vaginas or gets out as quickly as possible once it is in

---

31   Glover, Robert A. *No More Mr. Nice Guy* (Running Press, 2003) p. 157

Not having all that much sex - while unfortunate - is actually the least of the problems that can plague Nice Guys with vagiphobia. I've met countless Nice Guys whose vagiphobia caused them to:

- Develop crippling anxiety
- Put women on pedestals and develop unhealthy crushes
- Develop poor hygiene
- Develop an addiction to porn and masturbation
- Suffer from erectile dysfunction
- Unconsciously pick sexually unavailable partners

Take Adam, for example. Adam came to me in a self-acknowledged slump. He hadn't had sex in the three years since breaking up with his last girlfriend. So, Adam had one goal and one goal only: He wanted to end his three-year dry spell.

Impressively, Adam had little trouble meeting women. After just one coaching call, he began challenging himself to approach women on a daily basis, often sending me messages to inform me of his progress. He was having amazing conversations, getting phone numbers, and going on two - sometimes three - dates per week. Many of these women seemed to like Adam, and understandably so. Adam made his dates feel comfortable. He set the tone and took the lead. He exhibited strength and masculinity. He appeared confident.

That is until the opportunity for sex presented itself.

"It's so strange," lamented Adam, during one of our sessions. "I've gained so much confidence. I can approach a woman anywhere and strike up a conversation. I can go on dates. I flirt like a pro now. I can even get a woman back to my place. But as soon as things start heating up and clothes start coming off, I freeze up. I get anxious. I keep thinking: *Where is this gonna lead? What if she gets attached? What if I get attached? What if she's the one? What if she's not the one? What if I can't perform? What if she mocks me? What if she has a disease? What if I get her pregnant?* It becomes this endless loop. And it sucks. There I am, literally about to have sex, which I've been desperate to have for three fucking years…and I just end up talking myself out of the whole thing. So, I put the kibosh on it. Or she puts the kibosh on it. And then it's just uncomfortable and weird."

Clearly, Adam had a severe case of vagiphobia. The very idea of putting his penis in a vagina brought up all kinds of internalized shame and fear. Much of Adam's shame and fear came from beliefs he developed early in childhood, and it compounded during his three-year slump. As much as Adam wanted sex, his vagiphobia was keeping him trapped in a self-defeating cycle.

"Vagiphobia is really about much more than sticking - or not sticking - a penis in a vagina," expounds Dr. Glover. "It's about insecurities, shame, and fear. It's about men repressing their life energy. It represents a cornucopia of beliefs and behaviors that keep men from having the fulfilling sex lives they truly desire. Thankfully, with a bit of work, it's totally curable."

**INTEGRATED ACTION:**
✓ Do you crave sex yet find ways to avoid it? How do you avoid sexual situations? Write your answers in your journal.

# NEGATIVE NANCIES

"Well, I've been married for 17 years," divulged Carl during our introductory session. "But I've never been happily married. I mean, I love my wife, I guess. But we have nothing in common. We don't have sex. We haven't even kissed each other - like really kissed each other - in probably 10 years. She's gained a lot of weight. I'm not physically attracted to her, and I'm not sure I ever was. We don't go out or do anything fun. We just kind of exist together. We're basically just roommates."

"Why did you marry her in the first place?" I asked, unreservedly.

"We met in college," explained Carl. "We really liked each other back then. And I wasn't exactly a ladies' man. So, I was really excited when I got a girlfriend. And I loved the idea of being married."

"So, why do you *stay* married to this particular woman?"

"Because I don't want to be lonely," replied Carl. "I really doubt I'd ever meet someone else."

Carl seemed to be forgetting an important fact: There are literally billions of other women on the planet. But Carl's inability to see the world accurately came as no surprise to me. After all, Carl is a Nice Guy. And almost every Nice Guy suffers from *deprivation thinking*, also known as a scarcity mindset.[32]

---

32  Glover, Robert A. *No More Mr. Nice Guy* (Running Press, 2003) p. 183

Due to their childhood abandonment experiences, Nice Guys believed early on that there just wasn't enough of what they needed to go around. This became the lens through which they viewed the world. And this is how they view the world today – as a place of deprivation and scarcity rather than a place of abundance.

Deprivation thinking negatively affects how Nice Guys navigate every part of life. In relationships, it's part of what makes Nice Guys manipulative and controlling. It can make them excessively needy. It can lead to trust issues. And it can keep them in a constant state of fear. Like Carl, many Nice Guys believe that once they get into a relationship with a woman, they must hang onto her as tightly as possible; because, for Nice Guys, meeting another woman just isn't in the cards. Nice Guys believe that women are in short supply.

Generally, deprivation thinking is why Nice Guys play small. They don't believe they deserve good things. Or they believe that the Universe is a finite pie without enough good things. Nice Guys tend to resent anyone who seems to have what they lack.

This kind of mindset isn't just inaccurate, it can be downright debilitating. And Nice Guys are highly adept at finding ways to ensure their view of the world is never challenged. Thus, their deprivation thinking becomes a self-fulfilling prophecy. It keeps them stuck, wallowing in self-pity and unable to move forward.

"Deprivation thinking blinds Nice Guys to the beauty and bounty in this world," asserts Dr. Glover. "Nice Guys don't see glass as half empty; they see it as pretty much bone dry. This is why Nice Guys rarely live up to their potential or get what they want in life. They don't notice all the open doors of opportunity. And they definitely don't walk through them."

**INTEGRATED ACTION:**
✓ Do you engage in deprivation thinking? Do you believe there's not enough to go around? How does this affect your life and relationships? Write your answers in your journal.

# PITY PARTIERS

One of the more infuriating aspects of the Nice Guy Syndrome is that Nice Guys seem to have a crushing incapability to take ownership over their lives. Nice Guys constantly throw themselves pity parties. They play the victim, succumb to fear, and give away their personal power. This isn't necessarily their fault, however. Because of their childhood experiences, feeling like a victim is familiar to most Nice Guys.

Nice Guys tend to believe that others are the cause of all their problems in life. You can see it in their body language and hear it in their voices: *It's not fair. How come she gets to make the rules? How come everyone tries to take advantage of me? I always give more than I get.* The Nice Guy paradigm almost guarantees perpetual feelings of powerlessness.

Dr. Glover defines personal power as *a state of mind in which a person is confident that he can handle whatever may come.* Personal power allows one to successfully deal with problems and challenges. It isn't the absence of fear; it is the result of feeling fear but not succumbing to it. Unfortunately, Nice Guys are strangled by the memory of their childhood experiences and sacrifice their personal power by constantly giving into fear.[33]

"Pretty much everything Nice Guys do or don't do is governed by fear," says Dr. Glover. "Their thoughts are funneled through fear-encrusted neurons in their brains. Their interactions are dictated by the politics of fear."

---

33   Glover, Robert A. *No More Mr. Nice Guy* (Running Press, 2003) pp. 178-179

As Dr. Glover illustrates:

- Fear prevents a Nice Guy from asking for a raise.
- Fear keeps a Nice Guy from going back to school to get the education he needs to pursue a more fulfilling career.
- Fear prevents a Nice Guy from quitting a job he despises.
- Fear stops a Nice Guy from starting the business of his dreams.
- Fear keeps a Nice Guy from standing up for his values.
- Fear keeps a Nice Guy from honoring his own needs.
- Fear prevents a Nice Guy from being his authentic self.
- Fear prevents a Nice Guy from living the life he truly wants to live.

Certainly, everyone experiences fear – even those who seem to be fearless. Healthy fear provides a warning sign that danger is approaching. But this is different from the kind of fear that Nice Guys experience daily, which Dr. Glover refers to as *memory fear*. Nice Guys develop memory fear in childhood because their needs weren't met in timely and judicious ways. In adulthood, memory fear permeates the lives of Nice Guys.

"You know you are in memory fear when your emotional reaction seems out of proportion to the event," asserts Dr. Glover. "Nice Guys need to learn to ask themselves: *Hmmm, what's going on?* And use the event to help them clear out memory fear."

Due to their memory fear, Nice Guys interact with the world as though it is out to get them. They hunker down and play it safe. They avoid new situations, they procrastinate, they fail to finish what they start, and they try desperately to control the uncontrollable. As a result, they experience a great deal of needless suffering.

Additionally, Nice Guys often unconsciously reinforce the very behaviors they find intolerable. They don't take responsibility for how they let others treat them. Nice Guys never set boundaries; and boundaries – discussed in more detail later in this book - are essential for survival.

"Nice Guys must realize they can't insulate themselves from the chaotic, ever-changing realities of life," insists Dr. Glover. "All the Nice Guy paradigm does is create wimpy men who allow bullies to kick sand in their face. Nice Guys must stop playing the victim, embrace life's challenges, face their fears, and reclaim their personal power. Life isn't a merry-go-round; it's a roller-coaster. But when Nice Guys start taking back their personal power, they will begin to experience the world in all of its serendipitous beauty. It may not always be smooth or pretty, but it will be an adventure - one not to be missed."[34]

**INTEGRATED ACTION:**
- ✓ Are you throwing your self an endless pity party? Be honest with yourself, and write your answer in your journal.
- ✓ Do you give away your personal power? How so? Do you constantly play the victim? Do you succumb to fear? How does this affect your life and relationships? Be honest with yourself, and write your answers in your journal.

---

34  For more on how Nice Guys sacrifice their personal power, see Glover, Robert A. *No More Mr. Nice Guy* (Running Press, 2003) pp. 92-97

# TERRIBLE, HORRIBLE, NO GOOD, VERY BAD ENDERS

I t was a particularly humdrum afternoon when the following email came through from Jake:

*The last few years have been very difficult.*
*My life has been going downhill. I am engaged and the relationship isn't great.*
*I don't think I want to get married.*
*I got fired from my last job. I just started a new job.*
*I bury myself in work, even though I don't like it.*
*I get depressed. I have a lot of anxiety.*
*I desperately need to make some changes.*

Jake is in his mid-thirties and works as a mortgage broker. Born and raised in Manhattan, he has a delightfully thick New York accent. He now lives in West Palm Beach, Florida with his fiancee. They've been together for over five years.

"I'm pretty unhappy," admitted Jake, during our first coaching call, just a few days after I received his email. "But I don't really know what to do. My job is killing me. I guess I'm good at sales. But I don't really give a shit about mortgages. I'd much rather be doing something else. And my fiancée is constantly up my ass. She's really negative. She's relentless. She sees all her friends buying houses and getting married, and she feels she needs to do the same thing. So, all she does is nag me to get married and buy a house. But we can't even afford a house right now. And whenever we try to discuss a wedding, we just argue. Getting married isn't going to solve our issues. I mean, I don't even want to live in Florida. Basically, everything sucks. And the only way I know how to cope with it all is by drinking, which has caused me to do some shitty things in the past."

Jake let out a heavy sigh and buried his face in his palms. I allowed him a few moments of silence to collect his thoughts.

"How did it feel to share all that with me?" I then asked.

"Okay," he replied. "I definitely need to talk about it."

"Definitely," I agreed. "Do you mind if I ask you some questions?"

"Go for it," Jake insisted.

"Have you been looking for other jobs that you might like better?"

"No," said Jake.

"Why not?" I probed.

"Because I got fired from my last job. I can't just leave this one. My dad would probably kill me."

"But you're an adult. Have you told your dad how you're feeling?"

"No."

"What about your fiancée? Have you told her how you're feeling?"

"No."

"Have you told her how you're feeling about your relationship?"

"No."

"Why not?"

"I'm scared of how she'll react," acknowledged Jake.

"I understand," I said. "But can you see yourself marrying her? Getting a house with her? Spending the rest of your life with her? Is that what you want?"

"No, it's really not."

"So, why don't you tell her?"

"I mean, I love her. I care about her. I don't want to hurt her."

"But if you don't want to stay, isn't it more loving to leave?"

"I guess so," Jake muttered.

"So, do you want things to continue as they are? Is this the career you want? Is this the relationship you want? Is this the life you want? Is this the path you want to keep going down?

"No, it's not."

"So, why not change paths?"

"I'm not sure," answered Jake. "I obviously need to. It just seems like too much work. Like too many hard conversations. Like too much conflict. Like too many unknowns…"

For me, Jake's story was as relatable as it was heartbreaking. I know all too well what it feels like to be venturing down the wrong path. Tragically, though, Jake's story isn't unique. Nice Guys have been telling me similar stories - day after day, week after week - for years. And there's a reason. Nice Guys share an unfortunate characteristic: Nice Guys are terrible (horrible, no good, very bad) enders.

Nice Guys are especially terrible at ending relationships. When healthy people realize they are in a not-so-healthy relationship – or they have chosen a partner who lacks the qualities they desire – they move the fuck on. Not Nice Guys. Nice Guys double down on trying to fix the unfixable, and this just frustrates everyone involved.

Of course, being a terrible ender extends well beyond intimate relationships. Because of their flawed core beliefs, their need for approval, and their deprivation thinking, Nice Guys stay in all kinds of bad situations for way too long, even if they're miserable. They stay on the wrong path, despite the fact that it's leading them further away from where they want to go. Successful, self-assured people are good enders. But because Nice Guys are terrible enders, they almost never experience the success or the happiness they desire.

"Being a good ender might be the most important life skill for anyone who wants to live a kick-ass life," suggests Dr. Glover. "To be happy and successful, you must know how and when to remove yourself from toxic or dead-end situations. You must know when to cut your losses, backtrack, or take a mulligan. To paraphrase The Gambler,[35] good enders know when to hold 'em, know when to fold 'em, know when to walk away, and know when to run."

---

**INTEGRATED ACTION:**

✓ Are you a terrible ender? Do you stay in bad situations? How does this affect your life and relationships? Write your answers in your journal.

✓ Is there currently a situation in your life that needs to end? How can you be a good ender in this situation? Write down what you need to do, and then do it.

---

35 For you youngsters out there, "The Gambler" was a popular American song made famous by country singer Kenny Rogers. In 1980, the song won Rogers the Grammy Award for Best Male Country Vocal Performance.

# THE OPPOSITE OF A NICE GUY

Contrary to what many think when they first pick up *No More Mr. Nice Guy*, the book is not about being unkind. The opposite of a Nice Guy is not an asshole. The opposite of a Nice Guy is what Dr. Glover calls an ***Integrated Man***.

Being an Integrated Man means being able to accept all aspects of yourself.

As Dr. Glover describes, "an Integrated Man is able to embrace everything that makes him uniquely male: his power, his assertiveness, his courage, and his passion, as well as his imperfections, his mistakes, and his dark side."

- An Integrated Man has a strong sense of self.
- An Integrated Man takes responsibility for his own needs.
- An Integrated Man is comfortable with his masculinity and sexuality.
- An Integrated Man has integrity. He does what is right, not what is expedient.
- An Integrated Man is a leader. He is willing to provide for and protect those he cares about.
- An Integrated Man is clear and direct. He expresses his feelings with confidence.
- An Integrated Man can be nurturing and giving without caretaking or people-pleasing.

- An Integrated Man knows how to set boundaries. He is not afraid to work through conflict.

"An Integrated Man doesn't strive to be perfect or gain the approval of others," adds Dr. Glover. "He feels good about himself from the inside out. He seeks to improve himself – not so others will like him, but because he knows he can add value to the world.[36]

---

36  As Dr. Glover explains in *No More Mr. Nice Guy*, "Recovery from the Nice Guy Syndrome is not about going from one extreme to the other. The process of breaking free from ineffective Nice Guy patterns doesn't involve becoming "not nice." Rather, it means becoming **integrated**." For more information on what it means to be an Integrated Male, see Glover, Robert A. *No More Mr. Nice Guy* (Running Press, 2003) p. 28

# BREAKING FREE

If you believe you suffer from the Nice Guy Syndrome, there is an ever-growing wellspring of resources – thanks to Dr. Glover – to help you break free and become an Integrated Man. Dr. Glover has a number of certified coaches who are committed to helping Nice Guys start living the lives they want. There are men's retreats and support groups in cities all over the world. There are countless online forums, message boards, and communities. Of course, reading *No More Mr. Nice Guy* is the best place to start.

There is not a *right* way to break free from the Nice Guy Syndrome. Although, there might be a *wrong* way (trying to do it by yourself). There is not a specific timeline you need to follow, either. What's most important is that you make a lasting commitment to personal growth. And hopefully, you'll keep growing until the day you die.

Still, as Dr. Glover points out, Nice Guys tend to think strictly in black and white. They want all the ones and zeros to magically line up. They want precise, step-by-step instructions. They want to get rid of their Nice Guy Syndrome and they want to get rid of it *now*.

Nice Guys frequently ask things like: *What's the easiest way to break free from the Nice Guy Syndrome? Is there a guide I can follow? How long is this going to take?* The answers they get are rarely the answers they want.

In truth, breaking free from the Nice Guy Syndrome isn't easy. It requires a massive paradigm shift and major changes in behavior. It requires doing something different and facing your fears. It will almost certainly affect your personal relationships. There's no way around this.

*No More Mr. Nice Guy* is the closest thing you'll find to a guide. Use it as such for the rest of your life, because breaking free from the Nice Guy Syndrome is a journey that never ends. Based on my experience, however, I do believe that radical transformation is possible in a relatively short amount of time, as long as you challenge yourself and do the work. In fact, I believe that radical transformation is possible when you follow this simple roadmap:

# BUILD A FOUNDATION

Breaking free from the Nice Guy Syndrome begins with releasing toxic shame and breaking several bad habits. So, it is crucial that you build a solid foundation as you begin the process. Your foundation should consist of safe people. You must reveal yourself to and receive from these people. Because Nice Guys desperately seek the approval of women (and for a number of other reasons), your **safe people** should all be men, if possible.[37]

Dr. Glover has been leading men's groups for decades. He frequently acknowledges that the most significant aspects of his own recovery occurred in the context of a men's group. While you can certainly recover from the Nice Guy Syndrome without the help of an entire group, groups are probably the most effective tool for facilitating the recovery process. Based on my experience both attending and leading groups, I believe this to be true.

---

37   Glover, Robert A. *No More Mr. Nice Guy* (Running Press, 2001) pp. 33-34

# TAKE RESPONSIBILITY FOR YOUR OWN NEEDS (AND MAKE THEM A PRIORITY)

When I start working with a new client, I spend the first few coaching sessions trying to understand his world. I always ask: *What makes you happy? What lights you up inside? What do you need to live a rich and fulfilling life?* More often than not, he responds by telling me he has no fucking idea.

Nice Guys are terrible at getting their needs met. Most don't know what they're needs are or believe they're bad for even having needs. But taking responsibility for your own needs is a hallmark of maturity. As Dr. Glover likes to say, "Nobody was put on this planet to meet your needs except you and your parents. And your parents' job is done."

Treat yourself with love and respect. Learn to ask yourself: *What do I want? What feels right to me?* Then, do it. Ask others for help when you need it.

# TELL THE TRUTH, THE WHOLE TRUTH, AND NOTHING BUT THE TRUTH

Nice Guys are scared to tell the truth. They have an impressive ability to either withhold information or blatantly lie and still believe they are honest people. But Nice Guys are fundamentally dishonest. And dishonesty is childish and immature. It keeps you living in fear and perpetuates feelings of powerlessness and helplessness.

## THE FEAR-TRUTH FEEDBACK LOOP

The more you lie, the more fear you will have. The more fear you have, the more you will lie. When you start telling the truth, it reduces fear. And the less fear you have, the more honest you will naturally be. This is the **Fear-Truth Feedback Loop**.

"When I began I my Nice Guy recovery work, I committed to being honest," shares Dr. Glover.

"And my definition of honesty is: *the whole truth and nothing but the truth*. I made a commitment to myself and my wife at the time that when I noticed myself spinning up an untruth in my head, I would tell her the following: *I was going to tell you a lie. Here is the lie I was going to tell you. . . . And here is the truth...*

Learn to listen to that voice in your head that whispers: *Tell it this way, leave that part out, don't bring that up, look like you don't know what she is talking about, misdirect her attention, bring up her faults*. Then, tell the whole truth. This makes you more courageous. And it lets people get close to you.

People can handle a difficult truth. But they can't handle being lied to. Telling someone a difficult truth actually raises their trust level in you. If they catch you lying about little things, they will assume you lie about the big things as well."

When you tell the truth, you communicate to your unconscious mind that you are powerful and you can handle whatever comes your way. So, pay attention to the things you least want to reveal – the things you least want others to know. These are the things you most need to share. You may need to share a specific truth several times until you reveal all of it. If others react negatively, that's okay. Telling the truth is part of living with integrity. And it is far better than living a life of lies and deceit.

## SOOTHE YOURSELF

Because Nice Guy Syndrome is an anxiety-based disorder, Nice Guys must learn to soothe themselves. This is essential to breaking free. Here are three simple, yet effective ways to soothe yourself:

1. **Breathe**. When you're anxious, your breathing is shallow. Diaphragmatic breathing (deep, slow breathing) changes the oxygen content in your blood and calms your nervous system.

2. **Tell yourself you'll handle it**. Repeat it to yourself. No matter what happens, I'll handle it.

3. **Remind yourself of past successes**. If you're in a situation causing you anxiety, remind yourself that you've gotten through other similar situations.

## SET BOUNDARIES

As someone once said, "people only treat you one way, the way you allow them." When you start setting boundaries, you'll stop reinforcing the behaviors you find intolerable.

Dr. Glover frequently asserts that your power to set a boundary is predicated on your willingness to remove yourself from a situation, if necessary.

Don't defend yourself.

Don't argue over your boundaries.

Don't hang out with people who treat you badly. Ever.

# PRACTICE GRATITUDE

Because Nice Guys engage in deprivation thinking and believe there isn't enough to go around, they're often waiting for the other shoe to drop. They resent anyone who appears more blessed. But abundance is flowing all around us. Start living a life of gratitude. Each day, write down a few things for which you are grateful.

If you've made it this far, then you should have a solid understanding of the Nice Guy Syndrome. But we haven't even put a dent in Dr. Glover's work. In the pages that follow, you will learn about masculinity (and femininity), attraction, conscious dating, sex and sexuality, relationships, heartbreak, success, happiness, and more. Before you continue reading, though...

Take several deep breaths. Exhale slowly. Clear your mind.

Once relaxed, picture yourself living in an abundant world. In this abundant world, there are no limitations. Good things continuously flow. Imagine everything you have ever desired – a comfortable home, friends, love, joy, wealth, success, peace of mind. Picture yourself living your life surrounded by abundance.

Practice this visualization until it begins to feel real to you.

Open your arms, open your heart, open your mind.

Get out of the way and let it happen.

**INTEGRATED ACTION**

- ✓ If you feel so inclined, read (or-re-read) *No More Mr. Nice Guy*.
- ✓ Write down three safe people that might be able to provide support for you as you work to abolish your Nice Guy Syndrome. If nobody comes to mind, consider working with one of Dr. Glover's certified coaches or another men's coach.
- ✓ Look for a men's group in your area. If there isn't one, look for a virtual group that might work for you.

## WHAT IF IT WAS A GIFT?

In the epilogue of his first book, *Models*, number one *New York Times* bestselling author, Mark Manson writes:

*And in those times that it does become difficult, those times where you do get frustrated, and fall back to your unconfident beliefs, your desire for external validation, where you let yourself become swayed by the whims of others rather than your internal compass, you may feel lost or hopeless. This feeling of hopelessness may last for minutes, hours or days, but chances are if you push yourself, if you genuinely try to change yourself and re-orient how you interact with the world, then you will feel it at some point.*

*And for those times, let me share with you a phrase that has helped me and countless other men through those dire straits.*

*The phrase comes from Dr. Robert Glover and his book **No More Mr. Nice Guy**, one of the best books I've ever read on men's emotional health and development.*

*The phrase is: "What if it was a gift?"*

*Whatever happens to you, no matter how bad, no matter how bleak you feel. Ask yourself, "What if it was a gift?" And then try to rationalize a way it could be so.*

# PART II: MASCULINITY & FEMININITY

*The way a man penetrates the world should*
*be the same way he penetrates his woman:*
*not merely for personal gain or pleasure, but*
*to magnify love, openness, and depth.*
**- David Deida**

Boys have a pee-pee and girls have a woo-woo. This effectively sums up what I knew about men and women. If this is also the extent of your knowledge, you get no judgment from me.

Beyond our obvious biological distinctions, I never learned what makes the sexes so beautifully, curiously, and sometimes infuriatingly different. We never discussed it in Human Growth and Development class. My parents never sat me down and explained it. My older sister never enlightened me. My friends never gave me the inside scoop. But I don't blame them. I doubt they knew any more than I did.

Our culture teaches us about men and about women; but nobody teaches us what it truly *means* to be a man or a woman. Nobody teaches us the *essence* of the Masculine and the Feminine, and the energy that flows within each - perhaps because it's all a bit esoteric. Only the most enlightened seem to understand what defines Masculine and Feminine energies. The rest of us settle for just knowing that boys have a pee-pee and girls have a woo-woo.

The idea of Masculine and Feminine energies isn't new, nor is it all that abstruse. It is discussed most prominently, perhaps, by David Deida, spiritual teacher and author of *The Way of the Superior Man*. But I didn't come to understand it until I began working with Dr. Glover. And once I did, my world changed.

So, what are Masculine and Feminine energies?

What are these seemingly inexplicable forces in the cosmos?

And why does it matter?

We all have a Masculine and a Feminine side to us. And they can manifest differently within different contexts. Knowing this can raise you into higher consciousness and positively impact the quality of your life and relationships.

During his in-person workshops, Dr. Glover hands out his **Masculine Feminine Polarity Chart** (shown on the next page). Men pay good money to spend a few days with Dr. Glover. Yet, when they find this chart on their seats, many give it a quick once-over and then promptly toss it aside. But this is not the kind of information you should toss aside. It is the kind of information you should hang prominently on your refrigerator, allowing it to serve as a constant reminder for how to show up in the world.

In this section, you'll learn the characteristics that define Masculine and Feminine energy, and how to navigate between them. You'll learn what most women seek and why many of us are looking for love in all the wrong places. You'll also learn why it's important to embrace both your Masculine side and your Feminine side, and how this can help you become a better, happier, and more Integrated Man.

## Masculine and Feminine Polarity

*"What is most beautiful in virile men is something feminine;*
*what is most beautiful in feminine women is something masculine." - Susan Sontag*

| MASCULINE | | FEMININE |
|---|---|---|
| Does |  | Is Done To |
| Penetrates | | Penetrated |
| Internally validated through masterful action | | Externally validated through attention, praise, and desire |
| Seeks freedom | | Seeks security |
| Desires differentiation | | Desires fusion |
| Activated by challenge | | Activated by connection |
| Constant, solid, unwavering | | Ever-changing |
| The source of love (intention into action) | | The seeker of love (desire to be filled) |

| **Higher Masculine** (Conscious and Open) | **Higher Feminine** (Conscious and Open) |
|---|---|
|  | |
| Masterfully penetrates women and world (feminine) | Welcomes and opens to masculine penetration |
| Husbands own feminine and gives from the overflow | Reflects and reciprocates love received |
| Magnetically attracts all things feminine | Magnetically attracted to masculine consciousness |
| Keeps giving even when the world doesn't give back | Stays open even when hurting or feeling unloved |
| **Lower Masculine** (Fearful and Closed) | **Lower Feminine** (Fearful and Closed) |
| Controlling, rigid, dominating | Helpless, needy, insecure |
| Rageful and aggressive | Resentful and passive-aggressive |
| Defends and justifies behavior | Takes things personally and feels victimized |
| Attacks when frightened | Withdraws when frightened |
| Hurts before hurt | Hurts as hurt |

# THE MASCULINE

I f you remember one thing about the Masculine, remember this: **The Masculine does.** The Masculine penetrates. He penetrates his partner and He penetrates the world. He's supposed to, anyway.

Before you continue, please note that I will use the word "He" (capitalized) when referencing masculine energy; and the word "She" (capitalized) when referencing Feminine energy. This is merely a way to simplify the language.

Please also note that this is not intended to be a commentary on gender or gender roles. It is about energy - the polarities of the universe.

Men and women have both Masculine and Feminine energy. Women can penetrate from their Masculine and men can receive in their Feminine. If the words "Masculine" and "Feminine" carry too much weight for you, consider substituting them with whichever words you see fit.

The Masculine is internally validated through masterful action. He seeks freedom. He desires the ability to do what He wants, what feels right to him. The Masculine needs a mission. He is activated by challenge. He is constant, solid, and unwavering.[38]

Have you ever known a man without any kind of mission? A man without a mission is a man without purpose, a man without drive, a man without passion. A man without a mission is not constant, solid, or unwavering; he is lost and confused.

As Dr. Glover likes to say, "Men are most excited when they face a challenge and then conquer it. Bliss is when we conquer a challenge and then we rest into nothingness."

The Masculine builds dams, slays dragons, and cures disease. He sees everything as a problem to be solved.

But…He is something of a paradox.

He believes that perpetual calm will follow his victory. When the calm is inevitably disturbed by a new challenge, He becomes resentful. But He feels alive again when rising to face this new challenge.

When stressed, the Masculine often turns inward, thinking and analyzing, preferring to be left alone until he thinks of a solution. The Masculine brain is a problem-solving machine. Facts tend to replace feelings. In a relationship, the Masculine tends to see his partner's feelings as problems to be solved.

Because the Masculine is defined by doing - by passion and purpose - it rarely ends well when a man makes a woman his top priority.

"I've worked with countless men who have never discovered and pursued their passions, or who have sacrificed their passions to focus on pleasing other people," shares Dr. Glover. "I made the latter mistake for the first 25 years of my adult life. It cost me not only my relationships, but my own life

---

38  Glover, Robert A. "Lesson Five: Masculine & Feminine. Or, Why do Women do that?" *All The Way In* (TPI University. www.drglover.com)

energy. A man must make his passions his number one priority. By doing so he gives his woman (or women) something to be attracted to. Once he makes something else his number one priority, he loses the masculine energy that naturally attracts Feminine energy."

The day I learned what defines the Masculine was the day I began living differently. I stopped seeking validation from the Feminine and started focusing solely on my mission, purpose, and passions. In doing so, I vastly improved my relationships with women and, more importantly, my relationship with myself.

When you make your passions your number one priority, you will begin to align with your true Masculine nature. And you will be amazed by the beauty that starts to unfold.

---

**INTEGRATED ACTION:**

- ✓ Write down at least 20 things you would like to do before you die (otherwise known as a Bucket List). Plan to start doing these things.
- ✓ Practice living a life of passion. Shave with passion. Clean with passion. Work with passion. Fuck with passion. Try this for a week. Write down how it feels to live a life of passion.
- ✓ Make a copy of the Masculine and Feminine Polarity Chart. Or download it from bigstickbook.com. Study it and use it as a guide.

---

# THE FEMININE

While the Masculine does, **the Feminine is done to**. She is penetrated by the Masculine and the world. She is fluid and constantly changing.

The Feminine is validated by praise, love, and intimacy. Her deepest longing is for connection.

When the Feminine is stressed, she wants immediate resolution. She will talk to others about what is troubling her. The Feminine often sees change – quitting her job, rearranging the furniture, leaving a relationship - as the answer to most problems.[39]

"The Masculine can keep the same haircut for life," offers Dr. Glover. "But this would be hell for the Feminine."

The Feminine wants to feel good *right now*. She will paradoxically trade long-term comfort for short-term gratification. The Feminine will eat ice cream when She feels fat, or shop when She is stressed about money. She will sleep with the conniving, capricious Bad Boy. She knows he is trouble. She knows he's not a viable life partner. But he makes her feel something. And how she *feels* is everything.

---

39   Glover, Robert A. "Lesson Five: Masculine & Feminine. Or, Why do Women do that?" *All The Way In* (TPI University. www.drglover.com)

> *Don't analyze your woman. The feminine's moods and opin-*
> *ions are like weather patterns. They are constantly changing,*
> *severe and gentle, and they have no single source. No analysis*
> *will work. There is no linear chain of cause and effect that*
> *can lead to the kernel of the "problem." There is no problem,*
> *only a storm, a breeze, a sudden change in weather. And the*
> *bases of these storms are the high- and low-pressure systems*
> *of love. When a woman feels love flowing deeply, her mood*
> *can instantly evaporate into joy, regardless of the supposed*
> *reason for the mood.*
>
> **– David Deida, *The Way of the Superior Man***

For the Feminine, feelings can become facts. And because feelings can easily change, so can Feminine logic. Ever wonder why women so frequently seem to change their minds? What if you saw women as **the weather** like Deida suggests?

When we talk about the Feminine, however, we are not just talking about women. We are also talking about the Feminine within ourselves. The relationship we have with our own Feminine is part of the foundation upon which we can build fulfilling relationships with other Feminine creatures.

Because the Feminine is done to – and being done to is often far from enjoyable – the Feminine is always vulnerable. The #MeToo Movement, for example, was sparked by women standing up to say: *I've been done to, and it did not feel good.* Nearly all women – of all ages – have in some way been hurt by men. We men must learn to embrace and celebrate the Feminine while being consciously powerful and Masculine.

**INTEGRATED ACTION:**

✓ How would you be different – and how would your relationships be different – if you knew that women are like the weather? Write your answer in your journal.

✓ How can you embrace the feminine while being consciously powerful and masculine? Write your answer in your journal.

# DEFAULT STATES

Certainly, not all men are alike and not all women are alike. There are women who are more masculine than feminine, and men who are more feminine than masculine. There are women with more male-type brains (engineers, programmers), and men with more female-type brains (decorators, nurses). There are exceptions to every rule.

If we are conscious and present, we can fluidly access both our masculine and feminine sides.[40] Generally, though, most of us feel the best when we operate from our default state, particularly in relationships. But many of us have unknowingly been programmed to operate from our non-default state. As Dr. Glover points out, "this is likely why there are so many soft males and so many controlling women."

## HIGHER AND LOWER STATES

Knowing that we can consciously switch energetic states, let's revisit part of Dr. Glover's polarity diagram:

---

40  Glover, Robert A. "Lesson Five: Masculine & Feminine. Or, Why do Women do that?" *All The Way In* (TPI University. www.drglover.com)

| **Higher Masculine**<br>(Conscious and Open) | **Higher Feminine**<br>(Conscious and Open) |
|---|---|
| Masterfully penetrates<br>women and world (feminine) | Welcomes and opens<br>to masculine penetration |
| Husbands own feminine<br>and gives from the overflow | Reflects and reciprocates<br>love received |
| Magnetically attracts<br>all things feminine | Magnetically attracted to<br>masculine consciousness |
| Keeps giving even when<br>the world doesn't give back | Stays open even when<br>hurting or feeling unloved |
| **Lower Masculine**<br>(Fearful and Closed) | **Lower Feminine**<br>(Fearful and Closed) |
| Controlling, rigid, dominating | Helpless, needy, insecure |
| Rageful and aggressive | Resentful and passive-aggressive |
| Defends and justifies behavior | Takes things personally<br>and feels victimized |
| Attacks when frightened | Withdraws when frightened |
| Hurts before hurt | Hurts as hurt |

Now, let's examine an all-too-common scenario: You've just returned home from work and you're feeling stressed. You want nothing more than to have sex with your woman. But instead of leading her into her feminine and lovingly ravishing her, you *ask* her for sex. She declines. So, you start begging. When she declines again, you throw a temper tantrum and ask her why she never wants to have sex. Then, you retreat to the basement, turn on the television, and give your woman the silent treatment. In this scenario, where do you fall on the diagram?[41]

Healthy relationships consist of two healthy individuals – individuals who can move fluidly between their Higher Masculine (masterfully penetrating, giving without expectation) and their Higher Feminine (open to penetration, open even when hurt). This is a beautiful dance when two people – of any gender and sexual orientation – can consciously flow between their

---

41  The answer is: Lower Feminine.

Masculine and Feminine sides, both giving and receiving, doing and being done to. This is polarity.

Abusive and controlling people are generally in their Lower Masculine, while moody and insecure people are generally in their Lower Feminine. As you might guess, men and women who are generally in their lower energetic states co-create toxic, unhealthy relationships. But men and women who are generally in their higher energetic states can co-create magic.

Assuming you are a mature and psychologically sound person, if you find yourself in your Lower Feminine, for example, you can consciously move to your Higher Masculine, and aim to bring your partner into higher consciousness as well.

## A TOP & BOTTOM

In his decades working with men and women — both individually and as couples — Dr. Glover observed that the majority of intimate relationships seem to work best when the "default" masculine partner takes responsibility for setting the tone and taking the lead while the default feminine partner follows this lead.

"This doesn't actually have anything to do with what kind of genitalia someone has," asserts Dr. Glover. "And it does not mean that one person is burdened with making all of the decisions. But in every relationship, there does tend to be a natural top and a natural bottom, a default pitcher and a default catcher, so to speak. This is especially true in emotional terms."

Adds Dr. Glover, "Remember, this is about energy and polarity. The default Masculine partner tends to set the emotional tone in the relationship rather than reacting to or trying to fix the tone set by the default Feminine partner. Masculine leadership might involve managing the budget or deciding what is for dinner, but typically, these types of leadership tasks are best shared...or negotiated depending on the situation."

**INTEGRATED ACTION:**

✓ Do you think you've been operating from your non-default mode? Do you tend to operate from your Lower Masculine or Lower Feminine? Write your answers in your journal.

✓ Talk to a safe person about masculine and feminine energies, and how they manifest in your life.

# LOOKING FOR LOVE IN ALL THE WRONG PLACES

Due in part to societal conditioning – especially in America – both men and women seem to be looking for love in all the wrong places.[42] As a result, there are a lot of very unhappy people.

Men are constantly looking for fulfillment and validation from women. When Tom Cruise said 'You complete me' to Renee Zellweger in the film *Jerry Maguire*, it gloriously fucked us up. Many men now look to women to not only make them happy, but also transform and complete their lives. Men also look for love in cheap substitutes like strip clubs and porn.

Meanwhile, women are seeking fulfillment and validation from their careers. They spend each day in their Masculine – commuting, working, running errands, managing crises. Then, they return home only to make dinner, take care of the kids, and do household chores. From an evolutionary perspective, almost all work is Masculine because work is *doing*. And for many women today, the work never stops. Women rarely get to revert to their Feminine.

The point is, we are all operating in a way that goes against our very nature.

---

42  Dr. Glover frequently discusses this subject during his in-person and virtual Total Personal Integration (TPI) workshops. More information can be found on www. drglover.com.

After being in her Masculine all day, how do you think your woman feels when you come home and ask - or worse, *beg* - her for sex?

How do you think she views sex when you present it as one more chore for her to do?

How do you think she views *you* when you are in your Lower Feminine – when you are needy, resentful, and passive-aggressive?

How do you think She might feel if instead you ravished Her, showered Her with love, made Her feel wanted, and allowed Her to melt into your Masculine presence (without any attachment to outcome)?

As Dr. Glover insists, "If you consciously lead from your Masculine, your partner has the opportunity to open into her Higher Feminine. This is such a gift. In cisgender, heterosexual terms, a woman (default Feminine partner) cannot follow where a Man (default Masculine partner) does not lead. So, lead and see if She follows. Most importantly, lead and see if She likes it."

## THE SOURCE OF LOVE

Men are often surprised to hear Dr. Glover assert that the Masculine is the source of love. We tend to see women as mothers, as givers, and as nurturing caretakers, and can't help but assume they are the source of love. But as Dr. Glover points out: "Love is not a sentiment, not a feeling, not words. Love is action taken in the best interest of ourselves or other people. If the Masculine is action and the Feminine is reception, if the Masculine does and the Feminine is done to, how can the Feminine be 'love'? If somebody loves you, you know it because they act lovingly towards you. The Feminine is the seeker of love, activated by nurturing and connection."

Since we all have a Masculine and a Feminine side, we are capable of loving in an intentional, actionable way. But it is the Feminine side in all us that craves connection and the flow of love.

"If you are a man seeking love from default Feminine creatures, you might be in for some real disappointments," warns Dr. Glover. "And yes, this

might be especially confusing since most of us have been taught to look to
the Feminine for love."

---

**INTEGRATED ACTION:**

✓ How have you been looking for love in all the wrong places?
Do you seek fulfillment and validation from women? Write your
answers in your journal.

---

# HUSBANDING YOUR OWN FEMININE

Because we all have a masculine and a feminine side, men also need to be nurtured. You have a feminine bucket that needs to be filled. But you cannot rely on women to fill your feminine bucket. You must take responsibility for ***husbanding your own feminine***.[43]

As a man, you can repeatedly ask yourself:

*What do I need right now?*

*Do I need challenge* (a Masculine need)?

*Or do I need nurturing* (a Feminine need)?

If you are depressed or unmotivated; if you have low energy; if you are just wasting time, then you likely need challenge. You need to get out of the house and do something Masculine.

If you are seeking validation; if you are feeling hurt or victimized, then you likely need nurturing. In this case, you need to husband your own Feminine.

Husbanding your own Feminine requires slowing down, opening up, relaxing, and receiving. It is a way of giving to yourself. Almost anything you can do for yourself that is agenda-free qualifies as husbanding your own Feminine.

---

43 The term "husbanding your own feminine" was coined by author, intimacy coach, and spiritual teacher, John Wineland, in his book *From the Core*. Dr. Glover frequently discusses husbanding your own feminine during his in-person and virtual Total Personal Integration (TPI) workshops.

Do yoga, nap without guilt, walk mindfully, meditate, spend time in nature, soak in a hot tub, get a massage – while taking the word "do" out of the equation as much as possible. Add what you want to this list and start consciously planning these things into your day. Don't rely on anyone else to fill your Feminine bucket.

**INTEGRATED ACTION:**
- ✓ Practice asking yourself what you need – challenge or nurturing.
- ✓ Practice husbanding your own feminine. Do something today to fill your feminine bucket.

# WHAT WOMEN SEEK

I f you remember one thing about women (or the Feminine part of any person) remember this: **The Feminine is a security-seeking creature.**[44] This can be confusing because some of the most seemingly powerful women are actually highly Feminine. When the Feminine doesn't feel safe or protected by the Masculine, it tends to take charge – and this usually isn't pretty. Understanding this has forever changed the way I navigate my relationships with women. It has also changed how I navigate the world. It can do the same for you.

Think about it: Throughout our evolutionary history, women have been exceedingly – and horrifyingly - vulnerable. Generally, women are physically weaker. They carry babies and often have small children around them.

Women have never felt safe walking this planet.

In tribal times, women looked to men to be their providers and protectors. They relied on the tribe for physical and emotional security. But times have changed.

Women today can adequately take care of their own needs in society. They live on their own. They succeed on their own. They thrive on their own. They don't *need* men. Except that Mother Nature wired women to turn to men to be their primary security system. And you can't really argue with

---

44   See Glover, Robert A. Dating Essentials for Men (Robert A. Glover, Ph.D, Inc. 2019) pp. 74-75

Mother Nature. Whether they know it or not, most women today are seeking emotional security from men (more so than financial security).[45]

Sadly, most women have been repeatedly let down by men in their lives. This pattern often began with their fathers and continued to play out in their relationships with passive, unavailable, or abusive men. Women will often attempt to take the lead in relationships because they believe it's all they can do to feel safe, which can make them seem moody, controlling, and angry.

Women feel best when they feel secure - and for the Feminine, emotional security is often a fleeting experience. Let this sink in. Knowing this can bring you into higher consciousness. (It can help you let go of the expectation that once you've shown up in a way that creates a sense of security and well-being for a woman, it will last for more than a few moments.)

If you are anxious, if you are passive, if you are dishonest, if you are constantly seeking the approval of others, how do you think your woman feels around you? Do you think she feels safe and secure?[46]

The next time you find yourself arguing with your woman – or any woman – because she is behaving in a way you don't understand, pause and ask yourself: *Am I behaving in a way that makes her feel secure?* There's a good chance you're not. And there's a good chance she's behaving the way she is because her sense of security has been threatened.

---

**INTEGRATED ACTION:**
✓ Think back on the last time you had an argument with a woman. How was she acting? How were you acting? Do you think you were acting in a way that made her feel secure? Write about the experience in your journal.

---

45 Mother Nature is a real bitch sometimes.
46 Obviously not.

# CONSCIOUS MASCULINE LEADERSHIP

Now that you have a basic understanding of Masculine and Feminine energies, surely you have lingering questions. Like, now what? And how can I apply this information to my life in a practical way? You're wise to ask.

Foremost, let's acknowledge that in today's culture the terms 'masculine' and 'feminine' are often used in negative ways to trigger an emotional response. The public discourse around gender has become mired in controversy. That's not what we're talking about, however. So, let's not go there.

Let's also assume the 80/20 rule. Again, not all men are alike and not all women are alike. But let's assume that the majority (80 percent) of women want to be led by a conscious, masterful, open-hearted man. (This is the opposite of being *controlled* by a man.)

"The deepest Feminine desire is to be done to - in other words, to be opened and blissed," explains Dr. Glover. "But if a woman is in her Masculine all day - working, running errands, doing - it's hard for her to revert to her Feminine when she gets home. Most women aren't great at making that switch. So, part of our role in conscious Masculine leadership is to lead our partner back to her Feminine state - or at least give her a choice."

But what does that mean?

Foremost, it's vital to understand that Conscious Masculine Leadership does *not* mean "control." In relationships, it means lovingly giving your partner options that she either cannot give herself or would not instinctively choose on her own. It can also mean that you take charge of a situation so she has one less thing on her plate for which she feels responsible.

"Think of a male partner on the dance floor," illustrates Dr. Glover. "He leads his partner in ways that she will find both enjoyable and occasionally challenging. She has the choice to dance with him – follow his lead or not. He is not forcing anything on her – he is giving her a choice. And odds are, she will have more fun if she relaxes into his leadership and follows without resistance. Again, this is all a choice. And it's interesting how - in general - women sure do love to dance."

Leading a woman into her Feminine often means helping her slow down. This can be as simple as saying: *I've poured you a glass of wine. Let's talk and relax.* Or you might take her hand and say: *Let's go for a walk.* Anything that moderates the tempo, builds connection, and opens a pathway for the flow of love can be an effective way to lead a woman into her Feminine.

"Another way of leading a woman into her Feminine is by creating polarity, or a dynamic of dominance and submission," explains Dr. Glover. "Dominance and submission are two hot words, I know. But remember, this is all conscious and open-hearted, and involves choice. Any time the default Masculine partner leads and sets the tone in a conscious, loving way - that's the kind of dominance we're talking about. It invites the default Feminine partner to open and relax into the bliss of her Feminine, which is submission. And – wait for it – these roles can be consciously switched any time in a relationship. They are not gender specific."

Let's say, for example, that a woman comes home from the office and she's in a terrible mood. She's been in her Masculine all day. From the moment she woke up until the moment she pulled the car into the garage, she was *doing*. She was commuting. She was working. She was dealing with her boss, her co-workers, and her customers. Perhaps she ran errands. She was - to put it simply - getting things done. But now, she's home, and there are even more things to get done. As a default Feminine creature, she's out of her element. She's been out of her element all day. She can do it, of course. She can get things done. Most women do - every single day - at an impressively high level. But that doesn't mean it feels good.

It takes its toll.

"When women spend a lot of time in their Masculine, they tend to become irritable, pessimistic, negative, and controlling," explains Dr. Glover. "Unfortunately, most have never learned how to turn it off – how to transition out of their Masculine which requires 'doing' and slip into their Feminine which allows them to be 'done to' and  receive. Many cope by turning to junk-food comfort - television, social media, wine, food, drama – anything to medicate the pain of spending so much time in their Masculine."

So, if your woman walks through the door in a terrible mood - if she is irritable  or sullen - try giving her a loving command, as Dr. Glover suggests. A loving command might sound like:

*Go change your clothes and put on something comfortable.*

*Sit down and tell me about your day while I rub your feet.*

*I've put a glass of wine next to the tub and drawn you a bath. Go relax for a bit.*

*Come here so I can nibble your neck.*

"If you lead and she follows, you have created polarity," affirms Dr. Glover. "This is the kind of energetic interplay that makes it easy for her to relax, open, and experience the depths of Feminine bliss."

## THE POWER OF POLARITY

Indeed, women can open their own doors. They can draw their own baths. They can pour their own wine. They can decompress in their own ways. But creating polarity through conscious, Masculine leadership is a gift you can give to the women in your life.[47]

"There's almost always going to be polarity in an intimate relationship," affirms Dr. Glover. "Sure, in some relationships you might have two people who aren't stronger one way or the other. They resolve problems without arguing. They are more friends than lovers. But this is the minority. In the majority of relationships, there's a strong Masculine presence and a strong Feminine presence."

Unfortunately, many men - particularly Nice Guys - spend much of their time in their lower Feminine state. They feel victimized, they take things personally, they withdraw. And when men are in this lower Feminine state, they often attract women who are in their lower Masculine state. Is this kind of relationship you want? I suspect it's not what your partner wants.

---

### AVOIDING THE ROLLER COASTER

Men frequently ask Dr. Glover how they can avoid the emotional roller coaster of the Feminine.

His answer is: You can't. No matter what.

But here are some things to keep in mind:

In relationships, praise works better than criticism. Praise the things you like. Praise your partner's good behavior.

If something needs to be addressed, approach it as a team. Ask: *Do you have any ideas of how we can work on this?* Even if it's YOUR problem, approach it as a team.

Don't push for apologies or accountability. The Feminine apologizes by moving closer to you, by becoming more playful.

---

47  You can give the gift of conscious Masculine leadership to all the women in your life, not just your romantic partner. You can consciously lead your mother, your sister, your daughter, your granddaughter…

# SERENITY NOW

To help men better understand polarity - the Yin and Yang of Masculine and Feminine interplay – Dr. Glover points to the Serenity Prayer, which is often connected with 12-step programs like Alcoholics Anonymous. The prayer is simple yet profound:

*God grant me the serenity*

*To accept the things I cannot change;*

*The courage to change the things I can;*

*And the wisdom to know the difference.*

The Serenity Prayer folds neatly into Dr. Glover's interpretation of Masculine and Feminine polarity.

*God grant me the serenity to accept the things I cannot change;*

"This is conscious, higher Feminine, if you think about it," asserts Dr. Glover. "While many things in life may not feel good, they are out of our control. Resisting what is…causes suffering. There is a whole lot of shit we cannot change. Conscious surrender and acceptance, a higher Feminine trait, is a gift we can give ourselves or a loved one."

*The courage to change the things I can and the wisdom to know the difference.*

"This is conscious, higher Masculine," explains Dr. Glover. "Many things in life are not easy, but we do have options. And we can take action to alter our circumstances. We occupy our higher Masculine when we step up, take responsibility, and do what we can to change things around us for the better – even when it's difficult or frightening or inconvenient."

\*\*\*

The concept of Yin and Yang - of Masculine and Feminine polarity - has been with us for thousands of years. And it can still be beneficial today.

"Addressing the abuses of the patriarchy, challenging toxic masculine behavior, and releasing men and women from the tyranny of rigid and demeaning gender roles - these things are long overdue," affirms Dr. Glover.

"But these kinds of problems won't be solved by banishing terms like 'masculine' and 'feminine' or 'dominance' and 'submission' from our discourse. This only robs us of the depth of choice we have - the choice to consciously relax into our Feminine or consciously step up into our Masculine. Consciousness really is key."

**INTEGRATED ACTION:**
 Write down some ways you might be able to lead the women in your life into their Higher Feminine. Try one.

TONY ENDELMAN

# PART III: ATTRACTION

*All abundance starts first in the mind.*

**- Anonymous**

Throughout history, men have accomplished some truly remarkable things.

Jadav Payeng, for example, single-handedly (yes, single-handedly) planted a 1360-acre forest in Northern India, creating an entirely new ecosystem.

Scientists like Edward Jenner and Jonas Salk saved billions of lives by developing some of the world's most important medications.

Gutenberg developed the printing press.

Edison created the light bulb.

Farnsworth invented the television.

One guy even figured how to make a necktie that doubles as a flask.

Men have given us the wheel, the hammer and nail, the compass, paper, the steam engine, the internal combustion engine, the automobile, the airplane, nuclear fission, the Internet, and the smartphone. Men have fought and won wars, built cities, and explored the Universe well beyond Earth's atmosphere. Men have made mind-blowing technological advances that have solved some of the world's most complex problems. For most of human existence, men have been unyielding in their pursuit of greatness.

And yet, life still presents men with a seemingly impossible feat – an unsolvable mystery, an uncrackable code, an endlessly aggravating enigma. No matter how intelligent or imaginative they may be, many men haven't the slightest fucking idea how to attract high-quality women. The mere thought of approaching women fills them with existential dread.

Are you one of these men?

So was I.

And so was Dr. Glover.

After getting divorced for the second time, Dr. Glover faced a stark reality: He was single, middle-aged, and clueless. He hadn't dated since college, and he sucked at it back then.

"When I was younger and wanted to ask a woman out," remembers Dr. Glover, "I would first spend several weeks imagining what it would be like to be with her. Usually, my fear, my self-limiting beliefs, and my lack of social skills prevented me from ever actually talking to any women. If I ever did work up the courage to approach a woman, I would wait until the last minute, walk up to her awkwardly, and mutter something like, 'I don't suppose you might want to maybe go out with me tonight, would you?' When she would inevitably turn me down, I'd feel like an idiot, walk away in shame, and never talk to her again."

Occasionally, Dr. Glover did manage to get a girlfriend. He would then hang onto her for dear life - no matter how incompatible they were - fearing that he may never find another companion. This same pattern played out in both of his marriages. Dr. Glover frequently acknowledges that he shouldn't have gone out on more than three dates with either of his first two wives. He stayed married to each of them for more than a decade.

So, when Dr. Glover found himself unattached and in his mid-forties, he realized that if he was going to have a satisfying romantic life, he needed to go about meeting women differently. He began reading many of the classic books on attraction, dating, and seduction, while drawing insights from his own work in *No More Mr. Nice Guy.* He perused online forums populated by other seemingly clueless men. He listened to CDs and watched DVDs created by supposedly skilled pickup artists. Then, unlike most men, he actually *applied* what he was learning to determine what worked and what didn't. Dr. Glover approached the process of meeting women as a kind of scientific experiment. And it didn't take long to see positive results.

"To my surprise, I found that getting a woman to talk to me, give me her phone number, go out with me, and even have sex with me wasn't nearly as difficult as I thought it would be," recalls Dr. Glover. "I was frequently amazed by how easy it was when I applied the right principles. Eventually, many of my clients started to notice how much success I was having with women and begged me to teach them what I was doing."

Honoring the request of his clients, Dr. Glover launched four *Dating Essentials for Men* online courses in 2007. The courses quickly became successful and provided men with a breath of fresh air from much of the other dating advice circulating the internet. Several years later, in 2018, Dr. Glover compiled his insights around attraction and dating, and published them in his second book, *Dating Essentials for Men: The Only Dating Guide You Will Ever Need*. In 2022, he released the book's companion guide, *Dating Essentials For Men: Frequently Asked Questions*.

Today, there is no shortage of dating advice for the taking. The internet has given rise to an endless cavalcade of self-proclaimed attraction gurus promising to teach men how to become masters of seduction who, with just a few simple techniques, can get any woman to willingly open her heart... and her legs. Many of these "gurus" feed on the desperation of lonely and misguided souls who would do anything (and pay anything) to wake up next to the naked female form. Indeed, some pickup advice is helpful because it pushes men to step outside their comfort zones. But much of it is manipulative nonsense that requires men to be creepily inauthentic. It turns men into what Dr. Glover calls "geeks with techniques."

I am not a dating guru; nor do I want to be. In fact, I am much happier (and remarkably more productive) when chasing women isn't my primary focus. But I can confidently say that I enjoy an active dating life – the kind of dating life I never thought I'd have - because I decided to challenge my self-limiting beliefs, face some of my most ridiculous fears, and follow the basic principles that Dr. Glover teaches. Meeting women is an endeavor I once found equally terrifying and depressing. Now, I find it delightfully fun and easy. No canned openers, no rehearsed pickup lines, no DHV stories, no negging, no framing, no peacocking, no hypnosis, no cold reading, no aura reading, no magic tricks. No bullshit.

In this section, you will learn Dr. Glover's framework for meeting and attracting women. More importantly, you will learn to identify – and challenge – your self-limiting beliefs. You will learn what it takes to overcome your fear of rejection, soothe your anxiety, and cultivate more confidence. You might even learn to enjoy yourself along the way.

Most men make meeting women far too difficult. What you are about to learn is fundamentally simple. But it very well might challenge you in ways that you have never been challenged before, particularly if you are someone who constantly *thinks* about taking action but never actually does.

There is no substitute for taking action. As Dr. Glover likes to say, this shit works if you work it. And you can start working it today by simply doing what Dr. Glover commands at the end of every one of his *Dating Essentials* podcasts: *Get out of the house, expand your route, linger in public, talk to people everywhere you go, test for interest, and walk through the open doors.*

**INTEGRATED ACTION:**

✓ Does the thought of approaching a beautiful woman cripple you with fear? Why or why not? Write your answers down in your journal.

✓ When was the last time you approached a beautiful woman? What was the experience like? Write your answers down in your journal.

✓ How important is it to you to learn how to attract women? How would your life change if you solved this problem? Write your answers down in your journal.

✓ This week: Get out of the house, expand your route, linger in public, talk to people everywhere you go, test for interest, and walk through the open doors.

# YOUR DIRTY SLBS

Believe it or not, your mind is a fucking liar. It lies to you all the time. It lies to you about yourself, it lies to you about the world, and it lies to you about women. These lies usually take the form of Self-Limiting Beliefs (SLBs). Your SLBs are keeping you from having the romantic life you desire.[48]

*I'm too short.*

*I'm too inexperienced.*

*I'm not successful enough.*

*I'm not rich enough.*

*I have a small dick*

*I'm a loser.*

*Why would a good woman want me?*

*Women are just whores and gold-diggers.*

*All the good women are taken.*

*Blah, blah, blah.*

*Wah, wah, wah.*

Are these the kind of thoughts you have about yourself and about women?

You're not alone.

---

48  Glover, Robert A. *Dating Essentials for Men* (Robert A. Glover, Ph.D, Inc. 2019) pp. 17-21

I was completely ignored by women (or so I thought) in high school and college, and throughout my twenties. I believed that I was deeply unattractive. I believed this was my lot in life. I believed that because I don't look like a model or a movie star, beautiful women would never want to date me, let alone get naked with me. That is, until I decided to challenge those beliefs.

Your self-limiting beliefs have gotten you where you probably are right now – lonely and frustrated with your dick in one hand and a self-help book in the other. If you want to change your relationships with women, then you first need to change your relationship with your mind. It's time to stop believing the bullshit your mind tells you. It's time to get rid of your dirty SLBs.

---

**INTEGRATED ACTION:**
✓ In your journal, write down a list of your self-limiting beliefs. Writing them down will bring them to the forefront of your consciousness, allowing you to both challenge and overcome them. Keep this list handy because you will need to revisit it.

---

# THE PARADIGM EFFECT

Because you - like every other human being - grew up in an imperfect family and an imperfect world, you internalized certain SLBs during childhood. As you grew into adolescence and adulthood, you continued to add evidence that upheld your SLBs. This is the *paradigm effect*.[49] And it's likely intertwined with a bit of confirmation bias.[50]

Your life paradigm causes you to seek out, amplify, and retain any information that seems to support your SLBs. It also causes you to minimize, ignore, or deny the existence of any information that seems to challenge your

---

49  Glover, Robert A. *Dating Essentials for Men* (Robert A. Glover, Ph.D, Inc. 2019) pp. 21-22

50  Confirmation bias is the tendency to interpret new evidence as confirmation of one's existing beliefs.

SLBs. Odds are your life paradigm likes to rear its ugly head most often in the presence of beautiful women.

Let's say, for example, that an attractive woman flashes you a smile – or better yet, strikes up a conversation with you. You would probably assume that she is just being polite. She couldn't possibly be expressing interest in you. Such behavior would contradict all your SLBs, especially the belief that women aren't attracted to you.

If you see yourself as unattractive and unlovable, you will also assume that everyone else sees you the same way. So, why ask a woman out if you are convinced that she'll reject you? In fact, why let anyone get to know you if they are going to discover how fucked up you are? This is the insidious power of SLBs and a faulty life paradigm.

> **A VICIOUS CYCLE:**
>
> Your self-limiting beliefs have convinced you that women are not attracted to you.
>
> Because you believe this to be true, you don't interact with women you find attractive.
>
> Because you don't interact with women, they tend not to interact with you.
>
> You use this as evidence to reinforce your belief that women are not attracted to you.
>
> You continue to avoid interacting with women

## THE HARMFUL EFFECTS OF SLBs

What you believe to be true is what you will create. Your mindset determines how you interact with women and how they interact with you. If you think you're a worthless piece of shit, how do you think you will approach women? And how do you think women will respond if you do approach?

Furthermore, as Dr. Glover points out, your SLBs come with a variety of other harmful side effects:[51]

- **They encourage you to isolate and avoid**. Your SLBs whisper in the back of your consciousness: *Just stay home tonight. Don't approach her, she wouldn't be interested. Don't make eye contact; she'll think you're a perv.*

- **They create negative emotional states**. If your mind keeps telling you that you are shit, you will naturally feel like shit as a result. And because your SLBs prevent you from taking actions that might improve your life, you feel even worse. It becomes normal to feel like shit, and feeling like shit only reinforces your SLBs. Again, it's a vicious cycle.

- **They cause you to settle**. Because of your SLBs, you probably settle for women who either don't turn you on or who you don't even like. You know there are some amazing women out there, but you don't believe you could ever get one.

- **They prevent you from taking advantage of the opportunities presented to you**. Have you ever had a chance to take out - or take home - a woman you desired, only to squander the opportunity because of your SLBs? Exactly.

- **They keep you safe**. After all, if you don't take a risk, you can't get hurt. Right?

A belief is merely a thought you keep thinking. And your mind thinks your beliefs are true because you have always thought them. There's a good chance the beliefs you hold about yourself, about the world, and about women aren't even remotely accurate. But the mind strives for consistency. The good news is you can learn to replace your old, distorted beliefs with new, more accurate beliefs that serve you in a positive and productive way.

---

51 Glover, Robert A. *Dating Essentials for Men* (Robert A. Glover, Ph.D, Inc. 2019) pp. 22-24

**A SHORT CASE STUDY:**

During one of Dr. Glover's workshops in Puerto Vallarta, a young participant named Diego said, "If people see me sitting by myself on the beach drinking a Corona, they'll think I'm a fucking loser." So, Dr. Glover and the other workshop participants made Diego challenge this belief.

When Diego went down to the beach, sat at a table by himself, and popped open a Corona, nobody seemed to judge him. In fact, nobody seemed to care at all. Diego had a great time watching people and taking in the ocean breeze.

Diego continued to challenge himself over the next few days. On the last day of the workshop, he noticed an attractive woman sitting down by herself at his favorite spot on the beach. His SLBs reared their ugly head: *She's totally out of your league. She'll think you're a creep because you're by yourself. She probably has a boyfriend anyway.*

Diego decided to challenge his SLBs. He started a conversation with the woman, and she responded positively. He asked her to join him, and she did. He invited her to dinner, and she accepted. They ended up spending the entire night together.

The next day, while sharing his experience in the workshop, he recounted his original belief that people would think he was a loser if he was sitting alone on the beach. With an ear-to-ear grin, he proclaimed, "I guess I totally fucking destroyed that SLB!"

## IDENTIFYING YOUR SLBs

Perhaps you are keenly aware of your SLBs. If so, you're ahead of the game. But if you are like most men, your SLBs are probably whispering in the back of your subconscious (and have been since childhood) while you remain unaware that they are SLBs and they are causing you harm. It is imperative that you call your SLBs into consciousness so you can identify them... and then challenge the fuck out of them.

SLBs can take many forms and present themselves in many different situations, particularly when interacting with women. Your SLBs can be about you (*Attractive women don't want me. I'm too short. I'm a loser.*); about a particular woman (*She probably has a boyfriend. She's out of my league.*); about all women (W*omen only care about looks and money*); about sex (*I'm bad for wanting sex.*); or about the world at large (*Good things seem to happen to everyone except me. It's only a matter of time until the universe fucks me over... again*).

Having spent years working with Dr. Glover, mercilessly battling my own demons, and coaching hundreds of other men, I am now certain there is only one completely foolproof way to call your SLBs into consciousness, and it's **doing something outside your comfort zone**. When you do something outside your comfort zone, your SLBs will stop whispering quietly and start screaming maniacally at you. This makes it pretty goddamn easy to find out what they are.[52]

---

**INTEGRATED ACTION:**
✓ Make it a priority to go somewhere you don't normally go. Talk to people you wouldn't ordinarily talk to. Make eye contact and smile. Take a chance. Pay attention to the garbage your mind is shouting at you. Write about your experience in your journal.

---

# CHALLENGING YOUR SLBs

In *Dating Essentials for Men*, Dr. Glover writes, "Your mind can cause you great suffering. Your mind can also liberate you. Your mind can keep you stuck in the mire and your mind can help you attain everything you want

---

52  Glover, Robert A. *Dating Essentials for Men* (Robert A. Glover, Ph.D, Inc. 2019) pp. 30-32

in life. This is true because your mind is the source of your feelings and the conductor of your actions."

Your mind can do the following:

- Interpret your feelings and give them meaning
- Create feelings by what it attunes itself to
- Translate thoughts and feelings into physical responses
- Observe itself
- Correct erroneous beliefs
- Rewire old emotional programming
- Soothe itself
- Challenge itself
- Grow beyond its self-imposed limitations.

So, what does this mean? It means that your faulty paradigm doesn't have to dictate your life. You have the power to take charge of your mind. You can control how you think. You can reshape your emotions. You can create a new roadmap and start acting in new, more powerful ways. No longer do you have to be held hostage by your SLBs.

**INTEGRATED ACTION:**

✓ Revisit your list of Self-Limiting Beliefs. In your journal, answer the following questions:

- What belief has been holding you back the most?
- What stories do you tell yourself to justify this belief? What's your "evidence"?
- What's the payoff of this belief? What does it allow you to do (or allow you to not do)?
- How do you feel about yourself when you buy into this belief?
- What are the consequences of having this belief? What is the future cost if this belief continues? How does your life look in 5 years or 10 years if this belief keeps running the show?
- What could be untrue about this belief? Could it be a mis-interpretation? How could this belief be bullshit?
- Who could you be without this belief? What experiences could you have? Who could you date? How would it feel if this fucking parasite were finally out of your brain?
- What do you want more – your old belief or a new be-lief and amazing results? You can't have both. You must choose.
- What new belief – if you could feel it in your gut – would propel you towards the results you want?
- What are three pieces of evidence that your new belief is true?

✓ Talk to a safe person (or safe people) about your SLBs.

# MYTHBUSTING

If you buy into your beliefs about yourself, there's a good chance you also buy into your beliefs about women. And your beliefs about women are probably distorted. Do you believe a woman will transform and complete your life? Do you believe a woman holds the key to your happiness? If so, you have unrealistic expectations about what a woman (or women) can do for you. As a result:

- You are anxious around women.
- You find it difficult to approach women and talk to them.
- You care way too much about what women think of you.
- You hide your *perceived* flaws from women, making it impossible for you to be honest and transparent.
- You place women on a pedestal.
- You harbor feelings of anger and resentment towards women.
- You're afraid to set the tone and take the lead with women.
- Your relationships with women lack true intimacy.

Your distorted beliefs about women likely come from the preposterous feminine mythology that permeates our culture. Books, music, movies, magazines, television shows, marketing, advertising, and social media all perpetuate the idea that attractive women are virtually unattainable objects of mystery and desire.

"This does a serious disservice to both men and women," asserts Dr. Glover. "It makes it difficult for women to cultivate the deep connection they crave with men, and it keeps men confused and anxious around women."

In *Dating Essentials for Men*, Dr. Glover appropriately busts some of the common myths about women:[53]

**Myth: Women are Superior to Men**

Many men tend to be in awe of women (particularly *beautiful* women) as if they are the most sophisticated and highly evolved creatures on the planet. While many women do have their shit together, it is safer to assume that the average woman – no matter how beautiful - has a low opinion of herself and a fair amount of emotional baggage.

In Western culture especially, women are all but expected to maintain impossible standards of beauty. Even the most beautiful woman will look around and see other women who she thinks are more beautiful than her. Add in the modern trappings of things like social media, and this is likely why so many women are dangerously self-critical and suffer from body distortions.

Even more disturbing, over 80 percent of women in the United States experience sexual harassment or assault in their lifetime, while one in five women experience attempted or completed rape.[54] [55] Sexual abuse creates a great deal of emotional turmoil for survivors. It can affect everything from their mood to their ability to connect with men. It is one of the reasons that

---

53  Glover, Robert A. *Dating Essentials for Men* (Robert A. Glover, Ph.D, Inc. 2019) pp. 70-78

54  Kearl, H. (2018). The facts behind the #metoo movement: A national study on sexual harassment and assault. Stop Street Harassment.

55  Smith, S. G., Zhang, X., Basile, K. C., Merrick, M. T., Wang, J., Kresnow, M., & Chen, J. (2018). The National Intimate Partner and Sexual Violence Survey: 2015 data brief – updated release. Centers for Disease Control and Prevention.

women have higher incidences of depression, anxiety, personality disorders, and other psychosomatic issues like PTSD.[56]

Dr. Glover often shares these very sad and unfortunate truths to help men open their eyes and see women for who they really are - flawed human beings just like everyone else. Women are no smarter, no better adjusted, and no more emotionally evolved than you.

---

**EVERYONE SHITS:**

In his book, *Born A Crime*, comedian Trevor Noah writes:

*It's a powerful experience, shitting. There's something magical about it, profound even. I think God made humans shit in the way we do because it brings us back down to earth and gives us humility. I don't care who you are, we all shit the same. Beyonce shits. The pope shits. The Queen of England shits. When we shit we forget our airs and our graces, we forget how famous or how rich we are. All of that goes away. You are never more yourself than when you're taking a shit. You have that moment where you realize, 'This is me. This is who I am.*

So, what does this have to do with attraction and dating?

Everything.

No matter how beautiful, how graceful, or how flawless you think a woman is, she still takes a big, smelly dump just like everyone else. Admittedly, this little fact helped me tremendously in my dating life. And it can do the same for you.

Stop idealizing women. Remember: *Everyone shits*.

---

56   Kilpatrick, Dean G. Ph.D. National Violence Against Women Prevention Research Center, Medical University South Carolina (https://mainweb-v.musc.edu/vawprevention/research/mentalimpact.shtml)

### Myth: Women are Complicated

Many men believe women are so complicated that it makes them damn near impossible to understand. But this belief only keeps men feeling stuck and frustrated. Sure, women can be emotionally unpredictable – like the weather - but they aren't necessarily complicated.

Women only *seem* complicated because their brains are wired differently. In fact, researchers have found that women's brains are significantly more active than men's brains in the prefrontal cortex (which is involved in impulse control) and the limbic or emotional areas of the brain responsible for mood and anxiety.[57] Don't forget, the feminine often turns feelings into facts. Perhaps this is why men always complain that female logic is, well, downright illogical.

Female hormones can also play a role in why women befuddle the shit out of men. During a monthly cycle, a woman's brain can physically change up to 25 percent.[58] Suffice to say, sometimes a woman's unpredictability is simply the ebb and flow of female hormones.

### Myth: Women are Naturally Good at Relationships

In our society, much of the material about intimate relationships is aimed at a female audience and presented from the female point of view. Just try to wrap your head around the vast amount of television shows, books, and magazines specifically for women.

Men often think of women as experts in relationships and intimacy. But as Dr. Glover asks: "If women are so good at relationships, why are there so many television shows, books, and magazines about a subject they are sup-

57   Integrative structural, functional, and transcriptomic analyses of sex-biased brain organization in humans. Liu S, Seidlitz J, Blumenthal JD, Clasen LS, Raznahan A. Proc Natl Acad Sci U S A. 2020 Jul 20:201919091. doi: 10.1073/pnas.1919091117. Online ahead of print. PMID: 32690678.

58   Hagemann G, Ugur T, Schleussner E, Mentzel HJ, Fitzek C, Witte OW, Gaser C. Changes in brain size during the menstrual cycle. PLoS One. 2011 Feb 4;6(2):e14655. doi: 10.1371/journal.pone.0014655. PMID: 21326603; PMCID: PMC3033889.

posedly experts in? After watching these shows and reading these books, why do so many women have difficulty taking charge of their lives? Why do so many women pick terrible men...and stay with them? And why do women have such difficulty getting along with *each other*?"

Do the math, and it's easy to see that women aren't as skilled at navigating relationships as men believe they are. It is actually a man's job to set the tone and take the lead in a conscious, loving way. Women are not inherently wired to drive the bus of a relationship, nor do they want to.

**Myth: Women Expect Perfection from Men**

I regularly hear men explain that the reason they aren't dating is because women only want tall, good-looking, rich guys with power. I used to believe the same thing. (And I'm pretty fucking tall, by the way.)

The truth is: Women are a lot more forgiving than most men think.

This may be hard for you to accept, but you need not look much further than a woman's face for confirmation. When speaking to a crowd, Dr. Glover often asserts that "what attracts women the most is a man who is comfortable in his own skin, knows where he's going, and looks like he's having a good time going there." The women in the crowd then smile and nod, as they collectively let out an almost sensual moan in agreement.

"Your perceived shortcomings can be assets if you can accept them without judgment," says Dr. Glover. "A healthy woman wants a man who is real, honest, and confident in himself. She's not looking for and doesn't expect perfection. Besides, it's your rough edges that make you interesting."

**Myth: You Need a Woman to Complete You**

If you are looking for a woman to complete you - to give you meaning, purpose, and happiness - you are always going to be frustrated and resentful. As a man, you must take responsibility for creating an interesting life by pursuing your passions, leaning into challenge, and having meaningful relationships with other men. As Dr. Glover often says: *The more power you give a woman to make you happy, the more power you give her to make you miserable.*

**INTEGRATED ACTION:**

✓ Which myths about women have you been buying into? Write your answer in your journal.

✓ Do you have any other distorted beliefs about women? Write your answer in your journal.

✓ How do you think your beliefs have affected your ability to meet and attract women? Write your answer in your journal.

✓ How do you think your relationships with women might change if you took them down off the pedestal? Write your answer in your journal.

✓ Talk to a safe person (or people) about your distorted beliefs and how they affect you.

# EMBRACING ABUNDANCE I

I n 2002, Barnes & Noble asked Dr. Glover to write a series of lessons based on *No More Mr. Nice Guy* for an online class on career advancement. One of the lessons was on the topic of **abundance**.[59]

"This was one of the most difficult lessons I've ever written," shares Dr. Glover. "Intellectually, I could think of what to write on the subject, but emotionally, I was blocked. I realized that the beliefs I formed in childhood were preventing me from writing believably about abundance. Before I could teach others about abundance, I had to be tuned into it in my own life."

Dr. Glover decided to try an experiment. He asked a friend to join him in an abundance practice: Each morning and each night, they would kneel next to their beds, count their blessings, and think about the things for which they were grateful. Dr. Glover knew this could be a challenge, as it required both he and his friend to re-shape some of their old ways of thinking.

"In a short amount of time, we both noticed internal changes," recalls Dr. Glover. "We worried less. We were happier. We didn't dwell on past losses or mistakes and didn't obsess about future disasters. We didn't resent or envy other people's blessings. Judgment waned. Joy increased. We both began to experience an inner peace, knowing that everything would work out just fine, even if we didn't know how. I also discovered that developing an abun-

---

59  Glover, Robert A. *Dating Essentials for Men* (Robert A. Glover, Ph.D, Inc. 2019)
    "Chapter 4: Discover the Power of Abundance Thinking."

dance mentality is one of the most powerful ways to naturally attract great women to you – without having to learn silly pickup lines or magic tricks."

When Dr. Glover encouraged me to start an abundance practice, I was characteristically skeptical. It sounded like airy-fairy bullshit. But abundance thinking has positively impacted my life in a number of ways and continues to do so, primarily because it forces me to constantly challenge some of my deepest held self-limiting beliefs.

Many men do not have an abundance mindset. They have what Dr. Glover calls a "deprivation view," otherwise known as a *scarcity mindset*. Due to childhood experiences, they developed the belief that there just wasn't enough of what they needed to go around. If you're one of these men, this became the lens through which you viewed the world. And this is probably how you view the world today – as a place of scarcity rather than a place of abundance.

Having a deprivation view of the world can make you manipulative and controlling. It can prevent you from taking any chances in life. It can cause you to resent anyone who seems to have what you lack. It can keep you from seeing how blessed you truly are and from walking through the doors of opportunity in front of you.

Dr. Glover lays out several factors that likely contribute to your deprivation view of the world. These can include:

- **An obsession with fairness (or the lack of it)**: Though we live in an abundant world and you are already blessed, you likely tend to focus on anyone who seems to have more than you.

- **An obsession with women's looks**: Because men place so much emphasis on a woman's looks, we are all competing for the same women – the women with the best physical genes. Men have turned these women into sexual celebrities. This reflects immaturity, not scarcity.

- **A lack of understanding**: Most men don't understand women or what turns them on.

- **An unwillingness to take risks**: To get what you want in life, you must challenge yourself and take risks. Nowadays, most men take the path of least resistance.

- **Distraction**: Many men get caught up in distraction, which blinds them to opportunity. This is especially true for men who spend all their time at home, playing video games, watching porn, or otherwise wasting time.

A deprivation view of the world doesn't serve you in any way. If you believe that you're a loser and that no woman could ever want you, this will be your reality. Why would a woman be interested in a man with a deprivation view of himself and the world? And what will happen if you do meet a woman? Because you'll always be waiting for the other shoe to drop, you'll become possessive and push her away.

Abundance thinking is important in all areas of life, but it is particularly crucial when meeting and attracting women. There is no shortage of amazing women out there. You are surrounded by opportunity. In fact, any time you see a man with a girlfriend or wife, this is irrefutable proof that there is opportunity. As Dr. Glover frequently preaches (and admits he stole from the movie *The Edge*), **What one man can do; another can do.**

> **VISUALIZING ABUNDANCE:**
>
> Take several slow, deep breaths.
>
> Clear your mind.
>
> Once relaxed, picture yourself living in an abundant world. In this abundant world, there are no limitations.
>
> Good things continuously flow.
>
> Imagine everything you have ever desired – a comfortable home, friends, love, joy, wealth, success, peace of mind.
>
> Picture yourself living your life surrounded by this abundance.
>
> Open your arms, open your heart, open your mind. Get out of the way and let it happen.

Men of all ages, sizes, races, nationalities, and walks of life are enjoying love, sex, and great relationships. These men are no better than you. The next time you start to compare yourself to a seemingly average man with a seemingly great woman, just know that there is probably only one difference between him and you: He **takes meaningful action** because he has an abundance mentality.

*What one man can do; another can do.*

We often forget that there are four *billion* women on the planet. When you get hung up on one woman or think that all the good women are taken, you're operating purely from a scarcity mindset. You're also being fucking ridiculous. You must get out of your own way and let good things into your life.

Abundance is flowing by you like a river. Will you embrace it?

**INTEGRATED ACTION:**

✓ Do you think a great woman would prefer to be around a grateful, fun-loving kind of guy or a nothing-ever-goes-my-way kind of guy? Write your answer in your journal.

✓ Using a separate journal or notebook, start an Abundance – or **Gratitude** – Practice. Before you go to bed tonight, make a list of things for which you feel grateful. These can be small things (like seeing a beautiful sunset) or more significant things (like having a roof over your head). Do this every night for the rest of your life.

✓ Start an **Abundance Love Practice** in conjunction with your **Gratitude Practice**. Instead of obsessing over the people who have loved you inadequately, reflect on how people have loved you adequately. Do this every night for the rest of your life.

✓ If you are single, tell yourself: *Over the next 30 days I will meet at least three women who are looking for me, who are available, and who could all be a really great match.* How can you get out of your own way and run into these women? Write your answer in your journal.

# BECOME ATTRACTIVE

Modern men seem to have moved so far away from their inherent masculinity that most have completely lost sight of what turns women on. Nice Guys especially have an uncanny ability to make women feel absolutely nothing. They are overly domesticated table dogs who will dance and beg for a scrap of attention from almost any woman. It's no surprise, though. The world is full of falsities and misinformation regarding men, women, sex, and attraction.

If you want to meet and attract women, you must face reality. And the reality is that life isn't a cheesy romantic comedy. Sure, love and intimacy are appropriately coupled with feelings of warmth, comfort, and safety. But building *attraction* is far from comfortable or safe. Building attraction requires you to flirt, tease, be bold, take risks, and go after what you want. Put another way, building attraction requires you to stop being such a fucking Nice Guy all the time.

When you don't behave in a way that is true to your masculine self, when you place women on a pedestal, when you bend over backwards to attract women and win their approval, you'll end up driving them away. Perhaps you've experienced this in your life. I know I have. Many times.

In addition to believing that being nice is an effective way to attract women, many men also tend to believe that women are basically non-sexual beings who only engage in sex to please men and make babies. This is yet another giant myth.

If you believe that women don't like sex, it will behoove you to promptly dispel this belief from your mind. Women love sex just as much as men, if not more. From a purely biological perspective, women are sexual machines. I will spare you the anatomical diagram, but I will remind you that women have countless erogenous zones and can orgasm in a variety of ways. Researchers have found that women can have at least 10 different types of orgasms.[60]

You will also want to dispel the belief that you are somehow bad or disgusting for wanting to have sex with women. This is an idea propagated by modern political correctness, toxic feminism, and the occasional cheesy romantic comedy. You are not bad for wanting to have sex with women or wanting to have sex in general. You are normal. We are all sexual beings.

So, why is this relevant? Because embracing your sexual agenda is vital to building attraction. When you repress your sexuality, you are putting a lid on your life force. You are muffling your mojo, so to speak. You immediately extinguish any spark, any polarity, any sexual tension. And this does nothing to pique the interest of women.

Sadly, though, most men don't even give themselves an opportunity to build attraction because they are debilitated by what is perhaps the ultimate self-limiting belief: ***Women only care about looks, money, and status.*** Yes, if you're anything like I was, you believe that a man must be flawlessly handsome and filthy rich to be considered attractive. This just isn't true.

Of course, women aren't exactly much help to us men. You've probably noticed that women often say they want one type of guy and then get involved with the opposite type of guy. But women are not looking for physical beauty in the same way men are. Do looks matter to women? Sure. But only to a certain degree.

---

60   Canning, Kristin. "There are 10 Types of Female Orgasms - Here's How to Have Them." January 20, 2023. (https://www.health.com/condition/sexual-health/different-types-of-orgasms-0)

Women are looking for indicators of strength and confidence. They are evolutionarily wired to look for signs that a man can provide healthy offspring. And they likely do this at an unconscious level. This doesn't mean you need rock-hard abs, bulging biceps, and a perfectly square jawline. In fact, several studies, including one by The University of California, Davis, confirmed that women tend to focus much more on a man's behavior, attitude, and personality as opposed to his physical attributes.

If you want to become more attractive, you must first stop obsessing over things you can't control like your height and your age, which rarely make a difference anyway. Focus on what really matters, like your strength, confidence, and masculinity. Anything you can do to exude more masculinity will work tremendously in your favor. Again, women aren't looking for purely physical qualities in the same way men are.

All that said, here are some research-backed ways you can easily become more attractive to women:

**Strengthen your body.**

The way you present yourself to the world reveals a lot about your character as a man. How do you feel when you're in the presence of a man with a killer physique? Chances are he immediately has your respect. After all, you don't build a strong body by sitting on your ass all day.

One of the best ways to display a healthy reproductive system (what women are evolutionarily wired to look for) is to have a strong, toned body. Several studies have shown that women rate men with muscular bodies as more desirable.[61] Studies have also shown that women are more likely to pursue muscular men for short-term affairs and romantic relationships.[62]

---

61  Sell A, Lukazsweski AW, Townsley M. Cues of upper body strength account for most of the variance in men's bodily attractiveness. Proc Biol Sci. 2017 Dec 20;284(1869):20171819. doi: 10.1098/rspb.2017.1819. PMID: 29237852; PMCID: PMC5745404.

62  Frederick, David A., Haselton, Martie G. Why is Masculinity Sexy? Tests of the Fitness Indicator Hypothesis. UCLA (https://www.sscnet.ucla.edu/comm/haselton/webdocs/frederick%20and%20haselton%20pspb%202007.pdf)

By no means do you need to become the next Mr. Olympia; but for fuck sake, take care of yourself. Slim down and tone up. The benefits of exercise are universally agreed upon.

**Choose the right hairstyle.**

As a general rule, shorter hair projects a more masculine look while longer hair projects a more feminine look. Furthermore, if you spend hours trying to make your hair look perfect, you can come across as boring, predictable, and overly concerned with your appearance. Studies have shown that women seem to have a fondness for that slightly disheveled, just-rolled-out-of-bed, look.

Incidentally, if you are going gray, you might be interested to know that a Match.com study found that over 70 percent of women think men with gray hair look "distinguished" and "hot." Going gray doesn't mean you are no longer attractive – that's just bullshit your mind tells you.

If you are going bald, which seems to be man's greatest fear, the best thing you can do is shave your head and own it. Several studies, including one by the University of Pennsylvania, have shown that men with shaved heads are seen as more masculine than men with full heads of hair. Studies also show that men with shaved heads rank higher on strength, dominance, and leadership potential. (As you might already know, Dr. Glover has a shaved head.)

So, just shave your damn head. It's sexy.[63]

But don't shave your face.

Studies have shown that facial hair has a hugely positive effect on a man's appearance.[64] Men with stubble are seen as healthier, more masculine, and more attractive.

---

63 Beniaris, Katina. "Bald Men are More Intelligent, Successful, and Masculine, Says Science" (https://www.womansday.com/life/news/a57748/bald-men-study/)

64 Barnaby J. Dixson, Robert C. Brooks, The role of facial hair in women's perceptions of men's attractiveness, health, masculinity and parenting abilities,Evolution and Human Behavior, Volume 34, Issue 3, 2013, Pages 236-241, ISSN 1090-5138, (https://doi.org/10.1016/j.evolhumbehav.2013.02.003.)

Also, don't forget to shave - or more accurately, trim - your nose hair, your ear hair, and your crazy professor eyebrows. Women pay attention to these kinds of details. You should, too.

**Develop a deeper voice.**

Several studies have shown that deeper voices command significantly more respect than high-pitched voices.[65] And deeper voices resonate much more with women.

Many men tend to speak in a higher pitch when they are nervous, particularly around beautiful women. Obviously, you can't change the voice you were born with; but you can develop a more commanding tone by taking slow, deep breaths and speaking from your diaphragm instead of your throat.

Whenever you find yourself nervous or anxious, make a conscious effort to slow your breathing and relax your muscles, specifically the muscles around your shoulders. When you speak directly from your diaphragm, your voice will come out in its full, natural tone.

**Have a winning wardrobe.**

Mark Twain once said, "Clothes make the man." And he wasn't wrong. You can instantly become more attractive by wearing not just better clothes, but the right type of clothes for your body. Again, the way you present yourself to the world reveals a lot about your character as a man. What kind of image do you want to project?

There isn't one look that works for every man. But it's always better to dress well. A variety of studies have shown that women find well-dressed men more attractive. When you have a wardrobe that fits well and looks good, you will feel more confident, command more respect, and behave in a more attractive way. As a result, women will notice you.

---

65   Schild, C., Aung, T., Kordsmeyer, T.L. et al. Linking human male vocal parameters to perceptions, body morphology, strength and hormonal profiles in contexts of sexual selection. Sci Rep 10, 21296 (2020). https://doi.org/10.1038/s41598-020-77940-z

**Pursue your passions.**

Men often think that women are superficial for being attracted to things like toned bodies, facial hair, and nice clothes. But it's not actually superficial. All those things communicate strength, confidence, and masculinity. As does pursuing your passions.

Wholeheartedly pursuing your passions is the ultimate sign of ambition and masculinity. In the sexual marketplace, men who are lazy and lack passion are considered low value. And a study published in the journal *Evolution and Human Behavior* confirmed that unmotivated, unambitious men are considered less attractive.

The sad truth is that many men today take the path of least resistance in life. They don't take risks. They put little effort into accomplishing their goals - if they even have any. They don't take strides to improve themselves mentally or physically. They hang out in the nursery and engage in junk-food behavior – playing video games, scrolling through social media, and watching porn.

You don't need to be a power-hungry businessman or a well-paid celebrity to attract women. But you do need to show at least some degree of unrealized potential. Women want a man with persistence, drive, and a sense of purpose, not a fucking couch potato. Put another way, you don't have to be successful *right now*. But women like to know that you have what it takes to be successful in the future.[66]

# WHAT ABOUT MONEY?

Many men believe they don't have any value unless they have great financial wealth. It's easy to see why men might feel this way - particularly in America, a country obsessed with fame and fortune.

---

66 For more information on becoming attractive, see Glover, Robert A. *Dating Essentials for Men* (Robert A. Glover, Ph.D, Inc. 2019) "Chapter 11: Pay Attention to Detail (She Does)."

In a hilarious rant about divorce settlements, comedian Bill Burr proclaimed, "There is an epidemic of gold-digging whores in this country. And every night, I put on the news, waiting for someone to address it. Every night. Never see it."

No doubt, there are gold diggers. There are women with no discernible skills or talents other than using their looks to manipulate men out of money. There are sugar babies looking for sugar daddies to foot the bill for every aspect of their lives. It happens. And it happens all over the world.

> **HARSH TRUTH:**
>
> The world can be a shallow fucking place.

Most women, however, aren't after money. Women are attracted to the qualities and characteristics that make a man money, not the money itself. Money doesn't actually make a man more attractive. As someone once said: *An ambitious poor man is more attractive than a lazy rich man.*

Dr. Glover often points out this paradox: Focusing solely on money will never make you happy. In fact, it will likely keep you in a state of deprivation and living in relative poverty, neither of which are attractive to women. However, one of the most powerful things you can do to change your life - and your relationships with women - is to change your relationship with money.

"Get out of debt, save and invest, and enjoy the highest level of luxury you can afford," suggests Dr. Glover. "When you clean up your money stresses, you'll be a happier, more relaxed man, which is highly attractive to women. In other words, keep your mind on your money and your money on your mind."

Cue Snoop Dogg.[67]

---

67  "With my mind on my money and my money on my mind," is a line from Snoop Dogg's massive 1993 hit, "Gin and Juice." Damn, I hope you mothafuckas already knew this.

**INTEGRATED ACTION:**

- ✓ How can you exude more strength and masculinity? Write your answer in your journal.
- ✓ Pick one thing you can do to make yourself more attractive. Do you need a different hairstyle? Do you need better-fitting clothes? Do you need to trim your nose hair? Do you need to work on discovering your passions? Whatever it is, do it.
- ✓ Do you have money stresses? Are you in debt? Start making a plan to get a handle on your money problems.
- ✓ Check in with your safe person (or safe people). Tell them about your intention to become more attractive and clean up your money issues. Ask them to hold you accountable.

# THE LIE OF NICENESS

Take a moment to reflect on your time in middle school or high school – the age when you really started to notice girls. Your brain and your balls were telling you to get their attention. But chances are you weren't all that socially adept.

Understandable.

You were a budding teenager, after all. Chock full of hormones raging through your rapidly changing body. Pimples, pubes, and impure thoughts popping up out of nowhere and everywhere at the same time.

And you weren't in the cool crowd. You weren't a rich kid or the class clown or a star athlete. No, you were just plain awkward, trying to find your place in the world like almost everyone else.

So, you wondered how you could stand out from the pack. You contemplated how you could be different from the other bumbling, adolescent boys. You agonized over how you could get girls to notice you. Eventually, you came up with a seemingly brilliant and failsafe strategy: You would be *nice*.

Poor you. You just didn't know any better.

Neither did I.

Being nice wasn't just my strategy in middle school and high school; it was my strategy until I was over 30 years old. You'd think I would have learned by then. Because even in middle school, being nice got me nothing but a non-refundable, one-way ticket to friend-zone hell.

Whether you devised the strategy yourself, or you were convinced by others that being nice is a surefire way to succed with women, you fell victim to a big fucking lie. This is not to suggest that you become a raging douche-bag, which many men believe is the only alternative to being nice. There is another, far more effective option: **Become an Integrated Man.** Approach women with confidence and let your intentions be known.

Why do you want to interact with an attractive woman in the first place?

Is it because you want to listen to her talk about her problems?

Is it because you want to buy her drinks?

Is it because you want to spend your salary paying off her bills?

Is it because you really, really want to help her sister move?

Is it because you want to be her BFF?

No, it's because you want to get naked with her. You wanted to get naked with her when you were in middle school, and you want to get naked with her now. This is perfectly ok. It isn't demeaning, it doesn't make you bad or creepy, and it doesn't mean you're a douchebag. It means you're human.

Mother Nature made you want to put your penis in a vagina because it is the most effective way to maintain the human race. It also feels really, really good. Again, you can't argue with Mother Nature. And you can't really argue with Dr. Glover when he points out that *it is an evolutionary sin to repress your God-given sexual interest in women.*

"When you approach a woman with confidence," explains Dr. Glover, "she experiences the exact same chemical reaction in her brain - the release of dopamine and norepinephrine - that you would experience if she lifted up her shirt and showed you her tits."

For a woman, confidence is the ultimate aphrodisiac. Being nice, on the other hand, is the quickest way to make her labia shrivel.

**Being nice does absolutely nothing to turn a woman on.** Sure, when a woman is nice to you, it probably makes you hard. But when you are nice to a woman, it makes her bone fucking dry. And it makes her think of you as a buddy.

**Being nice is an obvious attempt to win her approval.** Seeking approval makes you appear weak and timid. It also increases your anxiety. When you don't care what a woman thinks about you, you can engage her with a calm detachment that projects confidence.

**Being nice makes you appear lower in status.** People generally only kiss the asses of those who seem to be greater in status. So, when you kiss a woman's ass by being passively pleasing and overly polite, how do you think she will perceive you?

**Being nice creates a terrible foundation for any ongoing relationship.** Once you start trying to win a woman's approval by being nice, chances are you'll never stop. If you end up in a relationship with her, you'll already be stuck in a pattern of trying to please her and make her happy. This is a recipe for disaster, not a healthy relationship.

Don't buy into the lie of niceness.[68] Most men who struggle with women do so simply because they are too nice, too passive, and too pleasing, which projects a general lack of confidence.

A confident, Integrated Man will hold an attractive woman's gaze instead of immediately looking away. He will flash her a playful smile instead of retreating. He will approach her and introduce himself instead of staying put and wondering what it would be like to talk to her. He will make his intentions known by testing for interest, flirting, and creating tension instead of repressing his sexuality.

---

68    Glover, Robert A. *Dating Essentials for Men* (Robert A. Glover, Ph.D, Inc. 2019) pp. 104-107

# TESTING FOR INTEREST

Immerse yourself in what is considered classic pickup and seduction material, and much of it reads like the assembly guide for a sizable piece of furniture from IKEA - a lengthy, overly complex set of instructions that no human could ever remember and that frequently leads to anger, frustration, and failure:

*Approach her at a 60-degree angle. Use a functional, indirect, opinion opener. Speak two octaves lower. Don't forget to add a time constraint. Stand with one foot pointed at a 45-degree angle. Keep your hands out of your pockets but minimize the use of gestures. Use the Triangular Gazing Technique. Do a cold reading. Demonstrate higher value using "The Cube" or "The Mouse Race." Do an Aura Reading but only after you've done a Cold Reading. Look for at least three Indicators of Interest. Neg her to create an emotional spike. Compliment her character, but don't mention her looks. Maintain frame control. Touch her precisely halfway between her elbow and her wrist. Create at least one more emotional spike. Go for the number close. Wait no less than 84 hours before texting...*

Huh?

The beauty of what Dr. Glover teaches lies not just in the fact that it works, but also in its inherent simplicity. His method of testing for interest[69]

---

69   Glover, Robert A. *Dating Essentials for Men* (Robert A. Glover, Ph.D, Inc. 2019) pp.165-173

is nearly impossible to forget. And it allows you to either build attraction or get to rejection quickly. It is refreshingly free of magic tricks, mind games, and other manipulative nonsense. It is also the foundation for nearly all social interaction. Test for interest everywhere you go with everyone you meet, and your life will unfold in ways you never thought possible.

As Dr. Glover illustrates, there are three levels of testing for interest:

**Level One – Social Pleasantries:**

These are what make the world go round. They are the lubrication of everyday interaction. Most men are perfectly capable of exchanging social pleasantries in any given situation. That is, until they see a beautiful woman and their brains turn to mush. They become bungling idiots, trying desperately to think of the right thing to say. But the right thing to say is what you would say to anyone else; because a beautiful woman is just like anyone else. She doesn't sleep on a rainbow and shit chocolate sprinkles. She's a flawed and imperfect human being. Your goal is simply to start a conversation.

Make eye contact, smile, and utter words like 'Hi' or 'Hello' (both work surprisingly well).

Ask her how her day is going.

Compliment her.

Share an observation about your environment.

For the love of God, mention the weather.

It doesn't matter.

What matters is that you open your mouth and say something. *Anything.* Whatever comes to mind. This isn't rocket science. You don't need a magic pickup line (there isn't one). You just need to find out if she is interested in having an interaction with you.

Using an example from Dr. Glover, let's say that you are in an elevator. The doors open, and an attractive woman steps in. She has her phone in her hand, as women often do. You greet her and ask her how her day is going. If she smiles, offers an answer, and then asks *you* how *your* day is going, this is a sign of high interest. If she grumbles something without ever looking up from her phone, this is a sign of low interest. Don't take it personally; you did nothing wrong. There are an infinite number of reasons why she has low interest. Move on with your life. It has nothing to do with you.

If she shows high interest, you can escalate to Level Two.

**Level Two – Conversation and Commonalities:**

Here, you will continue the conversation as you would with anyone else. You might ask her where she's from or what she does for a living. If she shows low interest in continuing the conversation, that's great. Don't take it personally. You did nothing wrong. There are still an infinite number of reasons why she has low interest. Move on with your life. It has nothing to do with you.

It's worth noting that at Level Two, a woman will usually let you know – sometimes subtly - that she's involved with a man. Some men get angry at this, which is unnecessary and immature. Women aren't stupid; they know why we're talking to them. It is actually considerate of a woman to tell you that she is involved with a man, even if it's not what you want to hear.

That said, if a woman shows high interest at Level Two and you are enjoying the interaction, you can escalate to Level Three.

**Level Three – Requiring Something of Her:**

By now, you should know if a woman wants to continue to interact with you. More importantly, you should know if *you* want to continue to interact with *her*. If so, you should require something of her. Most commonly, this is a phone number. Sometimes, it's an instant date.

Do not be vague at Level Three. Be bold and be specific. You might say something like, "Give me your number. I'll call you and we'll grab a drink next week." This lets her know why you're asking for her number. If she gives you her number, call or text her right then and there so she has your number. If she doesn't want to give you her number, don't take it personally. You did nothing wrong. Just say, "No worries, it was great meeting you." You'll still look like a confident and intriguing man. Then, move on with your life.

\*\*\*

While testing for interest, men tend to stumble the most when going from Level Two to Level Three. They overthink. They get attached to a specific outcome. They let their anxiety take over. And they seek the woman's approval, which is almost always the kiss of death. When you are testing for interest, you are not trying to get anyone to like you. You are merely...you know...testing for interest.

Again, Dr. Glover's method of testing for interest is the foundation for all social interaction. It is how you create new friendships, new business partnerships, and new relationships. It is also the foundation for all sales. You only need to observe one thing - the other person's perceived interest in having an interaction with you.

As you test for interest, be mindful of your tendency to overcomplicate and overanalyze. You're looking for either low interest or high interest. That's it. There is nothing in between. There is no gray area. There are no weird-ass sub levels. Keep it simple. If a woman shows high interest, that's great. Enjoy it and escalate. If a woman shows low interest, that's great, too. You found out what you needed to know. Don't waste anymore of your time. Move on so you can interact with women who have high interest.

The way others behave tells a story about them, not you. Taking their responses personally is what causes a lot of men to shut down. Don't try to figure out why people do what they do. But test for interest everywhere you go, with *everyone* you meet – not just beautiful women. Most of the people you meet either won't be interested or won't be available. That's okay. And that's life. Still, as Dr. Glover likes to say, *miracles happen around people*. If you don't leave your house and test for interest, you'll never experience any miracles.

**INTEGRATED ACTION:**

✓ Get out of the house and test for interest everywhere you go with everyone you meet. Test, test, and test some more. Don't take anything personally. Let go of attachment to outcome. Move on when you get low interest. Escalate when you get high interest.

✓ In your journal, write about your experiences testing for interest. Did any miracles happen?

# THE THREE TS

As you interact with women who display high interest, you must continue to build attraction. While building attraction does require you to be bold and take risks, it doesn't require convoluted techniques or elaborate routines. It is no more complex than testing for interest. You can build and maintain attraction by simply practicing what Dr. Glover calls *The Three Ts:* Touch, Tease, and Tell.[70]

**Touch:**

Touching a woman will ignite – and maintain - the spark of attraction. This obviously doesn't apply to a woman you just met three seconds ago. But if a woman has high interest – if she is flirting, if she is touching you, if you're dating, if you're in a relationship – then you need to touch her.

Touch her arm, caress her leg, put your hand on the small of her back. Grab her hand when crossing the street. Kiss her on the lips and elsewhere. Press your body up against hers. If you have an impulse, do it. Don't hold back. Especially if it's a woman with whom you've already been intimate.

Women frequently complain that their men only touch them when they want sex. This makes women feel used and unloved. So, touch your woman and touch her often.

---

70 Dr. Glover repeatedly mentions the 3 Ts in *Dating Essentials for Men*. But he discusses them in greater detail on one of his Dating Essentials Q&A Podcasts. See Glover, Robert A. "Podcast 137, The 3 Ts - Touch, Tease, and Tell." Podcast Audio. www.drglover.com

**Tease:**

Many men overlook the importance of teasing. Often, this is because they're afraid of how a woman might react. But teasing is a crucial part of building attraction. Don't insult a woman and make her feel bad about herself. Tease her with love as if she were your bratty little sister. If you're with a woman you've just met, teasing her is a great way to find out if she has a sense of humor. It can also drive up her desire to have sex. Why? Like the old song declares: *Girls just wanna have fun.*

Teasing keeps your interactions with women light and playful. Again, girls just wanna have fun. Don't be a fucking stick in the mud.

**Tell:**

Telling a woman what to do is a powerful way to establish what Dr. Glover calls "loving dominance." Women are evolutionarily wired to feel safe and aroused when dominated. Nice Guys damn near shit themselves when they hear this because they instantly relate "dominance" to control and abuse. But that's not what we're talking about here.

"A woman can't follow where a man doesn't lead," insists Dr. Glover. "Women want a man with a plan. So, tell your woman to do what she already wants to do."

*Put on a hot dress, we're going out.*

*Come over here and kiss me now.*

*Take off your clothes and meet me in the bedroom.*

Tell. Don't ask.

Practicing The Three Ts creates palpable sexual tension. It's also a way for you to set the tone, take the lead, and show that you are a confident, Integrated man. If you practice the Three Ts, you'll be the masculine presence that women want you to be. If you don't practice the Three Ts, you'll spend your life flailing around in the friend zone.

**INTEGRATED ACTION:**

✓ If there is a woman in your life, make a conscious effort to practice the Three Ts. Pay attention to how your woman responds.

✓ If you are single and dating, practice the Three Ts with the women you meet. Pay attention to how these women respond. Write about your experiences in your journal.

✓ Which of the Three Ts are you confident that you can excecute? Which of the Three Ts do you think you need to practice the most? Write your answers in your journal.

✓ Check in with your safe person (or people). Talk to them about the Three Ts.

# POSITIVE EMOTIONAL TENSION I

In the spring of 2009, Dr. Glover was on vacation in Puerto Vallarta, Mexico, the city he eventually made his permanent home. While catching his breath after a strenuous workout on the beach, he had a flash of inspiration that seemed to answer almost every question he'd ever had about women: Dr. Glover realized that women need tension – primarily **emotional tension** – to feel attracted and attached to a man. When he got back to his villa, Dr. Glover instantly began writing what would ultimately become his most popular online class, *Positive Emotional Tension*.[71]

Dr. Glover likely isn't the first person to realize that women need to experience tension. Others have undoubtedly put their own spin on the idea of tension, calling it polarity, friction, or uncertainty. Refer to it how you want, Positive Emotional Tension (PET) is a powerful concept that is fundamental to building and maintaining attraction. And Dr. Glover's class is chock full of insights.

Still, PET seems difficult for many men to understand. Nice Guys in particular want things to be smooth and predictable. They're afraid of doing something wrong or getting rejected. They're especially afraid of doing anything that might make a woman angry.

---

71  For more information on *Positive Emotional Tension*, see Glover, Robert A. Positive Emotional Tension (TPI University, www.drglover.com) or listen to Glover, Robert A. "Podcasts 37-41, Parts 1-5 of a Five-Part Series on Creating Positive Emotional Tension with Women." Podcast Audio. www.drglover.com

It's true: Create tension with a woman and she may not like it. But this makes creating tension a great way to get to rejection quickly, to find out what you need to know so you can move on. Also, a woman may *claim* she doesn't like tension when she actually finds it arousing. Whether or not a woman likes tension doesn't necessarily matter. You'll still create a strong emotional and physiological response in her.

Unfortunately, most men manage to kill all tension with women. Some men do it inadvertently because they don't know any better. But some men - like Nice Guys - do it because they can't stand it when things are, well, you know…tense.

Either way, men kill tension by:

- Trying to be nice
- Going way too slow
- Going way too fast
- Repressing their sexuality
- Failing to set the tone and take the lead
- Seeking approval and validation
- Letting the woman make all the decisions

Many men seem to be skilled at creating tension on the first few dates with a woman; but once these dates turn into a relationship, these men turn into floppy fucking doormats. When this happens, a woman will create *Negative* Emotional Tension (NET) to feel an ongoing attachment. Women often create NET unconsciously, by withdrawing, criticizing, nagging, or flirting with other men.

As a man, it is your job to create PET. Be bold, take risks, and step outside of your comfort zone. If you're always playing it safe, you'll never create any tension.

As Dr. Glover explains, you can create PET by:

- Practicing the 3 Ts
- Embracing your sexuality
- Blurting (or saying whatever comes to mind)

- Acting on impulse – especially if it scares you
- Setting the tone and taking the lead
- Having an opinion
- Being authentic
- Being mysterious
- Being unpredictable
- Being playful
- Having a life

Looking at this another way, uncertainty and *anxiety* can fuel attraction. But not anxiety in you, anxiety in *her*. Thus, it makes sense that neediness and niceness are the ultimate turn-offs to a woman.

If you are constantly texting or calling a woman, if you are always at her beck and call, if you bend over backwards to please her, how do you think your behavior comes across? Do you think you're creating any tension or uncertainty? Even psychological studies have shown that uncertainty can increase a woman's attraction for a man.[72] If a woman thinks she has to fight to be with you, she'll find you even more desirable.

> **HOW TO CREATE PET (IN JUST 3 SENTENCES):**
>
> Don't be too needy. Don't be too available. Don't be such a fucking Nice Guy all the time.

Ever wonder why women seem to be attracted to dickheads?

Tension.

Ever wonder why women can't get enough of those awful daytime soap operas?

Tension.

---

72  Whitchurch, E. R., Wilson, T. D., & Gilbert, D. T. (2011). "He Loves Me, He Loves Me Not . . . ": Uncertainty Can Increase Romantic Attraction. *Psychological Science, 22*(2), 172–175. https://doi.org/10.1177/0956797610393745

How about chick flicks?

Tension.

For better or worse, women want to experience the kind of emotional tension that makes them feel alive. Be the source of those feelings, and they'll keep coming back for more.

---

**INTEGRATED ACTION:**

- ✓ Think about your interactions with women. Do you create enough PET? How can you create more? Write your answers in your journal.
- ✓ How do you think a woman's evolutionary wiring basically makes it impossible for her to be attracted to a Nice Guy? Write your answer in your journal.
- ✓ How can you be bolder and take more risks with women? List at least five ways in your journal.
- ✓ The next time you interact with a woman, practice creating PET. Write about the experience in your journal.

# APPROACHING WOMEN

In the opening scene of the 2005 movie *Hitch*, Will Smith, who plays a high-end dating coach for men, proclaims that "No woman wakes up and thinks: *I hope I don't get swept off my feet today.*" Granted, *Hitch* was a formulaic rom-com vomited out by Hollywood to appeal to the masses. But its basic sentiment holds true. Women want you to approach them.

Of course, many men are terrified by the mere thought of approaching women. But in the current age of online dating, men who approach women are intoxicating. When you approach a woman, you exhibit boldness and confidence (even if you're nervous). And you immediately set yourself apart from most men - because most men never approach women in real life and resort solely to meeting women online.

As Dr. Glover explains, "A single woman essentially lives in a waiting state. She waits for a man to approach and show interest, giving her the opportunity to accept or reject the man. Approaching a woman does not make you a creep or a pervert – unless you lack common sense and act like a creep or a pervert."

Throughout history, it has primarily been angry, toxic feminists who think all men are creeps. This may be shocking to read in these politically correct times. But as Dr. Glover points out, "Rarely do we see a beautiful, sensual, fun-loving, Feminine woman at some kind of men-are-pigs rally. Most heterosexual women are familiar with the laws of nature, enjoy a man's company, and know that it is a man's job to approach. Women have evolved over thousands of years to respond to you as a man."

So, consider this: **It is creepier not to approach than it is to approach.**

Who do you think a woman might find more attractive? The man who walks up to her, gives her a compliment, and introduces himself? Or the man who sits in the corner and ogles her from a distance? The first man, though he may be nervous, exhibits confidence and charm as a man of action. The second man is just one big creepy turn-off.

# OVERCOMING APPROACH ANXIETY

There is one phrase that you are likely to find in almost every book, blog article, YouTube video, cheat sheet, guide, manual, and manifesto on meeting women, and that phrase is *Approach Anxiety*.[73] Every man who struggles to meet women seems to suffer from overwhelming Approach Anxiety, which is likely exacerbated by his equally overwhelming obsession with overcoming it.

Here is an age-old question: **What's the worst that could happen?**

I have never known a man to die from cordially introducing himself to a woman. I don't know any men who have been prodded, punched, or publicly shamed for engaging in the same activity. I don't even know a man who's had a drink thrown in his face.

If you were to approach a woman, smile, introduce yourself, and pay her a compliment, what's the worst that could happen? If she tells you that she's not interested or that she has a boyfriend, do you think you could handle it? Worse yet, if she tells you to fuck off, do you think you could go on to live a perfectly adequate life? I'm betting you could.

---

73  For more information on Approach Anxiety, see Glover, Robert A. *Dating Essentials for Men* (Robert A. Glover, Ph.D, Inc, 2019) "Chapter 5: "Overcome Your Anxiety with Women."

"As long as you're alive, as long as you're challenging yourself and putting yourself in new situations," affirms Dr. Glover, "you are going to feel some degree of anxiety. You can manage your anxiety by completely avoiding situations that make you anxious, in which case Mother Nature will still fuck with you. Or you can learn to soothe your anxiety and do what makes you anxious. At the end of the day, thinking causes anxiety, acting cures it."

Anxiety won't kill you. It's an electrical and chemical impulse in your brain. Your anxiety is likely caused by a few basic things: your inaccurate, internalized beliefs about yourself and the world, your lack of experience using effective social skills, your attachment to outcome, and perhaps your unwanted inheritance of an overactive amygdala.

"If you want something different, you have to do something different," says Dr. Glover. "It's really that simple. We make things way too complicated. There's no magic bullet. The alcoholic has to stop drinking. The porn addict has to stop watching porn. The phobic person has to do what frightens him. And the anxious person has to do what makes him anxious."

Unfortunately, many men are indeed looking for a magic bullet. They want an easy fix. They never want to feel anxious. They don't want to take risks. They want the gorgeous woman with no baggage, and they want *her* to make the first move. They don't want to set the tone and take the lead, they don't want to face rejection, and they don't want to have to break up. They don't make any changes. They keep doing what they've always done and keep getting what they've always got. Then, they feel worse about themselves because they know there are solutions. Usually, they know what they need to do, they just don't do it.

If you're like the men I just described, I feel a certain responsibility to tell you - just as Dr. Glover told me - that it's time to grow up and become an Integrated Man. It's time to start doing what you need to do instead of what's easiest. It's time to stop making excuses. If you want to overcome your approach anxiety, then you need to approach women. Approach women until it becomes instinctual. Approach women until you don't give a fuck about the outcome.

---

**DR. GLOVER'S**
**8-POINT PLAN FOR TACKLING APPROACH ANXIETY**

1. Get a therapist or coach. Work on your self-image, your toxic shame, your perfectionism, and any resentment you have towards women. Even if you're broke, there are ways. Find a way to get the help you need. You're worth it. And we all have issues.

2. Learn more effective social skills. If necessary, hire someone to teach you these skills.

3. Learn to soothe yourself from the inside. Even babies soothe themselves. And if babies can do it, so can you. Learn to calm the anxiety in your head enough so you can take meaningful action. Breathe. Take deep, slow breaths from your gut. Tell yourself you'll handle it.

4. Get out of your head. Thinking causes anxiety, acting drowns it out. Overanalyzing causes more anxiety.

5. Take action. There is no substitute for this. *Get out of the house, expand your route, linger in public, talk to everyone you meet, test for interest, walk through the open doors.*

6. Practice, practice, practice. And practice some more. Talk to everyone, not just beautiful women. *What amateurs call genius, professionals call practice.*

7. Let go of attachment to outcome.

8. Enjoy the adventure of life. Because that's what life is. Get up every morning primed for an adventure. Put yourself in new situations and soothe yourself. That's when the fun begins.

---

It's likely that 80 percent of men stay stuck, while the remaining 20 percent get the most out of life. The only difference between these groups of men is their willingness to do what makes them anxious. Which group of men do you want to be in? You get to decide.

# CONGRUENCE

What you are saying and doing should reflect what you are thinking and feeling. This is **congruence**.[74] And it's especially important when approaching women.

If you're not taking aligned action, if you're not acting in accordance with your thoughts and feelings, women can pick up on it. Women can sense whether or not a man is being congruent. If an available woman shows low interest in you, it's not because she thinks you're a loser. It's not because she can see right through you. She can, however, feel your incongruence.

This is one of the reasons that classic pickup techniques generally don't work and come across as inauthentic and creepy. Things like DHV stories, cold reading, peacocking, and magic tricks are dead giveaways to women. These are not authentic forms of communication. They are inherently manipulative, and they probably aren't congruent with who you are as a man.

As Dr. Glover offers, "Think about it: If you are not a magician, why the fuck would you do magic tricks for a woman?"

You are also being incongruent when you:
- Approach a woman but repress your interest in her
- Seek someone else's approval by being what you think they want you to be
- Hide your feelings, thoughts, or agenda
- Try to be a woman's friend when you really want to get her naked
- Play it safe to avoid upsetting a woman

---

74 Glover, Robert A. "Podcasts 77-80, Parts 1-4 of a Four-Part Series on Effectively Approaching Women: Congruence." Podcast Audio. www.drglover.com

- Lie or withhold information

Have you ever been spending time with someone and - while you can't quite put your finger on it - something just seems off about them? This is what incongruence feels like to a woman.

A woman will almost always have a negative reaction at an unconscious level when you are being incongruent. She will sense that you are not being you, that you are not being present, that you are holding back, and that you are trying to get her approval. Consequently, she won't want to get close. She'll want to run like hell, even if she doesn't know why.

Here are some things to consider as you work towards approaching women with congruence:

- **Begin with you.** Get comfortable with yourself and your sexuality. If you don't like who you are, it's no wonder you don't think a woman will. You must value yourself enough to consciously work on you. Change what you can and learn to accept the rest.

- **Live a congruent life.** Whatever you do, do it 100 percent and in the open. As Dr. Glover likes to say, *Nothing hidden, nothing half-assed.* If you have secrets, reveal them to safe people. Consciously work at being a man of integrity. Do the things that make you happy. Don't defend yourself to anyone. Stop seeking external validation. Pursue your passions. Live in a way that feels right to you.

- **Talk to everyone you meet.** Become a social animal. By being yourself with all kinds of people, you develop and project congruence.

- **Ask your friends how you come across.** Do you have any mannerisms that might be a turn-off? Do you send any uncomfortable signals? Does your body language make you seem unapproachable? Work on these things.

- **Practice being present and real.** Be in the moment. Say what comes to mind without apology. Be playful. Use humor. Acknowledge what you're feeling.

- **Don't try to hide the reason you're approaching a woman.** Again, women aren't stupid. They know why we're talking to them. There's no need to repress your sexuality.

Approaching women with congruence requires you to be honest and be yourself. Like Dr. Glover often commands, *Be a what-you-see-is-what-you-get kind of guy. Give women the chance to like you just as you are.*

## THE CONFIDENCE CONUNDRUM

If you are anything I used to be, then you are probably thinking: *If women are turned on by confidence but I don't feel even remotely confident when approaching women, what the hell chance do I have?*

Ah, yes, the ol' confidence conundrum.

If confidence is required to have success with women, and success with women is what you need to feel confident, you'll probably never get a woman. You might as well just stay home and jerk off, right?

Wrong, obviously.

This is a self-limiting belief that your mind has concocted to keep you safe - to prevent you from having to experience the anxiety that comes with approaching women.

Learning to approach women is undoubtedly like learning any other skill. You are probably going to suck at first. And you are probably going to feel unconfident. But the more you practice, the more confident you'll become. Eventually, you'll be able to do it with ease.

Until then, however, you can interact with women in a way that makes you appear confident, even if you're riddled with anxiety. And this is how:

- **Make eye contact**. What do you think you're communicating if you never look up, never look around, or never make eye contact? Or what if a woman makes eye contact with you and you immediately look away in shame? You need to maintain eye contact, and either smile or approach. Eye contact will trigger an evolutionary response in a woman. Not to mention that you will exhibit confidence. If she looks away or seems uninterested, you aren't doing anything wrong. (And, yes, there's a difference between making eye contact and staring. Don't stare. It's creepy).

- **Test for interest.** Again, this is the foundation for all social interaction. Test for interest everywhere you go with everyone you meet. You don't need to be a master conversationalist; you just need to be social. Women are typically attracted to men who are social.
- **Practice the Three Ts.** Naturally charismatic men touch women, tease women, and playfully tell them what to do.

Women may pick up on the meta signals of your anxiety, but most will cut you some slack. Your courage will almost always trump your anxiety. So, own it. Women generally welcome an anxious man if he is congruent and taking aligned action.

---

**INTEGRATED ACTION:**
- ✓ Do you suffer from Approach Anxiety? Write about your experience in your journal.
- ✓ What's the worst that could happen if you approach a woman with charm and confidence?.
- ✓ How can you act more congruently?
- ✓ Get out of the house, expand your route, linger in public, talk to people everywhere you go, test for interest, and walk through the open doors.
- ✓ Approach at least one woman you find attractive. Smile, introduce yourself, pay her a compliment. Let go of attachment to outcome.

---

# THE 'R' WORD

When it comes to meeting and dating women, one of the most pervasive issues among men is the ever-present fear of rejection.[75]

That's right. The "R" word.

Before you do anything, ~~strike it from your vocabulary.~~

Fear of ~~rejection~~ is usually what keeps men stuck in romantic purgatory. It leads to isolation. It leads to passivity. It leads to approval-seeking behavior. It leads to bad dates and bad relationships. In my case, it led to morbid thoughts, clammy hands, and vomiting in my mouth a little.

Just the idea of approaching (and being shot down by) a woman used to churn my stomach and send my mind plummeting down a rabbit hole: *What's the point of approaching her? She'll think I'm a douche. She's going to rip me to shreds. I should just avoid the humiliation. Why risk getting hurt?*

Sound familiar?

The truth is: Women aren't out to humiliate you. And ~~rejection~~ doesn't hurt.

Let me repeat that.

~~Rejection~~ **doesn't hurt.**

---

75 Glover, Robert A. *Dating Essentials for Men* (Robert A. Glover, Ph.D Inc, 2019) pp. 40-41. For more on rejection, see "Podcasts 14-15, Parts 1 and 2 of a Two-Part Series on Dealing with Rejection" and "Podcasts 58-60, Parts 1-3 of a Three-Part Series on Overcoming the Fear of Rejection." Podcast Audio. www.drglover.com

This is a fact that I have witnessed Dr. Glover attempt to hammer into the heads of countless skeptical men. At one point, I was one of these men, paralyzed by the thought of being "rejected" by a woman.

"The pain of rejection is purely a function of the mind," explains Dr. Glover. "It has nothing to do with being told 'No.' When we have emotional attachment to a specific outcome, then rejection hurts; not because of the actual rejection, but because of what we do with that rejection in our own minds."

How can a woman who is a complete stranger possibly know you well enough to reject you or validate you?

She can't.

A stranger can't know who you are. And being told 'No' does not in and of itself cause any pain. As Dr. Glover helped me understand, when a woman rejects you, it is not a reflection of who you are. It simply means that for whatever reason, she has low interest in interacting with you at that given moment. Usually, it has nothing to do with you. Not to mention that one person's low interest does not reflect what everyone else thinks.

When you take a woman's rejection personally, you are actually rejecting yourself. You have certain inaccurate beliefs about yourself, so you interpret a woman's low interest as proof that those beliefs are true. This is merely the Paradigm Effect doing its dirty work. A woman's low interest generally means that she is unavailable, distracted, busy, or that you are simply not her type. It doesn't mean that you are worthless and unlovable.

# TAKING A SCIENTIFIC APPROACH... TO APPROACH

Fear of rejection is likely caused by having an emotional agenda or being attached to a specific outcome like:

- Wanting a girlfriend
- Desiring a regular sex partner

- Not wanting to be lonely
- Not wanting to feel like a loser
- Getting validation from a desirable woman desiring you
- Not wanting to look foolish

But what if you were to entertain the idea of approach not as a way to get validation from women, but purely as a scientific experiment? This is precisely what Dr. Glover did when he became single in his mid 40s - he tried to figure out what works and what doesn't work. That's what scientists do.

By taking a scientific approach to approach, Dr. Glover not only appeared more confident and, subsequently, attracted more women, he also learned that:

- Women responded better when he was more direct.
- Women responded better when he was bold.
- Women responded better when he called back quickly instead of waiting three to five days like many self-proclaimed dating gurus recommend.
- Women responded better when he practiced the Three Ts.
- Women responded better when he consciously let go of attachment to outcome.

Men often experience low interest or ~~rejection~~ because they don't test boldly enough to drive up attraction. But taking a scientific approach to approach[76] will make you more willing to test boldly and try new things. It'll also lower your anxiety and temper your fear of rejection. It's just science, after all.

---

76  Glover, Robert A. *Dating Essentials for Men* (Robert A. Glover, Ph.D, Inc, 2019) p. 62 and "Podcasts 102-103, Parts 1 & 2 of a Two-Part Series on Treating Dating Like a Scientific Experiment." Podcast Audio. www.drglover.com

# TRYING TO GET ~~REJECTED~~

While treating approach like a scientific experiment usually strikes men as reasonable, one of Dr. Glover's most befuddling (yet ultimately life-changing) pieces of advice is to consciously *try* to get ~~rejected~~.[77] Most men wonder what the point of trying to get ~~rejected~~ might be, until Dr. Glover points out that the inherent paradox is what makes it so powerful.

Fundamentally, trying to get ~~rejected~~ is a form of Cognitive Behavior Therapy or, more specifically, Exposure Therapy. When you try to get rejected, you are facing your fear head on. Directly confronting your fear of ~~rejection~~ is one of the most powerful things you can do to overcome your fear and challenge your self-limiting beliefs.

"Trying to get rejected can help you let go of attachment to outcome and stop taking things personally," insists Dr. Glover. "It will help you realize that rejection doesn't hurt. It will help you stop trying to figure women out. And it will make you appear significantly more confident."

Of course, trying to get rejected doesn't mean you should approach women in a way that is crude, creepy, or offensive. It does, however, mean that you should be bold and straightforward. For example, you might say:

"Hi, you caught my eye and I wanted to come introduce myself. What's your name? I'd love to take you out for drinks."

If you get ~~rejected~~, just say, "Well, you can't blame a guy for trying."

Then, move on.

When you *try* to get ~~rejected~~, you'll likely discover that you don't get ~~rejected~~ nearly as much as you thought you would. Try to get ~~rejected~~ five times in one night and there's a good chance you won't get ~~rejected~~ all five times. Women are actually wired to say Yes. And they will often say Yes just

---

77  Glover, Robert A. *Dating Essentials for Men* (Robert A. Glover, Ph.D Inc, 2019) p. 41. And"Podcasts 14-15, Parts 1 and 2 of a Two-Part Series on Dealing with Rejection"

because you've asked. If a woman says No, rename it as low interest, and know that it has nothing to do with you or worth as a person.

---

**INTEGRATED ACTION:**
- ✓ Get out of the house and try to get five women to reject you. Soothe yourself, comfort yourself, challenge yourself, lean into your anxiety. It helps to do this assignment with a buddy. Don't have a buddy? Get to work on that.
- ✓ Check in with yourself regularly. Your anxiety levels will continue to drop. The very act of getting rejected lowers your anxiety around it.
- ✓ Write about your experiences in your journal. Talk to your safe person (or people) about these experiences.

---

# MORE ON THE FEAR OF ~~REJECTION~~

Many men don't feel all that good about themselves. As you've learned, we tend to share a plethora of common core issues. These include toxic shame, feelings of inadequacy, self-limiting beliefs, anxiety, inexperience, and ineffective social skills. But the primary issue most men have when it comes to ~~rejection~~ is *niceness*.

"Being 'nice' means that you are constantly seeking external validation, especially from women," explains Dr. Glover. "This perpetual need for approval can keep you stuck in a vicious cycle because it raises your anxiety, makes you passive, makes you uninteresting, and gives others the power to determine your desirability. So, when a woman doesn't desire you the way you would like her to, it only reinforces the flawed beliefs you have about yourself."

Again, you must strike the word ~~rejection~~ from your vocabulary and rename it as low interest. Because that's all it is. It has nothing to do with your worth as a person. If you didn't already have an issue around your self-worth, you wouldn't care about a woman's low interest in you.

Still, there's no denying that the fear of ~~rejection~~ affects the lives of countless men. Treating approach like a scientific experiment and trying to get rejected are undoubtedly the most effective ways to obliterate your fear of rejection. But here are some other things you can do:

- **Become an observer.** The essence of growth is learning how to become a non-judgmental observer of yourself, further explained in an upcoming chapter. Observe the process of approaching and testing for interest. Observe your feelings. Observe your attachments. Observe your actions. Don't judge, just observe.

- **Hire a coach to teach you new skills.** Find someone who will challenge you, encourage you, and hold you accountable. If what you're doing isn't working, enlist someone to show you what does work.

- *Get out of the house, expand your route, linger in public, talk to people everywhere you go, test for interest, and walk through the open doors.*

- **Be realistic.** Many men only want to interact with the most stunningly beautiful women. If you're one of these men, you're setting yourself up for failure, primarily because you likely don't yet have the skillset (or the mindset) to approach these women. Not to mention that you've turned these women into sexual celebrities. Practice talking to *everyone* until you can talk to *anyone.*

- **Remember that women are like the weather.** They change. They're emotional. That's just their nature.

You are not defective or unlovable. If a woman shows low interest in you, take one of Dr. Glover's favorite pieces of advice and "do a happy dance." Be glad you found out quickly that she wasn't interested. Then, move on. Don't waste your time pounding on closed doors when you can walk through open doors. As David Deida writes in *The Way of the Superior Man,* "choose a woman who chooses you."

## DR. GLOVER ON MAGICAL THINKING:

Many men seem to think there is some magical way to make a woman attracted to you, even against her will. This assumption has no basis in reality.

There is no magical way to make a woman interested in you - not hypnosis, not card tricks, not DHV stories, not the "Mystery Method."

As David DeAngelo, the creator of *Double Your Dating*, says, "Attraction is not a choice."

It's either there or it's not there. You can kill it or drive it up.

Additionally, many women are just plain flaky by nature - especially single women. This isn't a blanket generalization, nor is it meant to insult women. There are a lot of amazing women out there. The more quickly you can move on from a flaky woman, the more likely it is you'll meet an amazing woman.

# FUCKABILITY

Remember: When you approach a woman, you must show up with your sexual agenda intact. After all, you're trying to determine what Dr. Glover calls her *fuckability*.[78] And she's trying to determine *your* fuckability.

Does the idea of embracing your sexual agenda scare you? Confuse you? Make you squirm a little? There's a good chance it does, especially if you buy into the myth that women don't like sex. It's also important to note that many men have some degree of sexual shame or anxiety. Subsequently, they hide their sexual agenda from both women and themselves.

When appropriate, bring your sexual agenda to every woman you meet, and test for fuckability. You might be surprised by the chemistry that unfolds. You were born a sexual being and you were wired to have sex. The same goes for women. And the same goes for all your ancestors.

"Let the essence of who you are radiate out of you in the presence of the women you meet," says Dr. Glover. "If you are comfortable with your sexuality and are comfortable manifesting it with women, you will increase your odds of meeting an amazing woman who loves sex and would be thrilled to have a sexual adventure with you."

---

78  Glover, Robert A. "Podcasts 82-83, Parts 1 and 2 of a Two-Part Series on Bringing Your Sexual Agenda to the Table" Podcast Audio. www.drglover.com

You can start embracing your sexual agenda by simply being honest with yourself. The reason you are approaching a woman is because you want to find out if she is somebody with whom you can have some sort of relationship – a relationship that likely involves you getting naked with each other. She has tits and a vagina. You want to access them.

"Fuckability is not a term of disrespect," explains Dr. Glover. "Really, fuckability is nothing more than consciousness. It's loving good sex and not holding back."

---

**fuckability** [fuh-ka-bilədē]

*noun Sociology*

the quality of embracing one's sexuality, enjoying sex, and being comfortable with the idea of sex

a set of qualities and characteristics that make someone a viable candidate for a romantic relationship

---

Trying to determine a woman's fuckability doesn't mean you should be blatantly sexual or otherwise creepy upon first meeting her. Nor does it mean that you should try to sneak in your sexual agenda later, after you've acted like you just want to be her friend. But you must embrace your sexual agenda early on, create Positive Emotional Tension, and get to ~~rejection~~ quickly.

Fuckability relates to much more than physical appearance, by the way. If you're attracted to a woman, that's great. But…do you enjoy her company? Do you find her interesting? Does she show interest in you? Does she follow your lead? Is she receptive to your sexual energy? Is she a cool person?

You may be approaching women for sex, but hopefully you are evolved enough to know that women are far more than just sex objects.

# MOJO MANTRAS

Dr. Glover often points out an inescapable truth: *Most women want to be fucked. They want to be fucked often and fucked well.* How would you behave differently if you knew this?

All humans – including you – came to exist through an act of sexual intercourse. We are sexual beings. Are you comfortable with *that*?

You were put on this planet to fuck and procreate. Are you comfortable with that? Women love sex just as much as men. And women are biologically wired to have more orgasms than men. Are you comfortable with ***that***?

If you're not comfortable with these realities, get comfortable with them.

As Dr. Glover explains, "the man who isn't comfortable with these realities will try to become a woman's friend, hoping she will develop feelings for him. He hides his sexuality from himself and the woman. He does everything to get her to approve of him. As a result, there is no sexual tension and no sexual activity. Meanwhile, the man who is completely comfortable with these realities knows he is talking to a woman because he has a cock and she has a vagina. He knows that *she* knows this, too. He is relaxed and playful. He invites her into this space. If she obliges, he walks through the open door without hesitation."

Incidentally, if you find all of this sex-talk unsettling because of your religious convictions, you may want to consider that according to the book of Genesis, the first commandment God gave to Adam and Eve was basically to go fuck a lot.

"The Gospels do not contain even one instance of Jesus condemning anyone for having sex," points out Dr. Glover. "You can look it up yourself. Or you can take my word for it, given that I grew up in a fundamental Christian church and before I got my PhD, I was in the ministry."

It's time to get over the idea that wanting sex is shallow or that you are bad for wanting sex. If you are uncomfortable embracing your sexual agenda, consider using what Dr. Glover calls ***Mojo Mantras***.[79]

As you move about the world, repeat this to yourself: *I love to fuck and women love to be fucked by me.* Or try these:

- *I'm a fucking machine.*
- *Everywhere I go, women want me.*
- *I'll take a woman places she's never been.*
- *My cock is a weapon of mass destruction.*
- *Women want me and men envy me.*
- *Women get wet when I enter the room.*

These mantras may seem silly at first, but using them to shift your thinking can help you develop a healthier relationship with your sexuality and put you in the right frame of mind for talking to women.

> **INTEGRATED ACTION:**
> ✓ Are you comfortable with the reality that we are all sexual be-ings? If not, how might your life be different if you were com-fortable with it? How might your relationships be different? Write your answers in your journal.
> ✓ Pick one *mojo mantra* and repeat it to yourself every day for the next week. Or mix them up and practice a different *mojo mantra* every day. Make note of how you feel. Did you notice any women noticing you? Write about the experience in your journal.

---

79  Glover, Robert A. "Podcast 22, Parts 1 of a Three-Part Series on Sex" Podcast Au-dio. www.drglover.com

# WHY DO WOMEN LIKE ASSHOLES?

If women tend to be security-seeking creatures, why do so many women fall for liars, manipulators, narcissists, and even abusers? Are the women blind? Are they morons? Are they masochists? What's the deal? What the fuck? What is it about so-called Bad Boys? Why do women like assholes?[80]

These are questions routinely asked by frustrated Nice Guys from all walks of life. I used to ask the same questions, often baffled by the dangerously stupid decisions I'd see women make. But women don't always act in their own best interest. As Dr. Glover points out, "Women can be security-seeking creatures and still make bad decisions."

Maybe it's time for you to do something that has helped me tremendously, which is to let go of the need for everything to make perfect sense. As you've learned, a woman's brain is governed by the fluidity of her emotions, while a man's brain is governed by reason and logic. You can't make logical sense out of the seemingly illogical.

That said, women don't actually like *assholes*. They don't fantasize about *assholes*. And they don't seek out *assholes*. But assholes tend to exude masculinity and confidence (albeit a kind of pseudo-confidence), which are turn ons for women. As previously mentioned, assholes do what many men don't: They create *tension*.

---

80   Glover, Robert A. "Podcast 62: Why are Women Attracted to Jerks?" Podcast Audio. www.drglover.com

Let's look at a classic scenario:

A woman has recently started dating two men. She calls the first man, and he doesn't answer. So, she starts thinking about him. She wonders what he's doing. She questions whether he even likes her. She begins fantasizing, hoping he's not with another woman. After five or six hours pass, he calls back.

Later, she calls the second man. He answers immediately. They have a perfectly nice conversation that lasts around a half an hour.

As she goes to bed, which man do you figure she's thinking about more? Who do you think she finds more attractive? Who caused a stirring in her loins? Who created more tension? The second man may be healthier for her. But the first man created more tension.

*** 

Again, women often go for assholes because assholes create tension. Assholes may be constantly unavailable, they might lie or cheat, they might even be verbally or physically abusive. Sadly, though, this can keep women connected because it activates their biological programming.

My ex-girlfriend Katie, for example, is a bright, beautiful, kind-hearted woman. When we met, she had just ended a horrifically toxic and abusive relationship, which she stayed in for 18 years. Yes, *18 years*. 18 years with an absolute psycho. During moments of clarity, Katie knew she needed to find a way out. But the constant tension and ceaseless drama kept her hooked.

Meanwhile, Nice Guys never create any tension because they act like puppy dogs (and they hate tension). Assholes make women feel something. Nice Guys don't. Even if an asshole makes a woman miserable, at least she feels *something*. Does this mean you should be an asshole? Of course not. It means that you should be an Integrated Man who creates tension in positive, healthy, and loving ways.

If there is one thing that ultimately separates the assholes from the Nice Guys, it's that assholes are not completely weak and ineffective around women. In fact, the next time you are in a predicament with a woman, ask yourself: *What's the strongest course of action here?*

If a woman tries to put you in the friend zone, for example, the weakest course of action is to accept friendship and become what Dr. Glover likes to call "a girlfriend with a penis." The strongest course? Say 'thanks but no thanks' and walk away.

---

**INTEGRATED ACTION:**
- ✓ Do you know any assholes who are infuriatingly good at meeting and attracting women? Why do you think women find them so attractive? Write your thoughts in your journal.
- ✓ Think about your relationships with women. Where are you exhibiting weakness? How can you exhibit more strength? Write your answers in your journal.

---

# NEGATIVITY & RESENTMENT TOWARDS WOMEN

When Dr. Glover started writing *No More Mr. Nice Guy,* he was still married to his second wife – a woman who didn't treat him very well, to put it mildly. As Dr. Glover describes, "If you made a list of anything that a person could do to another that would be a legitimate reason to get divorced, my second wife did them all."

Understandably, Dr. Glover harbored feelings of negativity and resentment towards his second wife. But once he realized that he'd been projecting those feelings onto all women, he knew that he needed to make some shifts.

"I kept getting feedback on some of those early book chapters that I seemed to have a lot of anger towards women," shares Dr. Glover. "So, I decided that I needed to look inside myself. Then, when a woman I was dating asked me about my mother and I described my mother as a 'passive-aggressive cunt,' I realized that I probably needed to work on my mommy issues, too."

Dr. Glover's story is hardly uncommon. Many men have some degree of resentment and negativity towards women.[81] This is especially true for single men who struggle to find success in dating, or for men who tend to get

---

81 Glover, Robert A. "Podcasts 100 & 101: Parts 1 & 2 of a Two-Part Series on Overcoming Resentment and Negativity Toward Women." Podcast Audio. www.drglover.com

involved with damaged women. Add to that our current reliance on dating apps, which have paved the way for ghosting, mosting, cloaking, cricketing, kittenfishing, and a bunch of other ridiculously stupid terms we've invented to describe appalling human behavior. These kinds of experiences can leave men with emotional scars, causing them to resent not just one woman but women in general.

As Dr. Glover illustrates, here are some other reasons a man might have negativity and resentment towards women:

- **Insecurity and social awkwardness as a teen:** Most young boys are not socially adept. In fact, girls' brains form earlier and in more ways that allow them to negotiate social situations. So, if you weren't the captain of the football team or the kid with the Camaro, you likely didn't have much luck with girls. This can be especially damaging because your brain is being flooded with hormones during a time when you are developing your identity and your beliefs about yourself. You are driven by sex hormones when getting sex feels damn near impossible.

- **SLBs:** You believe your SLBs to be true, and then act as though they are true. Thus, you get results consistent with your SLBs.

- **Lack of boundaries:** If you spend time with women who behave badly or treat you badly, it's your fault. (If you let *anyone* treat you badly, it's your fault.) But you will develop negative beliefs about women based on your experiences with them.

- **Lack of understanding:** Not understanding how women are different from men can cause a lot of issues. Again, men try to use the male brain to understand the female brain. But the female brain isn't wired like the male brain. Men are constantly trying to solve the unsolvable. If you keep doing what doesn't work, you'll always walk away feeling resentful.

- **Using Covert Contracts:** Do you believe that because you're a Nice Guy people should like you and love you, and women should want

THE BIG STICK

to sleep with you? Remember: Covert contracts don't work, and they almost always lead to frustration, resentment, and anger.

- **Seeking the approval and validation of beautiful women:** Wanting only the most attractive women is purely about your ego. Only an insecure man feels he *needs* a beautiful woman on his arm. But the very act of putting a woman on a pedestal and trying to get her validation leads to resentment. "You've given her all the power," explains Dr. Glover. "As a result you will always feel powerless. And this tends to create a shitload of resentment."

Be conscious of your projections and generalizations. Just because a woman (or even a few women) have treated you badly, it doesn't mean all women will.

Indeed, there are badly behaved women in the world. There are mean women. There are gold-digging women. There are women who go on dates purely for the free meals. There are women who trade their beauty for material things. There are women who take their husbands to the cleaners because they want *his* things. There are women who think they have free reign to behave badly because they have big fake tits and nice round asses. But you can't blame women.

*Men* have created this monster.

Men have created the culture of worshiping beautiful women.

It's no wonder so many men have so much resentment towards women.

Generalizing all women doesn't serve you. Your projections are what keep you safe. They allow you to blame others for your situation. They allow you to stay victimized. You then find comfort in your negativity and resentment. And you probably find other men who share your feelings so you can support each other's paradigms.

Is this how you want to live?

If you harbor negativity and resentment towards women, work at letting those feelings go. When feelings of negativity and resentment towards women bubble up, just observe your feelings without resistance or criticism. And the next time you're interacting with a woman, try humanizing her. Ponder who she is as a person. What are her life experiences? What are her parents like? What might her fears and insecurities be?

Don't walk the planet with negativity and resentment. There are a lot of truly amazing women out there – cool, open-hearted, down-to-earth, fun-loving, beautiful women who take accountability for their own shit. And many of them are just waiting for you to walk up and introduce yourself.

---

**INTEGRATED ACTION:**
- ✓ Be honest with yourself. Do you have negativity and resentment towards women? What story is the resentment telling you about yourself? How is this story keeping you stuck? Write your answers in your journal.
- ✓ Talk about your feelings of negativity and resentment with a safe person (or people).

---

# PART IV:
# CONSCIOUS DATING

*Dating is about finding out who you are*
*and who others are. If you show up in*
*a masquerade outfit, neither is going to*
*happen.*
**- Henry Cloud**

Two divorces and more than thirty years as a marriage and family ther-apist gave Dr. Glover a valuable insight: ***The way that most people date pro-vides the worst possible foundation upon which to build a healthy long-term relationship.***

"People tend to date unconsciously," explains Dr. Glover. "They try and get their new crush to like them, they seduce, they fuse, they rush into sex, they ignore all sorts of red flags. They often live in a fantasy world about what a relationship with someone would be like. Time and time again, I've seen first-hand how people begin their relationships and what they end up with months or years later. I've also experienced this myself in my first two marriages."

Given how most of us approach dating, it's easy to see why nearly all re-lationships go down the shitter, that half of all marriages end in divorce, and that only a small fraction of married couples report being happy.[82] The way you date determines the kind of relationships you have. And the typical man approaches dating like this:

He doesn't have a plan. Nor does he have any idea what he wants. He just knows he's lonely. And he believes that a woman is the remedy for what ails him. Maybe he gets lucky and meets a woman who shows interest - probably on a dating app. She isn't all that bad looking; so, he works up the nerve to ask her out. He does his best to make a great first impression. If they hit it off, he starts texting and calling her regularly. He then gives up most of the things that are important to him to spend as much time with her as possible. If she's willing, they start having sex. All the while, he turns the other cheek at every warning sign that comes up. The relationship inevitably starts to go south, but he does everything he can to keep it together. He becomes needy. He panics. He's riddled with anxiety. He can't imagine feeling lonely and having to start the dating process all over again.

Sound familiar?

This is largely how my dating life played out for years. If you've been down the same road - or you're currently stranded alongside it with no help in sight - then you know how frustrating it is. Most of the time, your approach to dating probably leads to heartache, or it leads to getting stuck with someone who either disappoints you or drives you nuts. But you can reengineer your dating life by taking a more *conscious* approach, which Dr. Glover details – and adamantly recommends – in his second book, *Dating Essentials for Men: The Only Dating Guide You Will Ever Need*.

There's no denying that modern dating can be an infuriating, time-wasting, mind-boggling clusterfuck. If done consciously, however, dating can be a vehicle for profound personal growth.

"Conscious dating is like standing naked, completely exposed in front of every woman in the world and asking if they find you interesting enough

---

82  Shapiro, Dana Adam. *You Can Be Right or You Can Be Married* (Scribner 2012)

to spend time with - and maybe get naked with – despite all your visible and invisible flaws," describes Dr. Glover. "But this doesn't mean it's about being judged. It's about making yourself vulnerable and challenging your self-limiting beliefs. If you set the tone, take the lead, and date with consciousness, you'll increase your odds of meeting a Really Great Woman."

Principally, though, Conscious Dating[83] is about going slow. It's about keeping your mind and your eyes open. Much like Dr. Glover, I have seen and experienced first-hand how both men and women date unconsciously and then end up in a world of shit months or years later. I've worked with far too many clients whose lives are in shambles solely because they got involved with the wrong person. Whether you are single, actively dating, or in a relationship, the information in this section can positively change your life. If you're an exceptionally bad dater, I believe it can *save* your life.

---

83   Dr. Glover frequently discusses the importance - and the power - of dating consciously. *Dating Essentials For Men*, in its entirety is about Conscious Dating. Although Dr. Glover doesn't use the phrase "conscious dating" until page 212. For additional information on Conscious Dating, see Glover, Robert A. "Podcasts 81: The Power of Conscious Dating" and "Podcasts 134-136: Parts 1-3 of a Three-Part Series on Attachment to Outcome and Conscious Dating." Podcast Audio. www.drglover.com

# EMBRACING ABUNDANCE II

If you haven't yet figured it out, I'll go ahead and spill the beans: **Abundance** is a recurring theme throughout this book. And there's a reason. Of all the tips, tricks, tools, and techniques I've learned on my self-development journey, Abundance thinking was perhaps the hardest for me to adopt. It has also been the most life-changing.

A lot of men struggle to internalize the concept of abundance, not because they don't understand it, but because they simply don't believe it. For much of their lives, they've been gathering evidence that supports their deprivation view of the world – or their scarcity mindset. They believe there just isn't enough to go around. Or they believe that good things never come to them. It can take a significant amount of work and dedicated practice to undo this kind of thinking.

If you have a deprivation view of the world, make the effort to start embracing abundance. (Meanwhile, I'll make the effort throughout this book to pound the idea into your head.) Abundance thinking is important in every area of life. But it is perhaps nowhere more important than it is in modern dating, as it can save you from a great deal of anger, bitterness, and frustration.

When you venture into the world of modern dating – especially if you use dating apps – you are going to encounter a lot of rude, flakey, immature, or otherwise bad behavior. You might be ghosted, stood up, or catfished. You might fall victim to benching, breadcrumbing, roaching, or cloaking. You might be friend zoned. You might be love-bombed, devalued, and discarded. These kinds of things are almost guaranteed to happen, no matter who you are or what you look like or how much status you have. When these things do happen, they aren't much fun. But they are a hell of a lot easier to stomach when you have an abundance mindset.[84]

How do you think your dating life would change if you knew, without a shadow of a doubt, that the world is a place of abundance?

How might your behavior change if you knew that there are endless opportunities for you?

How might you respond to bad behavior if you knew that there are eight *billion* people on the planet and "another bus comes every 15 minutes?"

Dr. Glover frequently shares how a shift in mindset positively impacted his own dating life. While successful in meeting and attracting women, he was struggling to find his Really Great Woman - a woman who was available to get all the way into a committed and sustained relationship.

"I was always throwing myself a pity party," remembers Dr. Glover. "I was constantly wallowing in deprivation, wondering why it was so hard to love me. But then, one dark night of the soul, I had a Come-to-Jesus moment. I realized that if I wanted to experience a shift in my life, I had to break out of my deprivation thinking. I had to open up to abundance."

Dr. Glover immediately did two things: First, he started a gratitude practice that required him to think of every person in his life who loved him imperfectly – Mom, Dad, ex-wives, a few girlfriends, some friends. He then focused on how each of these people had blessed his life despite their inability to love him perfectly or completely. As a result, Dr. Glover's mood began

---

84    For more information on the concept of abundance, see Glover, Robert A. *Dating Essentials for Men* (Robert A. Glover, Ph.D, Inc, 2019) "Chapter 4: Discover the Power of Abundance Thinking," and Glover, Robert A. "Podcasts 4 & 5: Parts 1 & 2 of a Two-Part Series on Abundance." Podcast Audio. www.drglover.com

to shift. He became grateful and optimistic, eventually opening his eyes to the abundance in the world.

Dr. Glover then began repeating a mantra to himself: *In the next 90-days, I am going to cross paths with at least three women who have the potential to be my Really Great Woman.* He wholeheartedly committed to clearing out any residual negativity – and anything else in his life that could prevent him from intimately connecting with these women. To increase the odds of meeting these women, he also committed to getting out of the house and becoming a social animal.

You may be wondering if these simple abundance practices did in fact help Dr. Glover reshape his dating life and ultimately connect with a Really Great Woman. Well, as I write this, Dr. Glover is about to celebrate his sixth wedding anniversary with his spunky, strong-willed, stunningly beautiful, Spanish-speaking wife, Lupita.

When you adopt an abundance mindset, you'll begin to behave differently. Thinking abundantly will prevent you from acting needy, from seeking approval and validation, and from getting hung up on one woman. You'll exude confidence and masculinity. You'll let go of attachment to outcomes. You won't take a woman's low interest personally. And you'll no longer tolerate intolerable behavior. With an abundance mindset, you'll know that each day provides yet another opportunity to meet a Really Great Woman.

---

**INTEGRATED ACTION:**
- ✓ If you knew, without a shadow of a doubt, that the world is a place of abundance, how would your dating life change? How would you respond differently to women's low interest? Write your answers in your journal.
- ✓ Have you started a Gratitude Practice yet? How about an Abundance Love Practice? If so, keep going. If not, start now. It's time for you to shift how you see the world.

---

# THE PURPOSE OF DATING

Because most of us date unconsciously, we tend to overlook (or forget) the real purpose of dating. Many men seem to have just three criteria when evaluating a woman:

- She's not bad looking
- She seems to like me.
- She's willing to have sex with me.

But even if a woman meets all these criteria, a man can still end up living in some version of relationship hell. After all, the *real* purpose of dating is to **discover another person's nature.**[85]

Being attractive and wanting to have sex with you are undoubtedly wonderful qualities, but they aren't the only qualities that make someone worth dating long-term. Instead of trying solely to determine whether or not a woman will spread her legs for you, you'll be much better off trying to find out the answers to questions like:

- Is she cool?
- Does she share your values?
- Does she come from a good family?

---

85  For more information on discovering a woman's nature, see Glover, Robert A. *Dating Essentials For Men* (Robert A. Glover, Ph.D, Inc, 2019) pp.141-142, Glover, Robert A. "Podcast 26 & 29: Parts 2 and 5 of a Seven-Part Series on Finding a Really Great Woman," and Glover, Robert A. "Podcast 81: The Power of Conscious Dating." Podcast Audio. www.drglover.com

- Does she have the characteristics you are looking for in a partner?
- Do you enjoy spending time with her?
- Are there any red or yellow flags?

This is not to discourage you from having fun. If you are looking purely for sex, there are plenty of women out there who are looking for the same thing. But even a casual sex partner can fuck up your life if you're not mindful. (Just watch Fatal Attraction[86]).

Let's assume, though, that you are looking for a relationship with a Really Great Woman – a woman who blesses your life, who brings out the best in you, and who isn't a lunatic. If you want to find your Really Great Woman, you must do something different than what you've been doing. You must leave behind your old, bullshit criteria and date more consciously. Test, test, test, and test some more. As Dr. Glover loves to say, *go as slowly as possible to find out as quickly as possible what a woman's nature is.*

Put any woman you date into a variety of situations that allow you to discover her nature. Do this consciously. Observe her to determine if she has the characteristics of a woman who could bless your life.

"To discover a woman's nature," asserts Dr. Glover, "you need to see how she behaves in a lot of different scenarios. Have her ride a bus with you. Take a short trip together. Cook together. Run errands together. Do a lot of different things together in a lot of different settings. You have to do this to find out if someone is going to make a quality long-term partner."

Dr. Glover offers several other ways you can go as slowly as possible to find out as quickly as possible what a woman's nature is:

---

86  Released in 1987, *Fatal Attraction* is an Academy Award-nominated film starring Michael Douglas, Glenn Close, and Anne Archer. In the film, Daniel "Dan" Gallagher (played by Douglas) is a successful, happily-married lawyer whose work leads him to meet Alexandra "Alex" Forrest (played by Close), an editor for a publishing company. While his wife, Beth (played by Archer), and daughter, are out of town for the weekend, Dan has an affair with Alex. Alex begins to cling to him. A shit show ensues.

- **Always be working on your Great Cake of a Life.** Invite her to be the icing on your cake. Welcome her into your world to do the things you love to do. See how she responds. Don't get caught up in doing things *she* likes to do. Keep living *your* life.

- **Introduce her to your friends and family and spend time with her friends and family.** Pay attention to how she interacts with them and how they interact with her. How she acts with them is eventually how she will act with you.

- **Stay off the phone.** Don't chit-chat, don't text. These are forms of pseudo-communication that create an intense bond without you really getting to know each other. Use the phone (and that includes texting) only to set up in-person dates.

- **Always pay attention to what a woman does and not what she says.** "She may tell you who she perceives herself to be or who she wants you to perceive her to be." explains Dr. Glover. "But what she tells you may not match who she really is. Her behavior will tell you a lot more."

- **Resist any temptation to fuse, to become enmeshed, or to get really close really quickly.** The temptation to fuse is a Feminine trait, but many men want to fuse just as much as women. Don't fuse with someone who you don't actually know very well.

Much of this may dampen your love-at-first-sight fantasies of whirlwind romance. Admittedly, there are few things in life as exhilarating as meeting someone with whom you feel an instant and indescribable chemistry. But love-at-first-sight is often just *lust*-at-first-sight, and almost never leads to happily-ever-after. Conscious Dating may require you to go slowly, but it will dramatically increase your odds of meeting a Really Great Woman.

**INTEGRATED ACTION:**

✓ How have you ignored the real purpose of dating in the past? How did it work out? Write about your experience(s) in your journal.

✓ How many of your past relationships have blessed your life? Write your answer in your journal.

✓ Have you started your Abundance Practice yet? Have you been learning to think more abundantly?

# YOUR REALLY GREAT WOMAN

Here's a golden rule of life: *Whenever you settle, you get exactly what you settled for*. Of course, settling is easy. Finding **your Really Great Woman,** on the other hand, requires work and perhaps a bit of luck. But it is entirely possible. And it is worth the effort.

"It's understandable that you might settle," acknowledges Dr. Glover. "Even though it's not the relationship you really want, maybe you think it's the best you can do. Maybe you think you're being too picky. Or maybe you don't want to be alone or go through the dating process again. I suggest you work to give up that line of thinking. Do not settle for less than a Really Great Woman. If you do, you'll probably regret it."

A Really Great Woman is the kind of woman who will lighten your load and won't add to your burden. She will challenge you in healthy ways. She will bring out the best in you. She's not perfect – nobody is. And she's not your "soul mate." She's just an amazing human being with whom you absolutely love spending time.

While your Really Great Woman could be any number of women walking the planet, this number is relatively small. The vast majority of women will not be your Really Great Woman. This is not meant to discourage you; nor is it meant to give you one-itis.[87] But it is the truth. Consider the odds

---

87    "One-itis" is a term commonly used by the pickup community to describe a man's unhealthy obsession with one specific woman

that you and a Really Great Woman meet in precisely the right place at precisely the right time, when you're both ready, available, and open for commitment. It's a statistical rarity.

Indeed, you could stumble across a Really Great Woman following the traditional dating model and doing what you've been doing (unless you've been doing nothing). But why leave something this important purely to chance? Serendipity can happen, but you'll be much more likely to meet a Really Great Woman with the following roadmap:[88]

**Create a Great Cake of a Life:**

A Really Great Woman – a woman who has her shit together – will want you to have your shit together, too. She'll want you to have a life. It's your responsibility to create a rich and fulfilling life for yourself – the kind of life that naturally attracts women to you. As you've already learned, Dr. Glover calls this a **Great Cake of a Life.**

If you don't have a Great Cake of a Life, don't wait until you meet a woman to do something about it. Do something about it now. Get off the internet, get out of the house, and work on your Great Cake. That said, don't let your mind convince you that you must create a perfectly Great Cake before you can work on your dating skills. This is a common excuse men make to avoid doing what scares them. But you can do both at the same time. You can look for your Really Great Woman while making your really Great Cake.

"Start with a simple bucket list," advises Dr. Glover. "Make a list of things you want to do, classes you want to take, skills you want to learn, places you want to go. Start checking these things off your list. If you can, find other men to do some of these things with. Don't give up any of this stuff once you meet a woman. Many men lose sight of everything in their lives when they meet a woman. But this is a recipe for disaster. Don't try to adapt to a woman's life.

---

88  Glover, Robert A. *Dating Essentials for Men* (Robert A. Glover, Ph.D, Inc, 2019) "Chapter 18: Follow This Roadmap to Find Your Really Great Woman."

Invite a woman to join you in your life. Invite her to be the icing on your Great Cake."

When you create a Great Cake of a Life, you'll dramatically increase your odds of meeting a Really Great Woman. You'll expand your social world and sharpen your emotional intelligence. This puts you in the position to meet more interesting people. And as Dr. Glover frequently proclaims, *miracles happen around people.*

**Make Your 5 & 5 List:**

If you don't know what you're looking for, you'll probably never find it. Many men never think about what they're looking for beyond someone with a nice ass and great tits who fucks like a porn star. This is exactly why so many men end up in bad relationships.

"To find a Really Great Woman," asserts Dr. Glover, "you need an objective way to evaluate the women you meet. You need a way to determine whether or not she is a good match for you. You could be with someone who is very wrong for you, and you won't find out until it's far too late."

One of the simplest and most effective ways to evaluate the women you meet is by using what Dr. Glover calls a **5 & 5 List.** To create your list, get out a sheet of paper and draw a line down the middle. On the left side, write down at least five characteristics you ***must have*** in a partner. On the right side, write down at least five characteristics you absolutely ***will not tolerate.***

For a woman to be your Really Great Woman, she must possess all the characteristics on the 'Must Have' side of your list. There is no right or wrong here. Your Must Haves are based on your personal preferences – your wants and needs – and they may change over time with experience (both good and bad).

Most men list characteristics like honesty, intelligence, emotional stability, fidelity, humor, passion, and sexuality. Of course, most men also list physical traits, too - and that's okay. But your Really Great Woman should be someone you're attracted to on a multitude of levels.

The 'Will Not Tolerate' side of your list is non-negotiable. These are deal-breakers. **No exceptions**. This side of your list might include things like dishonesty, anger issues, mood disorders, addictions, emotional instability, laziness, and little to no interest in sex. Again, these are deal-breakers. If a woman demonstrates any of these characteristics, move on. Immediately.

"Don't give a woman the benefit of the doubt," advises Dr. Glover. "These are the kinds of characteristics that will destroy you and destroy your relationship, no matter what. It's that simple. *How you find them is how they are.*"

Men often fool themselves into thinking that once a woman overcomes her depression, conquers her addiction, resolves her money problems, or gets over her abusive ex, she will turn into the perfect life partner. This almost never happens, which men usually learn the hard way.

"Don't choose a woman based on her *perceived* potential," asserts Dr. Glover. "Investing in a diamond in the rough is not a good dating strategy."

If you are actively dating, making your 5 & 5 List is an essential exercise. You might find that the characteristics you must have and the characteristics you will not tolerate are just the opposite of each other. This is perfectly fine. In fact, observing the characteristics from both sides can help you get even clearer on what you want and what you don't want.

Your 5 & 5 List will very likely evolve as you evolve. Put your list where you can see it. Review it regularly, especially when you start dating someone new.

If you've had several dates with a woman, consider showing her your 5 & 5 List. Most men are quite reluctant to do this because they think it will either piss off the woman or scare her away. But this is unlikely to happen.

"If she does react negatively, that's great," affirms Dr. Glover. "Do you really want to be with a woman who thinks it's a negative thing that you put some conscious thought into what you want in a relationship? Now, if your list just says you want a woman who is 20 years younger and has big tits, then the woman might be offended. But if your list says things like honesty, integrity, and intelligence, then a healthy, mature woman will appreciate your list. And she'll probably tell you that she has a list of her own."

---

**INTEGRATED ACTION:**

✓  Make your 5 & 5 List. Evaluate your most recent relationships to see how they match up with your list. Think about how your list reflects dynamics from your past relationships that you would like to change moving forward. Also, remember that '5' is not a magic number – you can write more than 5 characteristics on your list.

✓  Share your 5 & 5 List with a safe person and ask for feedback.

---

# THE RELATIONSHIP PYRAMID

Remember, you need a roadmap – an objective way to evaluate the women you meet. Without it, you're likely to get involved with someone who could be very wrong for you, particularly if you're a bad dater who tends to repeat the same patterns. So, in addition to working on your Great Cake of a Life and creating your 5 & 5 List, you can make use of what Dr. Glover calls the *Relationship Pyramid*.

Again, you'll be evaluating women based on your own preferences and from your own perspective. But every woman on the planet falls somewhere inside the relationship pyramid:

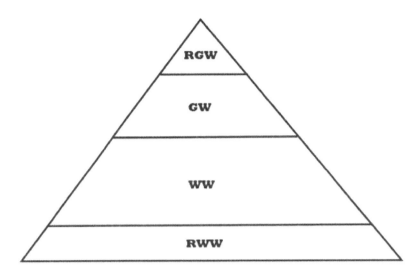

At the top of the pyramid, you'll find your **Really Great Woman (RGW).** Your Really Great Woman matches perfectly with your 5 & 5 List. Fundamentally, there's nothing about her you would change. A Really Great Woman is the only kind of woman with whom you should be in a long-term relationship. This doesn't mean you should hunt for unicorns (or get one-itis), but it does mean you should be unwilling to settle.

Beneath your Really Great Woman (on the pyramid), you'll find **Good Women (GW).** There are a hell of a lot of Good Women out there. A Good Woman, however, is not someone you want to spend a large part of your life with. There are things about her you would like to change. But you can't change someone. It's unloving. And it's not possible.

"Because you'll always be trying to change a Good Woman, you'll become manipulative," explains Dr. Glover. "And you'll always be somewhat disappointed. You'll wish she was different. You'll fantasize about being with someone else. You'll start seeing women everywhere who look like they are a better fit. You'll become resentful. And you'll probably start to act out by watching porn or having affairs because you settled."

Next on the pyramid are **Wrong Women (WW).** Most of the women you meet will be Wrong Women. This is not necessarily a judgment of character.

A Wrong Woman just isn't a good match for you, and this could be for any number of reasons. Maybe she's already in a relationship. Or she is too old. Or she speaks Cantonese (and you don't). Or maybe you're just not attracted to her. Don't waste your time with a Wrong Woman.

Lastly, at the bottom of the pyramid, you'll find **Really Wrong Women (RWW)**. Avoid these women like the fucking plague. Really Wrong Women include dishonest or deceitful women, drama queens, insecure and jealous women, angry, rageful, resentful, vindictive women, abusive women, emotionally unstable women, cheaters, alcoholics, addicts, women with mood disorders, and toxic feminist man-haters. Should you meet a Really Wrong Woman, move on as quickly as possible.

> ### THE QUEEN MOTHERS OF REALLY WRONG WOMEN:
>
> Unfortunately, the Queen Mothers of Really Wrong Women have a hard-to-recognize, commonly misdiagnosed condition: **Borderline Personality Disorder**. Nice Guys especially tend to get involved with Borderlines. Borderlines can be incredibly seductive and charismatic. But you will always feel crazy with a Borderline.
>
> As Dr. Glover illustrates, "Borderlines turn their feelings into facts. They can't separate their dream states from reality. They re-write history. They make you question your own sanity. They can't be alone. They often exhibit compulsive behaviors. They lie and cheat. They push you away and pull you back in. Ultimately, they'll make your life a living hell."

Unfortunately, many men get involved with Really Wrong Women and stay way too long. Dr. Glover explains that this usually happens for two reasons:

1. **Her dysfunction matches his dysfunction.** It's not uncommon for a man to be attracted to the worst kind of woman for him because she gives him the opportunity to act out his own dysfunction.

2. **Really Wrong Women can be very seductive.** They frequently use their sexuality, neediness, and intelligence to manipulate. But they often feel defective inside. They don't believe anyone could love them just as they are. So, they go out of their way to seduce.

As Dr. Glover likes to tell men, "If a woman tries to give you a blow job in the front seat of your car on the first date, run like hell. She's fucked up. A healthy woman might be turned on by you, but she'll invite you to take her. She won't seduce you with cheap tricks. A Really Wrong Woman learned a long time ago how to hook the average guy. It's up to you if you want to run before or after the blow job."

**Warning:** A Really Wrong Woman might initially seem like a Really Great Woman. She might be funny, smart, and successful. Don't be fooled. Keep your 5 & 5 List handy. As soon as you notice intolerable behavior, get the hell out of there.

## RED & YELLOW FLAGS

In traditional dating, both men and women expend a hell of a lot of energy trying to make a good first impression. Most of us try to put our best foot forward. We've got our game faces on, as we work to win the approval and acceptance of the other person. We do our best to demonstrate what a great catch we are. Basically, we're all fucking phony, which is why traditional dating can make it difficult to find a Really Great Woman.

"It isn't until somewhere down the line that you start discovering who the person you've been dating really is," says Dr. Glover. "By then, you're enmeshed, you're having regular sex, maybe you're talking about the next steps in your relationship. Making corrections at this point can be problematic."

The point of the Relationship Pyramid and your 5 & 5 list is to help you keep the purpose of dating top of mind. Always be testing – testing for honesty, testing for passion, testing for open-mindedness, testing for any characteristics that are important to you. *Go as slowly as possible to find out as quickly as possible what a woman's nature is.*

Your 5 & 5 List will help you identify glaring Red Flags. Don't ignore these. Don't think that a woman will change or that troublesome behaviors will magically disappear. And don't try to rationalize behaviors you don't want to put up with.

Don't ignore *Yellow* Flags, either. These are the little things that may not be on your 5 & 5 List but that catch your attention as you get to know a woman. Make a mental note of these things to determine if they are indicative of larger problems.

Is she always running late?

Does she have old boyfriends constantly sniffing around?

Does she have trouble keeping track of her finances?

Does she drink a little too much every time you are together?

These kinds of behaviors are not to be swept under the rug. Remember: Always pay attention to what a woman does, not what she says. If a woman tells you something about herself, observe how she behaves to see if it's true. A woman's behavior defines her.

"Never dismiss bad behavior of any kind," advises Dr. Glover. "If it shows up early, it will show up frequently as the relationship evolves. Ask yourself if you can envision spending the rest of your life with the woman just as she is right now. If you hesitate to answer this with a resounding 'Yes,' then you probably need to move on."

Dating is indeed a numbers game. And Really Great Women are few and far between. Know what you're looking for. If you are actively dating, there is no way to avoid meeting Good Women, Wrong Women, and *Really* Wrong Women. But your 5 & 5 List and the Relationship Pyramid can prevent you from getting into ongoing dysfunctional relationships with them. Eventually, your Really Great Woman will present herself. And when she does, you can walk right through the open door.

**INTEGRATED ACTION:**

- ✓ What kind of women do you tend to date? RGW, GW, WW, or RWW? Write about your experiences in your journal. And share them with a safe person.
- ✓ How have your past relationships allowed you to act out your own dysfunction? Write your answer in your journal.
- ✓ Moving forward, use the Relationship Pyramid as a guide when evaluating women.

## THE 12/12 CHALLENGE

If you want to become skilled at anything, you need to prac-tice – a lot. Dating is no exception.

This is why Dr. Glover often challenges men to **go on 12 dates with 12 different women in 12 weeks.**

The 12/12 challenge is perfect for men who have little ex-perience dating, lack confidence, or need to practice their dating skills. The challenge can't be half-assed. It requires a commitment, even if you have no idea how you are going to meet 12 women. But this is purely for practice. So, it doesn't matter what kind of women you date. Women of all kinds will do.

Approaching the challenge this way frees you to focus on improving your skills instead of trying to get someone to like you. The 12/12 allows you to practice approaching women, asking women out, having conversations with women, test-ing for interest, setting the tone and taking the lead, and cre-ating Positive Emotional Tension.

Men who commit to the 12/12 Challenge often find a wom-an they want to keep dating. This is great. But the beauty of the 12/12 Challenge is that it allows men to fail repeatedly. And each time they fail, they learn something new they can apply to their next date.

**So, what about you? Are you up for the 12/12 Challenge?**

# FIRST DATE BASICS

Many men think they know how to date. So, they end up scratching their heads when a first date doesn't transpire the way they'd hoped. But a lot of men don't actually know how to date as well as they think they do. Often, they gloriously fuck up the basics.

If you're one of these men, don't feel bad. Most of us were never taught how to date. We just bumble our way through, trying to figure out what works and what doesn't. Perhaps the only difference between those who experience success and those who repeatedly fail is the willingness to learn from one's mistakes.

If you want to increase the odds that your next first date will lead to a second, consider following the basic strategies that Dr. Glover prescribes in *Dating Essentials for Men*[89]. He prescribes them for a reason: They work.

**Have a plan.**

Know when and where you want to meet the woman. Your plan can be adjusted, of course. But having an initial plan is a powerful way to start setting the tone and taking the lead. Ideally, your first date should be on a week-night (Monday-Thursday). When you plan a first date for Friday or Saturday night, you give the impression that you might not have a social life.

---

89 Glover, Robert A. *Dating Essentials for Men* (Robert A. Glover, Ph.D, Inc, 2019) "Chapter 13: Commit to Going Out with 12 Women in 12 Weeks

### Tell. Don't Ask.

Most of us like to think it takes balls to ask a woman out. And it does. But *asking* a woman out actually lowers your status and makes you appear weak. **Telling** her when and where to meet you raises your status and makes you appear confident. Dr. Glover offers these two examples:

- *Let's grab coffee Thursday night at the Starbucks on Main Street. Meet me there at 7.*
- *I'm going to Carlo's on Tuesday night to check out a great Latin band. You should join me.*

Either way, you'll come across like an interesting guy with an interesting life. And you're simply inviting her to join you. Remember: Every interaction you have with a new woman is a test of her nature – how cool she is, how fun she is, how well she follows. Of course, she'll be testing you, too. And if she's a healthy woman, she won't want a man she can push around.

### Stay off the phone.

When you meet an enticing new woman, it can be difficult to resist the temptation to talk on the phone and text her regularly, even if you haven't been on a date yet. But these forms of communication don't allow you to discover the woman's nature. This is especially true for back-and-forth messages on dating apps. There is no point to these exchanges. You can't get to know a woman (or her nature) until you actually spend time with her. Use the phone only to set up dates.

### No gifts.

Never bring your date gifts or flowers. When you do this, you make it seem like you are trying to buy her affection and win her approval. It's worth repeating that this is not the purpose of dating. You are not trying to win the woman's approval; you are trying to discover her nature. Give her gifts or flowers only after you have been dating for at least a few months.

### Be a gentleman.

Whether it's your first date or your fiftieth date, you should always strive to be a gentleman by doing the following:

- Remember what she likes. When possible, order for her.
- Open the door and let her enter first.
- Open her car door. If necessary, tell her to wait for you to do so.
- On a city sidewalk, walk between her and the street.
- Stand when she enters or leaves the room (in public).
- Let her be seated first.
- Help her put her coat on and take it off.

Try not to be glaringly obvious about any of these things. To the best of your ability, make them look second nature.

**Pony up.**

In addition to planning your first date, you should pay for it. And because your first date should be casual and inexpensive, you can go on plenty of first dates (if you want) without breaking the bank. Paying isn't just the right thing to do, it's also a way for you to set the tone, take the lead, and test her nature.

Does she offer to pay while allowing you to set the tone?

Is she gracious?

Is she appreciative?

If she resists letting you pay, just tease her a little and hold firm.

If you go on a second date with a woman, you should pay for this, too. She may offer to pay because you paid for the first date. In this case, you can let her know that if there's a third date, she can plan it and pay for it. This is yet another way to set the tone, take the lead, and test for interest. If she follows up with an invitation for another date (the date she gets to plan), she has high interest. If she doesn't, she has low interest, and you should move on.

**YOUR FIRST DATE CHEAT SHEET:**

✓ Get to the location early. Scope it out, find a table, get comfortable.

✓ Stand up when your date arrives and wait as she walks toward you.

✓ Be attentive. Pay attention to detail.

✓ Make plenty of direct eye contact. Don't look around, look at her.

✓ Share things about yourself but keep it brief.

✓ Don't be negative or critical.

✓ Don't talk about your exes.

✓ Be curious and ask questions, but don't interrogate her.

✓ Make fun of yourself. Tell her an embarrassing story.

✓ Don't try to impress her.

✓ MAKE HER LAUGH.

✓ Practice the 3 Ts.

✓ Breathe. Relax your shoulders.

✓ Smile.

✓ Give yourself permission to make mistakes.

✓ Imagine the best.

✓ Have fun.

✓ If you have the impulse to kiss her, don't ask. Just go for it.

**Be a good ender.**

Being a good ender is an important life skill, and it's especially important in dating. You must be able to recognize when a woman isn't a great match and then end things quickly, especially if you are meeting and dating a variety of women.

If you don't intend to see a woman again after a first date, walk her to her car, shake her hand, smile, and say something like, *It was great meeting you. Good luck with your dating.* As Dr. Glover points out, "Most people understand this as code. You don't actually need to say you're not going to call again."

If the woman says she would like to see you again, tell her that she's a terrific person but you don't feel any romantic chemistry. Don't tell her you're going to call when you know you won't. Be a good ender.

**Remember: It's all practice.**

Dr. Glover wrote a portion of *Dating Essentials for Men* in Sayulita, Mexico, a small, coastal town just north of Puerto Vallarta. While in Sayulita, Dr. Glover decided to take surfing lessons. On his first day, after a 15-minute introduction on land, he followed his teacher into the water, brand new surfboard in tow. During the next hour, Dr. Glover approximates that he rode at least 20 waves. He wiped out on all of them.

After each ride, Dr. Glover's instructor gave him something new to try. On some rides, he focused on pushing up on the board. On others, he thought about where to place his back foot or how far up to place his front foot. Occasionally, everything Dr. Glover was learning seemed to come together. Most of the time it didn't.

"None of my wipeouts were proof that I am a failure or a loser," explains Dr. Glover. "None were proof that I lack the ability to surf. None were proof that surfing was too difficult for me to learn. They were just a part of the learning curve. Eventually, I figured it out. The same goes for dating. If you ride enough waves, if you go on enough dates and learn from them, you develop skills that lead to more confidence and more success. Remember, it's all practice."

---

**INTEGRATED ACTION:**

- ✓ If you're single, consider taking on Dr. Glover's 12/12 Challenge. Practice the first date basics. Let go of attachment. Remember, it's all practice. Write about your experiences in your journal.
- ✓ If you're in a relationship, take your partner out on a date. Practice first date basics all over again. You might be pleasantly suprised by what unfolds.
- ✓ Revisit your 5&5 List and the Relationship Pyramid. Continue to get clear on what you're looking for in a relationship. Who is your Really Great Woman?

---

# SETTING THE TONE & TAKING THE LEAD I

S o, what exactly does it mean to **set the tone and take lead**? This is a question commonly asked by Nice Guys who spend their lives trying to please others, especially women. But when you bend over backwards to please a woman, you're not setting the tone and taking the lead.[90]

- When you try desperately to make a woman happy, you're not setting the tone and taking the lead.
- When you force a woman to make all the decisions, you're not setting the tone and taking the lead.
- When you change your life to fit into a woman's world instead of inviting a woman into your world, you're not setting the tone and taking the lead.

As Dr. Glover loves to say, *A woman cannot follow where a man doesn't lead.*

Many men have trouble grasping the idea of setting the tone and taking the lead because they equate it with being controlling. But setting the tone

---

90  Dr. Glover frequently discusses the importance of setting the tone and taking the lead with women. It is a common theme throughout *Dating Essentials for Men*. Additionally, see Glover, Robert A. "Podcasts 18 & 19: Parts 1 & 2 of a Two-Part Series on Setting the Tone and Taking the Lead in Dating." Podcast Audio. www.drglover.com

and taking the lead is not controlling; it's Masculine and loving. Given that women tend to be security-seeking creatures, how do you think a woman feels when she's with a man who doesn't lead?

"Certainly, there are women out there who like to be dominated by men, even if those men treat them like shit," explains Dr. Glover. "But imagine if you were to lead with love and consciousness. Make it easy for a woman to follow by having a plan. Always treat a woman with respect. Setting the tone and leading is not about being selfish, manipulative, or abusive. Nor is it about having everything go your way. It's about deciding what you want and inviting a woman to join you. Making all the decisions feels burdensome to a woman."

Set the tone and take the lead before a first date, during a first date, and beyond. Be decisive from the very beginning. Tell your date when and where to meet you. Don't bombard her with countless options. Don't force her to make a lot of decisions. She should only have to decide one thing - whether or not she is going to meet you at the time and place you proposed. If she wants, she can make a counter proposal.

Again, every first date is a test. You are testing to find out as much as you can about her nature. You are testing to determine how well she follows your lead. You can take the lead by teasing her, by making her laugh, by playfully telling her what to do. You can take the lead by telling her to wait until you open her door. By ordering for her. By being a gentleman. By deciding when the date ends. By leaving her wanting more. After all, she is testing you, too. Don't let her set the tone and take the lead. If you do, you will likely fail *her* test.

Concurrently, it's important to keep in mind that setting the tone and taking the lead means setting the *emotional* tone of your date (or your relationship).

"Most men – especially Nice Guys – tend to follow a woman down her emotional rabbit hole," explains Dr. Glover. "She complains and they try to problem solve. She's unhappy and they try to figure out how to make her happy. She picks a fight and they either defend themselves or fight back. None of these show good emotional leadership. As a man, it is your job to set the emotional tone and take the lead. If you don't, she will. And you probably won't enjoy where she goes with it."

# OPENING A WOMAN'S DOOR

While learning to date again after getting divorced from his second wife, Dr. Glover began seeing a European woman with distinct European sensibilities. This was exciting for Dr. Glover, who was born and raised in Bellevue, Washington.

"The west coast of the U.S. is extremely casual," describes Dr. Glover. "But after high school I lived in the southern U.S., in Arkansas, which is fairly traditional. That's where I first learned to say 'Yes, sir' and 'No, sir;' 'Yes, maam,' and 'No, maam.' It's also where I learned to stand up when a woman enters the room, open the door for a woman, and wait for a woman to walk through the door first."

It wasn't until he began seeing a European woman, however, that Dr. Glover would learn a simple yet life-changing lesson.

"I remember visiting her in Europe," shares Dr. Glover. "As we traveled around and did things together, we were basically on her turf. So, she was setting the tone and taking the lead in a big way. But she liked that I took the lead on the smaller things, like opening her door. The thing is, I wasn't consistent. And that's when she turned to me one day and said very directly: *I love when you open the door for me. You don't have to do it. But if you are going to do it - and again, I love it - please do it consistently. Do it all the time. That way, I'll know. Then, I won't stand there waiting, wondering whether or not you're going to open the door.* From that moment forward, I decided I was going to consistently open the door for all the women in my life."

Opening the door for a woman may reek of the patriarchy or a kind of old-school mentality. But that's because we simply don't practice the manners nor the civility that we once did. Opening the door for a woman may also reek of Nice Guy Syndrome. But if there's no covert contract attached - if there's no hidden agenda - opening the door for a woman is a simple way to set the tone and take the lead. It can keep you conscious. It builds trust. It makes most women feel safe and secure. And remember: Women tend to be security-seeking creatures.

"I consistently open the door for a woman," affirms Dr. Glover. "No matter who it is - my mother, my granddaughter, my date, my romantic partner. If we are getting in a car, I will open the door for her. If we're getting out of a car, I will tell her to wait because I will open the door for her. If we're walking into a building, I will open her door for her. I've essentially trained all the women in my life to wait for me to open the door. This isn't patronizing or demeaning, it's loving. And it helps me stay in my role as a provider, protector, and leader."

So, try consistently opening the door for a woman.[91] You might just open the door to a magical relationship.

**INTEGRATED ACTION:**
- ✓ Examine your relationships with women. Do you set the tone and take the lead? How can you improve the way you lead? Write your answers In your journal.
- ✓ How do you think women feel when you don't set the tone and take lead? Write your answer in your journal.
- ✓ Practice setting the tone and taking the lead with the woman (or women) in your life.

91   Glover, Robert A. "Podcast 123: "Why You Should Always Open a Woman's Door & How to Approach Waitresses" Podcast Audio. www.drglover.com

# BANTERING & FLIRTING

Most of the men who enroll in Dr. Glover's *Dating Essentials* courses and programs frequently lament that they don't know how to talk to women.

*I don't know what to say.*

*I'm not funny.*

*I'm afraid of saying the wrong thing.*

*I'm not a natural.*

It's likely that many of these men actually do know how to talk to women. They just don't know how to banter and flirt. Thankfully, you don't have to be a so-called natural to banter and flirt. These skills can be learned.

Bantering and flirting are the manifestation of a certain mindset. They demonstrate confidence, intelligence, and social competence. They also demonstrate that you are comfortable with your sexuality. And because women find this combination of traits to be a turn-on, bantering and flirting can supercharge your dating life.

Dr. Glover defines bantering simply as "a playful repartee," and flirting as "adding sexual innuendo and energy to bantering."

"Bantering and flirting are all about being yourself," explains Dr. Glover. "They aren't about putting on a show. You are inviting a woman to get to know you. You don't have to be amazingly clever, and you don't have to entertain her. You just have to relax, take the lid off, and let the real you come out."

Of course, this is terrifying for those of us who live in our heads. Nice Guys especially tend to overthink and overanalyze damn near everything. They are constantly worried about looking foolish. They obsess over what could go wrong. They worry far too much about what others think of them. If this describes you, then STOP IT.

"Stop worrying," asserts Dr. Glover. "Less than 10 percent of a woman's initial impression of you is based on what you say. The rest is based on appearance, energy, and body language. So, just say something! When you walk into a room, own it. Tell yourself that you are The Man and that women want to get to know you. It is better to present this kind of image than the one you present when you are spinning in your head, consumed by anxiety and self-doubt. Stop worrying. And present the very best You."

Bantering and flirting require that you see yourself as a fun person. If you think you are dull and boring, this will come across to women. There is a reason Dr. Glover recommends that you become a social animal and talk to people everywhere you go. When you practice bantering with everyone, you'll be far more relaxed when you meet a potential Really Great Woman.

There is no need to memorize lines or techniques. It's inauthentic. But you'll be amazed what transpires when you practice just a few of these bantering and flirting basics:[92]

**Eye contact:**

One of the easiest and most effective ways to flirt is to make strong eye contact. Your eyes transmit high interest. Looking directly into the eyes of another person is a powerful form of communication, so much so that we often resist it. Or we restrict it to very brief glances. But prolonged eye contact between two people creates intimacy.

"Eye contact is a great first level test," says Dr. Glover. "When you are in a public place, for example, look around. Check people out. If a woman

---

92  Glover, Robert A. *Dating Essentials for Men* (Robert A. Glover, Ph.D, Inc. 2019) "Chapter 17: Banter & Flirt Like a Pro (Even if You're Shy or Introverted)

notices you, look her in the eye and hold your look for just a moment longer than you might be comfortable with. Look away confidently, as if you have something else important to look at. Then, look back again and smile. If she holds your gaze, smiles, or sends other indicators of interest, approach her."

This is where I'm obligated to point out that there's a fine line between being confident and being creepy. Don't ogle a woman. Don't stare at her body parts. Make the kind of playful eye contact that you would want a woman to make with you.

**Blurting:**

You may tell yourself that you can never think of anything to say to a woman, or that you aren't funny or clever, but these are self-limiting beliefs. And they probably aren't true. Chances are you think of plenty to say. You just don't say it. You've been trained to censor yourself. Plus, you have that oh-so-common fear of saying anything that might upset a woman.

Perhaps it's time you practice what Dr. Glover loves to call **blurting**. Start saying the things that come to your mind without editing yourself. These things might be funny, dirty, unexpected, off-the-wall, even inappropriate. Great. If a woman has high interest in you, you'd have to say something pretty goddamn offensive to kill that interest. But saying nothing almost guarantees that women will never show interest in you.

As an example, one of Dr. Glover's clients was buying clothes at a popular men's store in the mall. The woman ringing up his purchase asked for his phone number so she could process the transaction. Without thinking (or overthinking), he blurted, "You just want my number so you can call me and ask me out." He immediately felt uncomfortable because he thought he made too bold an assertion.

The woman blushed and then said, "I get off work at 5."

**The Three Ts:**

There is perhaps no better way to banter and flirt than by practicing The Three Ts. In case you forgot, The Three Ts are: Touch, Tease, and Tell. Do these things regularly – and playfully – to build and maintain attraction. '

Teasing seems to create the most anxiety for men, particularly men who were bullied and teased as children. Now, as adults, they are sensitive to being teased and tend to avoid teasing others. If this is true for you like it was for me, you may have difficulty distinguishing between teasing that is hurtful and teasing that is loving.

"When you tease a woman, always do it with a smile," asserts Dr. Glover. "Invite her in, and open her up with your humor."

In a poll he conducted, Dr. Glover asked a considerable number of women why they like men who can make them laugh. The women responded with answers like:

- *It relaxes me.*
- *It creates comfort.*
- *It makes me feel known.*
- *It releases anxiety.*
- *It implies intimacy and familiarity.*
- *It creates a bond.*
- *It implies strength and confidence.*

You can tease a woman about almost anything, as long as you do it in a playful and loving way. Don't aim to offend or insult a woman. Aim to make her laugh.

### Asking (Better) Questions:

If you've ever been, let's say, talking to your Grandma and she bombards you with questions about the most mundane parts of your life, then you know this isn't much fun. So, how do you think a woman feels when you interrogate her with similar questions? There's nothing fun or polarizing about mindless, mundane small talk. It's a great way to bore the fuck out of a woman.

Still, if you want to get to know a woman, you do need to ask questions. But your questions should make for good flirtatious banter. And they should reflect your personality. Dr. Glover offers the following example:

*Suppose I call you up and tell you that you have 30 minutes to pack your bikini and your passport, and you get to pick our destination. Where are we going?*

As Dr. Glover illustrates, this question accomplishes a lot:

- It allows you to lead (in both the question and the fantasy) and see how she follows.
- It allows you to find out if she has an imagination.
- It allows you to test for interest.
- It provides the opportunity to ask follow-up questions that allow you to get to know her better.
- It forces her to think about the two of you together, creating a bond in her mind.
- It allows you to find out if she is comfortable with her body and her sexuality.
- It allows you to find out if she is spontaneous.

While it's good to have some thought-provoking questions in your back pocket, don't just memorize routines and run them mechanically. Ask questions as they come up. Then, use her answers to continue to thread the conversation.

**Humor:**

Numerous studies have shown that people who use humor in social situations are perceived as more likable.[93] Humor stimulates trust and attraction. It can also reduce anxiety and promote a relaxed mood. Of course, you can't exactly learn to be funny – either you are or you aren't. But this isn't about crafting and telling jokes; it's about bantering and flirting. And there are a variety of ways you can integrate humor and playfulness into your interactions with a woman:

---

93   Marc M., & Dunbar R. I. (2008). Naturalistic observations of smiling and laughter in human group interactions. Behaviour, 145, 1747-1780

- Alternate between serious and silly. Tell her you need to ask her a personal question. Lean in, look intense, and then ask her something completely ridiculous.
- Boast about yourself with a twinkle in your eye.
- *Flip her shit.* Example: "You've been making my drink every morning for a week, and you can't even remember what I order? I must not mean much to you!"
- Give her a nickname. Keep calling her by said nickname. If you ask her out, use her nickname.

**Fun and Games:**

Remember: *Girls just wanna have fun.*

Nobody likes a stick in the mud. Especially women. When you're on a date with a woman, it's in your best interest to make sure you are both having fun. Ask her to dance, ask her to thumb wrestle, ask her to tell you her favorite dumb joke. Play games, make bets, issue a dare. There's no end to the fun you can have with a woman as long as she's fun, too. If she's not, move on.

In fact, if you seriously can't think of what to say to a woman, move on. She probably has low interest. When a woman has high interest and you're enjoying each other's company, your conversations should flow. The bantering and flirting will come naturally.

---

**INTEGRATED ACTION:**
✓ Practice bantering and flirting. Practice everywhere you go with every woman you meet. Practice making eye contact. Practice saying what comes to mind. Practice, practice, practice. Journal about your experiences and share them with your safe person.

# THE EARLY PART OF DATING

So, you've met a woman.

You've been on a date.

Maybe, you've even been on a few dates.

Now, you're in that early part of dating.[94] And it feels good.

Unfortunately, this is when many men - especially Nice Guys – want to fuse as quickly as possible. Nice Guys tend to have a strong feminine side, and the Feminine wants to bond. Not to mention that Nice Guys don't think abundantly. A Nice Guy believes he must fuse with a woman quickly, otherwise he'll lose her and may never meet someone else. But fusing too quickly is a recipe for disaster. You can't know if a woman is your Really Great Woman after just a few dates.

"It's a man's job to stay conscious and slow things down," explains Dr. Glover. "Someone has to stay on deck and watch for the icebergs. Someone has to stay mindful. Someone has to look out for the best interest of everyone involved."

Perhaps the best way to resist the temptation to fuse too quickly with one woman is to date a few women at a time. Dating a few women naturally slows down the fusion process. It can keep you conscious of whether you need to slow things down. And while you may struggle with the idea of entertaining

---

94  Glover, Robert A. "Podcasts 34-46: Parts 1-3 of a Three-Part Series About the Early Stages of Dating." Podcast Audio. www.drglover.com

multiple women - either because of fear or guilt - consider that any woman you meet is likely entertaining other men.

"If a woman asks you if you're seeing other people, soothe yourself," advises Dr. Glover. "You aren't doing anything wrong if you are seeing other women. Don't defend yourself and don't lie. Look her in the eyes and calmly set the tone by saying: *Until you and I have a conversation about dating exclusively, you should assume that I'm seeing other women.* If she continues to question you, just repeat the exact same sentence."

Observe the woman's reaction. If she gets upset, throws a fit, or angrily declares that she has taken down her online profile for you, calmly tell her one more time: *Until you and I have a conversation about dating exclusively, you should assume that I'm seeing other women.* If she continues to argue, politely excuse yourself. Again, you aren't doing anything wrong. And you are not a bad guy because you didn't give her what she wants.

As Dr. Glover frequently reminds men: *A woman's reaction to something you did does not determine the rightness or wrongness of what you did.*

Be willing to walk away.

During the early part of dating, don't give in to please a woman out of fear that she'll quit seeing you. Telling her she should assume that you are seeing other women (whether you are or not) makes you seem more desirable in her eyes because she will know that you are not at her beck and call.

"When you start giving in to please a woman, things will only get worse from there," affirms Dr. Glover. "If she quits seeing you because you won't commit after just a few dates, let her go. Hold onto yourself. Don't get all the way in with a woman until you feel totally ready. Set the tone, be the decider, and invite her to be the icing on your Great Cake of a Life."

## KEEP SETTING THE TONE

As the early part of dating progresses and a new relationship begins to develop, you must keep setting the tone and taking the lead.

"There is a direct correlation between how desperate a man is and how willing he is to give a woman everything she wants," says Dr. Glover. "There is also a direct correlation between how much a man wants to please a woman and how little respect she will have for him."

Don't let a woman set the tone of the relationship. Especially at the beginning. This may sound odd to you, but letting a woman set the tone isn't loving. Nor is it an effective way to maintain attraction. Let the woman into the driver's seat of your relationship and she'll likely drive it off a cliff, telling you how "nice" you are the whole way down.

Here are some ways you can keep setting the tone during the early part of dating:

- **Don't chit-chat**. When you talk on the phone, text, and email, you are letting the women set the tone. Men get little value from chatting on the phone. You run the risk of becoming her "girlfriend with a penis." Indeed, talking is important, but keep your conversations live and in-person.
- **Don't allow a woman to tell you that you can't see your friends or that you can't spend time enjoying your hobbies.**
- **Don't engage in conversations you don't want to have.**
- **Don't argue** and don't try to convince her of anything.
- **Don't defend yourself**. She'll think you're weak.
- **Don't let her (or anyone) treat you badly**. Ever. Be willing to walk away.

Remember how important it is to embrace abundance. There are plenty of amazing women out there. When you let a woman treat you badly, you've established a precedent for the rest of the relationship. So, set the tone, take the lead, and see if she follows. If she likes the way you lead, she might just be your Really Great Woman.

**INTEGRATED ACTION:**

✓ How have you navigated the early part of dating in the past? Do you tend to fuse really quickly? Write about your experiences in your journal.

✓ If you're single, challenge yourself to go out on at least one date this week. If you've been doing the 12/12 challenge, keep it up. Plan your dates and pay for them. Practice building attraction. Set the tone and take the lead.

✓ If you're in a long-term relationship, take your partner out on another date night. Plan the entire night. Set the tone and take the lead.

# THE MIDDLE PART OF DATING

While many men struggle to navigate the early part of dating, there seems to be just as many men who struggle with another part of dating – that sort of middle part when you are regularly communicating, you've gotten to know each other, you see each other often, and you're regularly having sex. This part of dating can be especially challenging because you're trying to make an important decision: *Should I stay or should I go?* Cue The Clash.[95]

Maybe the woman you are dating is a good woman. And maybe there is a good connection. But it's just not…great. It's just not what you want it to be.

Maybe you feel a little smothered.

Or you're constantly thinking about other women.

Or you're just not yelling "Fuck Yes!" about the relationship.

Or maybe there isn't one identifiable reason.

As confusing as this part of dating can be, it is undeniably crucial. Because you really do need to decide if you should stay or you should go.

"Be willing to get all the way in at this stage," recommends Dr. Glover. "This doesn't mean you're making a serious, long-term commitment. But you honestly can't find out if she's a really great match for you until you get all the

---

95  Hopefully, I don't need to tell you that in 1982, hugely influential punk band The Clash released the song "Should I Stay or Should I Go" and it quickly became their biggest hit.

way in. So, this is when you need to look at yourself. How are you holding back? How are you not setting the tone and taking the lead? Where are you not showing up? Then, get all the way in."

Getting all the way in will allow you to fully determine her nature. Keep revisiting your 5 & 5 List. Don't avoid sensitive matters. Don't ignore character flaws or red flags. Don't overlook her issues and insecurities.

---

### THE SECOND DATE RULE

The closer you get to a woman, the more you are going to run into her defense mechanisms. If she starts to display an undesirable behavior, apply what Dr. Glover calls **the Second Date Rule**.

Ask yourself: *If this behavior had occurred on the second date, would there have been a third?*

---

During the middle part of dating, be willing to bring your full presence to the relationship. This scares the shit out of a lot of men. They think if they get all the way in they won't be able to get out. But you're never stuck. Every relationship is a choice.

The middle part of dating[96] is where you must step up and be the decider. Decide what works for you and what doesn't. Make it a practice to ask yourself: *How would an Integrated Man handle this?*

"There's no reason to drag a relationship on longer than necessary," asserts Dr. Glover. "Dragging a relationship on too long is not a loving thing to do. Not to her and not to yourself. It's best to be honest and tell her that she's a great woman but you just don't think you're a great match. It's best to end things in a timely and loving way."

---

96  Glover, Robert A. "Podcast 124: The Middle Part of Dating: When to Stay and When to Go" and "Podcast 141: The Middle Stages of Dating." Podcast Audio. www.drglover.com

**INTEGRATED ACTION:**

- ✓ How have you navigated the middle part of dating in the past? How has it served you? Write about your experiences in your journal.
- ✓ Do you tend to half-ass relationships? Write your answer in your journal.
- ✓ If you're currently in the middle part of dating, challenge yourself to get all the way in. If it's not a great fit, don't be afraid to get all the way out.

# SHIT TESTS

If you've read any sort of dating or pickup material - or you've even just poked your head inside the manosphere - then you've almost certainly heard the term **Shit Test**.[97] A Shit Test is generally defined as the way a woman evaluates a man. A woman might use a Shit Test to determine your strength, your resilience, and your masculinity. If you're like most men – and especially if you're a Nice Guy – then you probably hate Shit Tests.

Women really do test us. A woman wants to know if you are strong enough to be her man. (Cue Sheryl Crow.[98]) And she'll be sorely disappointed if you fail her test. But many men can't understand why women would test them. As Dr. Glover often jokes, "It's almost like men think women went to some sort of girls' school to learn how to drive us crazy."

To understand why women test men, remember that women tend to be security-seeking creatures. Thousands of years ago, when we lived in tribes, men were the security system for women. Now, women don't actually *need* men for security. But you can't change their evolutionary wiring. Women

---

97  Glover, Robert A. "Podcast 3: Part 2 of a Two-Part Series on General Questions About Dating," Podcast 12: How to Deal with Strong and/or Controlling Women," and "Podcast 126: Applying Principles of Conscious Dating to Long-Term Relationships Part 2: Shit Tests." Podcast Audio. www.drglover.com

98  American singer and songwriter, Sheryl Crow, had a smash hit called "Strong Enough," in which she repeatedly asks the question: "Are you strong enough to be my man?"

still walk the planet feeling emotionally vulnerable. And when a woman gets involved with a man, he becomes her security system by default.

A woman typically doesn't want to be the strongest person in the room. So, she will test you. She will test you to find out your strengths and weaknesses. She will test you to find out how dependable you are. She will test you to see if you have your shit together. Put yourself in a woman's shoes. A woman must trust you in order to feel safe.

Women aren't looking for perfection. And they aren't looking for your weaknesses just so they can fuck with you. But they need to know where you're vulnerable. If a woman knows where the kinks in your armor are, she can be prepared when the shit hits the fan.

"Let's say that you're the castle," offers Dr. Glover. "The castle is her place of security, away from all the evil outside. Well, your woman has to go poke around the castle, looking for holes and cracks and secret back doors she doesn't know about. She isn't doing this to be mean. She's doing this to find out how strong or weak the castle is. If she's poking around to find out how strong you are, every time you give in, or withdraw, or pout, she's disappointed. If she finds a weak spot, she will keep poking it. She's got to find out how weak it is. Instead of getting insecure or angry, you've got to stay conscious and notice your weaknesses. Be aware of when you're triggered."

You may never truly know the rationale behind a specific woman's Shit Tests. Don't try to figure it out. Remember: The male brain isn't wired to understand the female brain or why women do what they do.

A woman might test you for any number of reasons. Maybe she's feeling unloved. Maybe you're not creating enough tension. Maybe she is indeed looking for your weaknesses. Maybe she's just bored.

Sometimes, women are just *the weather*.

A woman might test you in any number of ways. She might repeatedly show up late. She might try to corner you into having long conversations. She might flirt with your best friend. She might pout. She might accuse you of things you haven't done.

Look at a Shit Test as your time to shine. If you pay attention to where you get triggered, you can pass almost any Shit Test. A Shit Test gives you the opportunity to show a woman what kind of man you are. Don't back down from a Shit Test. Respond with strength, humor, and playfulness. And don't take anything personally.

Additionally, learn to ask yourself: *Does this woman's heart seem open or closed?* A woman with a closed heart is just plain mean. She'll insult you, threaten you, and belittle you. Don't hang out with a woman who has a closed heart.

"It's a man's job to be the ascertainer," asserts Dr. Glover. "To be a good ascertainer, you can't be codependent. You can't be a fixer. You have to allow your partner to be who they are, to have a bad day or be in a bad mood, and not feel the constant need to fix it. You need to soothe yourself. You need to be non-attached. You need to be conscious. You need to have empathy. Understand that your partner can feel and act differently than you. You also need to be able to walk away."

---

**INTEGRATED ACTION:**
- ✓ How have women shit-tested you? How have you handled it? Write about your experiences in your journal.
- ✓ Do you have a tendency to take things personally, especially shit tests and rejection? Write your answer in your journal.

---

# THE FRIEND ZONE

Chances are you are no stranger to the Friend Zone. It's not a terribly fun place to be. I too have spent a significant amount of time in the Friend Zone, wondering why so many women put me in it. But as Dr. Glover loves to say, *Women don't put us in the Friend Zone, we put ourselves there.*

Men end up in the Friend Zone for a variety of reasons:

- They think women are creeped out by men who want sex.
- They think women don't like sex.
- They're afraid of ~~rejection~~.
- They're afraid of doing anything that might piss off a woman.
- They don't know how to act with any sort of finesse. (They're either too blunt or too assertive too early, or they're not assertive enough when appropriate.)
- They don't embrace their sexuality.
- They spend too much time listening to a woman talk about her problems
- They make themselves available at all times.
- They buy women gifts.
- They act like a fucking friend.

Sadly, many men are so clueless that they don't even realize they are in the Friend Zone. So, perhaps it's worth noting some of the tell-tale signs:

- You're not having sex (obviously).

- You regularly get what Dr. Glover calls "the hug of death."
- She always wants to talk on the phone instead of doing things in real life.
- She always wants to tell you about her problems.
- She doesn't express any affection for you through her words or actions.
- She tells you that you're such a Nice Guy and that any woman would be lucky to have you.

> **hug of death** [həg əv deTH]
>
> *noun Sociology*
>
> When a woman hugs you in a non-sexual way, the way she might hug a good friend or family member.

If you want to become intimate with a woman, avoid the Friend Zone at all costs. When you allow a woman to put you in the Friend Zone, you are basically telling her that you don't have the confidence to be the man, to ask her out, to make a move and seduce her. Remember: Women are attracted to strength and confidence. "If you act like a woman's girlfriend with a penis, you look weak," affirms Dr. Glover. "Period."

Nice Guys especially tend to surround themselves with more women than men; they have more female friends than male friends. And while men and women can certainly be friends, you'd be wise to quit hanging out so much with women you're not sleeping with.

"Get out of the nursery," asserts Dr. Glover. "Particularly if you want to improve your dating skills and have a more fulfilling sex life. Work on cultivating your male friendships. Hanging out with women you aren't having sex with just kills your sexual mojo."

Staying out of the Friend Zone[99] doesn't have to be complicated. If a woman ever tells you she just wants to be friends, just say, "Thanks but no thanks." Or consider using one of Dr. Glover's two favorite responses: "That's okay, I already have enough female friends," or "Great, I have two kinds of female friends – those who fuck me and those who introduce me to their friends who want to fuck me. Which type do you want to be?"

---

99  For more insight into staying out of the friend zone, see Glover, Robert A. "Podcasts 32 & 33: Parts 1 & 2 of a Two-Part Series on Staying out of the Friend Zone." Podcast Audio. www.drglover.com

# BEING AN INTEGRATED MAN-WHORE

D r. Glover thinks you should be a man-whore.

And so do I.

This may sound strange, but I stand behind it.

You should be a man-whore.

Yes, a total fucking man-whore.

At least for a while.

You should meet, date, and sleep with as many women as possible.

Only if you want to, of course.

But here's the thing: Going through a man-whore phase can be both powerful and therapeutic, if you do it with love, consciousness, and integrity – in other words, if you're an *Integrated* **Man-Whore.**

Evolution has wired us to need people and need sex. Throughout most of our history, our ancestors enjoyed connection by being part of a tribe. Everything was shared, including sexual partners. Now, modern culture expects us to match up with one person and stay monogamous for life. This is kind of insane. Just look around. How many relationships actually work?

Human beings aren't biologically programmed for romantic, monogamous love that lasts forever. Our ancestors were…whores. So, like it or not, man-whore is actually our most natural state. And there are plenty of advantages to being a man-whore, including:

- Sexual variety
- Freedom to live as you want
- Freedom from having to make sacrifices to accommodate one person
- Knowing that one person doesn't 'own' your body (which is essentially what monogamy is).
- More time to pursue your passions
- More adventure (When you're not in a committed relationship, you're more likely to travel, meet new people, try new things, and have a more interesting life.)

Furthermore, getting into a relationship with one woman does not even remotely guarantee bliss, companionship, regular sex, or having someone at your bedside when you die.

You can learn a lot about yourself as an Integrated Man-Whore.

"Every dating and relationship experience provides an opportunity to grow," says Dr. Glover. "When I went through my man-whore phase after my second marriage, I learned that I am naturally attracted to long-term relationships, that I stay in them way too long, and that once I get in, I start looking for ways out. I realized my pattern of getting involved with unhappy women and trying to make them happy. I discovered that I was a terrible ender. I learned that I'm generally happier when sleeping alone in my own bed. I also found that I don't like having to fit into another person's schedule. My man-whore phase allowed me to realize that I don't actually *need* relationships to enjoy life."

Going through a conscious, Integrated Man-Whore phase is also an amazing way to get out of your comfort zone, especially if you're a Nice Guy. It provides a way for you to overcome your sexual shame and insecurities, and challenge your self-limiting beliefs around sex. It can help you break an addiction to porn and masturbation. It can help you embrace your sexuality and bring it out into the open. It's great practice for sex and sexual exploration with real, like-minded women. And it can help you become a really good ender.

You might be wondering how long you should be an Integrated Man-Whore. Well, that's up to you. It is your responsibility to remain conscious and ask yourself: *Why did I decide to go through a man-whore phase? Have I learned what I needed to learn? Am I happy?*

Seek the formula for your life that allows your happiness to flow without restraint. Minimize exposure to people and situations that tend to block the flow of your happiness. Be a man-whore for life or for just a little while. There's nothing wrong with either when you act with integrity.

If you do choose to be an Integrated Man-Whore,[100] you just might stumble across a woman with whom you decide to have a conscious, monogamous relationship. That's okay. In fact, that's wonderful. But don't force anything. Set the tone, take the lead, and be the decider. Do what makes you happy.

---

**INTEGRATED ACTION:**
 Get out of the house, expand your route, linger in public, talk to people everywhere you go, test for interest, and walk through the open doors.

---

100 For more insight into being an Integrated Man Whore, see Glover, Robert A. "Podcasts 8 & 9: Parts 1 & 2 of a Two-Part Series on Being an Integrated 'Man-Whore.'" Podcast Audio. www.drglover.com

# TAKING A BREAK FROM DATING

It stands to reason that the men who enroll in Dr. Glover's dating courses (or *any* dating courses, for that matter) do so because they want to improve their dating skills. And many do improve their dating skills. Some become so remarkably skilled at dating that they experience the kind of romantic lives about which most men only fantasize. After all, Dr. Glover doesn't teach his principles for chuckles; he teaches them because they work.

Still, even if you do it consciously, dating can be time-consuming, expensive, and emotionally draining. It can lead to negativity and resentment towards women. It can lead to a distaste for the dating process itself. It can also get in the way of other important things in life.

Once you get good at dating, you might start to wonder if you should take a break.

I constantly - and consciously - cycle on and off from dating. When I'm in an off cycle, I don't even think about dating. Regularly taking a break from dating can be incredibly healthy, even transformative. Funny enough, it can also make you more attractive to women.

Single men – especially single Nice Guys – tend to have illusions about being in a relationship. They notice all the couples in the world and assume those couples are blissfully happy. If you have this tendency, I can assure you that most couples are not as happy as you think they are. In fact, almost all the relationships you're observing will come to end, likely in the near future. This may sound negative, but it's reality.

Many men also think they should be in a serious relationship by a certain age. And if they're not, they better double down on trying to find a partner. This too is a false assumption. We're not all on the same path. There is no magical age by which you need to settle down. You don't need to settle down *at all* if it's not what you want.

So, if you've been actively dating and you feel burnt out or frustrated, or you're not enjoying it as much as you once did, take a break.

Learn to be in and appreciate the now.

Work on your Great Cake of a Life.

A woman is never going to complete you.

If you think a woman will complete you, if you make a woman (or trying to find a woman) the cake of your life, you're going to be miserable. And when you do meet a woman, you're going to make her miserable.

Taking a break from dating[101] will help you let go of any built-up negativity. It's perfectly okay to have quiet nights alone. You will get so much benefit from taking a break that when you decide to start dating again, you will feel wholly refreshed and revitalized.

"We often mistake loneliness for the need for a partner," says Dr. Glover. "But actually we've lost touch with ourselves. Learn to be comfortable with yourself. Aloneness is normal. You need to enjoy your own company. Embrace your alone time as an opportunity to be creative, to pursue your passions, to cultivate your interests, to spend time with guy friends. Seek an adventure, not a woman."

# THE IRONY OF IT ALL

There's a good chance that when you're consciously taking a break from dating, you'll end up meeting some of the most interesting women. Dr. Glov-

---

101 For more insight into taking a break from dating, see Glover, Robert A. "Podcasts 108 & 109: Parts 1 & 2 of a Two-Part Series on Going on a Dating Hiatus." Podcast Audio. www.drglover.com

er often shares that his two most recent long-term relationships began when he wasn't actively seeking a partner. This includes his relationship with his current wife, Lupita.

Taking a conscious break from dating to focus on the other parts of your life can unexpectedly lead to exciting relationships with some amazing women. Just because you aren't proactively dating doesn't mean you can't walk through the doors that open up in front of you.

---

**INTEGRATED ACTION:**

✓ Do you believe a woman will complete you? If so, how has this line of thinking affected your life and relationships? Write your answers in your journal.

✓ Are you or have you ever been frustrated with dating? Why or why not? Write your answers in your journal.

✓ There is nothing wrong with going on a hiatus from dating. If you are currently dating and you're feeling burnt out, frustrated, and resentful, take a fucking break. Work on your Great Cake of a Life. Spend time with other men. In your journal, write about your experience.

✓ Talk to your safe person about your frustrations with dating and why you think you need a break.

---

# PART V: SEX & SEXUALITY

*Intimacy is a totally different dimension. It
is allowing the other to come into you, to see
you as you see yourself.*

**- Osho**

There's nothing quite like sex to bring up our fears, our insecurities, and our self-limiting beliefs. Nice Guys especially tend to have a smorgasbord of issues around sex and sexuality. And let's not ignore that when it comes to sex, many cultures do far more to confuse us than they do to enlighten us. American culture in particular is maddeningly schizophrenic. It uses sex to sell damn near everything, and then tells us that sex is naughty and dirty and you should save it for the one you love.

What the fuck?

If the very subject of sex is awkward for you, if you have sexual shame and sexual anxiety, you're not alone. It's also not your fault. So, before we proceed, perhaps I can make you slightly more comfortable by sharing a bit about my own experience with sex, starting with the fact that I didn't have any for an embarrassingly long time.

During high school and college, it seemed like everyone I knew had a shockingly active, Bonobo-like sex life.[102] But not me. Whenever my friends would talk about sex – or their sexual escapades – I'd have to smile and nod and pretend like I knew what they were talking about.

As badly as I wanted sex, I had no idea how to get it. Girls just didn't seem to be attracted to me (or so I believed). At some point, the thought of having sex began to scare me. I would imagine myself meeting a girl, only for her to find how grossly inexperienced I was. She would laugh, the rumors would spread, and I would be ruined.

Not until my junior year of college, when I was 21 years old, did I meet a girl who did seem to be attracted to me. I wasn't terribly attracted to her, but we dated for a short time, anyway. She was the first girl I got naked with. It was a clumsy affair, though none of my worst fears came true. In fact, having a real-life sexual experience put a little pep in my step. Unfortunately, it didn't lead to more sex.

When I was in my mid-20s, I began to notice that women were looking at me much more than they previously had. But given my insecurities, I assumed they were looking at me with disgust, not lust. I started reading all the dating and pickup books that were popular at the time, but none of them helped. I don't blame the books, necessarily. I blame myself for not having the balls to apply anything I was learning. It's no wonder that by the time I was 26, I could probably count on one hand how many times I'd been laid.

I was horny all the time. Practically 24/7. Weekdays were particularly unbearable. I'd sit in my office cubicle with a raging hard-on, unable to work because I was so consumed by my sexual desires. When lunchtime came around, instead of joining my colleagues in the break room or at a nearby restaurant, I'd rush home so I could rub one out.

---

102 Bonobos are often cited as the most sexually active creatures on the planet. Supposedly, they are the only apes that engage in many of the same sexual activities as humans. This includes having sex purely for pleasure.

In my late 20s, I managed to gain a bit more sexual experience. I was in a relationship for nearly a year. I had a handful of one-night stands with some spectacularly beautiful women. (Thanks, alcohol!) I even had a fuck-buddy, a voluptuous blonde in an open marriage who came by my apartment two - sometimes three - nights a week just to sit on my penis. No doubt these experiences were enjoyable. More importantly, though, they opened my eyes to the fact that women want sex just as much as men.

Upon turning 30, I couldn't stand the thought of being sexually unfulfilled for the rest of my life. So, when I decided to move out of my hometown to a much livelier city, I also promised myself that I would unreservedly explore my sexuality, overcome my sexual insecurities, and enjoy as much sex as I could. And that's what I did.

I dated and slept with a variety of women. I had my first threesome. I spent time with strippers and porn stars. I went to sex clubs and play-parties and the largest swingers' convention in the world. I learned Tantra and other more artful ways to experience sex. I fulfilled all my fantasies. Sewed my wild oats. Got my ya-yas out, so to speak. Cue the Rolling Stones.[103]

I tell you about these things not because I'm proud of them (I'm not ashamed of them either), nor to suggest that you follow the same path (choose a path that works for you). I tell you about these things because they served a purpose. They helped me get comfortable with my sexuality. And if you want to become a more Integrated Man, it's important that you get comfortable with your sexuality, too.

Growing up in certain cultures can make it difficult to maintain an untarnished perspective around sex. We receive too many conflicting messages - from society, from religion, from our families, and so on. No matter what messages you internalized, however, the truth is: Sex is not a bad thing. It is a healthy, natural, wonderful part of being human.

---

103 Recorded in 1969 and released in 1970, *Get Yer Ya-Ya's Out!* is the second live album by the Rolling Stones.

Many men find creative and unconscious ways to avoid sex: They isolate, they don't approach women, or they find women who, for whatever reason, have an unhealthy relationship with sex. These men also tend to distract themselves from their sexual shame and guilt, usually by putting themselves in a trance with fantasy or attachment-oriented masturbation. They spend hours on the internet looking for porn while completely ignoring the consequences of such addictive and fruitless behavior.

"They call it a 'sex drive' because it's supposed to drive you to other sexual beings, not to a computer screen," asserts Dr. Glover. "We are alive today because every one of our ancestors had sex with another human. We are wired to have sex. Sex can be an amazing way to challenge yourself to grow. It can allow you to connect intimately with another person. And of course, it can be a hell of a lot of fun."[104]

---

104 Glover, Robert A. "Podcasts 22-24: Parts 1-3 of a Three-Part Series on Sex." Podcast Audio. www.drglover.com

# SEXUAL SHAME

Attend one of his workshops and there's a good chance Dr. Glover will ask you to visualize your very first sexual experience. This doesn't mean the first time you had sex. Your first sexual experience likely occurred before adolescence. Maybe it was the first time you realized it feels good to touch your penis, or your first wet dream, or the first time you snuck a peek at your mom's Victoria's Secret catalog.

Dr. Glover will then ask, "Did this experience occur in the open where it could be seen and known and celebrated? Did you run and tell your parents about it? And did they say, 'That's great! That's a milestone in development! Let's go get pizza!' Or was your first sexual experience shrouded in secrecy?"

For pretty much all of us, our first sexual experience was shrouded in secrecy.

"What happens is that sex, which is the most amazing gift to the human race, gets cross-wired with things like shame, guilt, secrecy, clumsiness, anxiety, and fear," explains Dr. Glover. "So, sex only feels normal if it's hidden and shame-filled. That's how most of us grow into adulthood. And yet, we think we're going to have normal, healthy sex lives. This is why probably 80 percent of men have a porn habit or some other sexual issue."[105]

---

105 Bet-David Patrick. Valuetainment "No More Mr. Nice Guy - Robert Glover Interview." January 1, 2021. https://www.youtube.com/watch?v=mjXWzseQ8Ug

For many men, sex is like a magnifying glass for their insecurities and toxic shame. Nearly all the men who reach out to me for coaching are quintessential Nice Guys with at least one major sexual problem. Most commonly, these men are not getting enough sex, settling for bad sex, engaging in sexually compulsive behavior, or suffering from sexual dysfunction. Generally, these things can all be traced back to sexual shame.

"We have to start uncoupling sex from shame," says Dr. Glover. "Then, sex can be an honest, transparent, amazing adventure we can share with another person."

As mentioned in Part I, if you were to look inside the average Nice Guy's head and find the part of the unconscious mind that controls sex, you are likely to find some of the following:

- Memories of childhood abandonment experiences
- Pain from not getting his needs met in healthy ways
- Residual effects from growing up with sexually wounded parents
- Sexual illusions and distortions from living in a fucked-up society
- Sexual guilt and shame from years of religious influence
- Trauma from sexual violation
- Memories of early (highly secretive) sexual experiences
- Unrealistic images of sex from porn
- Shame from hidden and compulsive behaviors
- Memories of any sexual failures and rejection

Sexual shame is…well, nothing to be ashamed of. But you can start your healing journey now. Here are some things you can do to put yourself on the right path:

- **Identify the root cause**. Where does your shame come from? Does it come from messages you received from your parents? What about your religion? Once you've identified the root cause of your sexual shame, reveal it to a safe person (or people).

**POP QUIZ:**

**Think back to your first sexual experience. Was it:**

a) A joyous experience that you eagerly shared with your family and friends?
b) Secretive, rushed, guilt-ridden, or in a less than ideal situation?
c) Painful, abusive, or frightening?

**When it comes to masturbation:**

a) Do you and your partner talk openly and comfortably about it?
b) Would there be a crisis if your partner caught you doing it?
c) Do you do it compulsively or in secret?

**When it comes to your sexual experiences, thoughts, or impulses:**

a) You are comfortable revealing everything about yourself to your partner.
b) You have secrets that you have never shared with anyone.
c) Some aspect of your sexuality has caused problems in your relationship.
d) At some point in your life, you have tried to eliminate or limit some problematic sexual behavior.

**If you answered anything but "a" on any of these questions, you have sexual shame and fear.**

- **Work on your sexual relationship with yourself.** Even if you have a partner, it is vital that you reclaim your relationship with your own body. Practice *healthy masturbation*, explained in an upcoming chapter.

- **Find a loving, non-shaming partner.** Tell your partner what you are trying to work through and ask them to help you work through it. Communication is key. If you're not actively dating, there's nothing wrong with rekindling an old relationship or even hiring an escort. Professional sex workers (who have willfully chosen this career) often love doing this sort of thing. The key is that you feel safe, and that you know you won't be shamed.

- **Be patient and compassionate with yourself.** Your sexual shame is not going to disappear overnight. Feel any emotions that come up. Let the energy move through you. It's all welcome. And it's all okay.

"I began my Nice Guy recovery journey in a 12-step group for sex addicts," shares Dr. Glover. "I quickly found out that I wasn't having enough sex to qualify as a sex addict, but I loved having a safe space consisting of all men to begin revealing myself, releasing my toxic shame, and healing my sexual wounds. At one point, I had a dark sexual impulse that I didn't act on. But I shared it with my 12-step group. Then, I shared it with my therapist. Then, I shared it with my wife. It was incredibly healing."

Don't put off your healing journey. The sooner you start to tackle your sexual shame, the sooner you'll be able to enjoy a beautiful and fulfilling sex life. As the late fitness expert and motivational speaker, Jack LaLanne, once said, "Sex has to do with the imagination, so the sky's the limit. As long as you're not doing bodily harm, why shouldn't you do what turns you on?"

**INTEGRATED ACTION:**

✓ In your journal, describe your first sexual experience of any kind. Was it out in the open? Or was it shrouded in secrecy? How did it feel? Do you remember?

✓ From where (or from whom) did you receive your earliest messages around sex? What is the root cause of your sexual shame? Write your answers in your journal.

✓ Do you avoid sexual situations? If so, how? What problems around sex do you want to fix? How important is it to you to have a fulfilling sex life? Write your answers in your journal.

✓ Talk to your safe person (or people) about your sexual shame.

✓ How else can you start overcoming your sexual shame? Do you have a loving, non-shaming partner? Do one thing to start your healing journey. Write about your experience in your journal.

# OPENING UP A WOMAN SEXUALLY

D r. Glover likes to say: *The way men do sex is the way they do life. And the way they do life is the way they do sex.*

This is an astute declaration that has opened the eyes of countless men, planting the seed for both sexual and spiritual growth. Men often approach sex and life in much the same way – by constantly seeking approval, by trying to please others, by neglecting their own needs, and by avoiding risk. But this shit doesn't work in life, and it doesn't work in sex.

As a man, you evolved to penetrate your partner and penetrate the world. Remember, the Masculine *does* and the Feminine is *done to*. This is true both physiologically and emotionally. As Dr. Glover explains, sex can be an amazing laboratory for becoming an Integrated Male.

- Sex can allow you to practice setting the tone and taking the lead.
- Sex can help you clear out your shame and self-limiting beliefs.
- Sex can allow you to be passionate and take risks.
- Sex can allow you to embrace your masculinity and explore sexual polarity with your partner.
- Sex can help you stop seeking approval.
- Sex can help you learn to be completely vulnerable with another human being.

"All of your ancestors had sex," says Dr. Glover. "You are a sexual being. But I have a hunch that our forefathers would laugh at the passive, approval-seeking way a lot of us have sex today."[106]

Many men mistakenly believe that women think like they do. But women are not turned on by the same things that turn men on. By now, you should know that most women need to experience *tension* to feel attraction and attachment, and that women tend to be security-seeking creatures. For a woman to open up and let go, she needs to trust you. As Dr. Glover also likes to say: *Trust equals lust.*

To open up a woman sexually, you must establish a foundation of trust. Any man can establish this foundation through:

- **Presence.** When you're with your woman, goddamnit be with your woman. Be present. Be in the moment.
- **Confidence.** Be the Masculine presence your woman wants and needs. Stand up for yourself, set boundaries, take risks.
- **Integrity.** Tell the truth and follow through. This is important for maintaining a sexual bond with your woman. When you don't act with integrity, she will start to lose the ability to trust you.

"If you want your woman to experience bliss, fuck her well," insists Dr. Glover. "That means you fuck her with your head and your heart and all of your Masculine presence. Fuck her with your humor and your intellect and your imagination and your words. Fuck her with your physical strength, your hands, your mouth. It's not just about your cock. Use your whole being to heat her up throughout the day, every day."[107]

---

106 Glover, Robert A. *All The Way In.* "Lesson Eight: Transform Your Sex Life in 24 Hours or Less By Following Three Simple Rules." (TPI University, www.drglover. com).

107 Glover, Robert A. *All The Way In.* "Lesson Eight: Transform Your Sex Life in 24 Hours or Less By Following Three Simple Rules." (TPI University, www.drglover. com).

**INTEGRATED ACTION:**

✓ Do you think you've been successful at opening up your sexual partners in the past? How could you have been more present, more confident? Could you have shown more integrity? Write your answers and detail your experiences in your journal.

✓ What about establishing trust? Do you use your whole being to open up a woman sexually? Write your answer in your journal.

# THE SEX TALK

Getting naked with a person for the first time brings up a hell of a lot of questions: *Does she have an STD? If I have an STD, how should I break the news? Is she on birth control? Is she fertile or not? What if she gets pregnant? Is she also thinking about these things? Is she as nervous as I am?*

Again, it's your job as a man to set the tone and take the lead. Before clothes start coming off – or at least before you start having sex – consider having a conversation with your partner about what's going to happen. Dr. Glover calls this *the Sex Talk*.[108]

At an appropriate moment, tell your partner that you want to be sure you both feel safe and that you both have a great experience. Remember: Women tend to be security-seeking creatures.

"Most likely, any new woman you're having sex with will also be wondering about things like STDs, pregnancy, and protection," says Dr. Glover. "She may not bring them up. And you shouldn't force her to because it puts her in the Masculine position. When *you* bring them up, you are setting the tone and taking the lead and making her feel safe."

Women often trade their long-term security and well-being for short-term gratification. If a woman wants you inside her *right now*, there's a good

---

108 For more on the sex talk, see Glover, Robert A. "Podcast 1: The Sex Talk." Podcast Audio. www.drglover.com

chance she'll ignore the potential consequences. Don't let her do this. An Integrated Man will look at the big picture. Use some form of protection until you're in a monogamous relationship. Have the Sex Talk. Show your partner that you are both consistent and trustworthy. This will only make her feel safer.

The Sex Talk is also a great way to discover a woman's nature. Does she have sexual shame? Is she open-minded? Is she a good communicator? If you have the Sex Talk and it goes over like a ton of bricks, she's probably not a woman with whom you should have sex. If you do have sex with her, you'll pay a price for it sooner or later.

"It's just not worth it," asserts Dr. Glover. "Be willing to kill a woman's buzz. If she shuts down or gets irritated, don't stick your penis in her vagina. Take her home and move on. So maybe you didn't get to have sex. Not having sex is a hell of a lot better than getting a nasty STD or paying a shitload in support for an unwanted child."

---

**GOLDEN RULE:**

*A woman's reaction to something you said or did doesn't determine the rightness or the wrongness of the thing that you said or did.*

---

In addition to talking about STDs, unwanted pregnancy, and protection, Dr. Glover also suggests asking the following question: *What does us having sex mean to you?*

This question raises consciousness; it lets you discover more of a woman's nature. And it can protect you from the woman later claiming that the sex was non-consensual. When she answers your question, she must also consent to being sexually intimate with you.

"Consent is sexy," affirms Dr. Glover. "Never have sex without it. And try not to have sex with a woman if either of you are impaired, even slightly.

Many men don't believe they can get a woman to have sex unless she is at least a little bit drunk. But this strategy is often a recipe for disaster. Sex is best when sober and consensual."

The idea of having the Sex Talk may make you squirm, but a healthy, mature woman will welcome the Sex Talk and respect you for initiating it. She'll appreciate that you took the time to make her feel safe and comfortable. *Trust equals lust.* The more she trusts you, the more she'll be inclined to let go as you embark on a wondrous sexual adventure.

# THREE RULES FOR AMAZING SEX

L ogically-minded men want rules. A roadmap. A step-by-step plan. A manual for how to get from A to Z. Even when it comes to sex.

But sex is supposed to be messy and fun and unrestrained.

Knowing this, Dr. Glover came up with a way to give men what they want without sucking all the fun and spontaneity out of sex. So, forget the complex formulas and procedures, throw away your diagrams and blueprints, put the books and pamphlets back on the shelf. Dr. Glover's *Three Rules for Amazing Sex* are all you need.

These rules may be contrary to the way you've always thought about and approached sex. Some men get panicky and anxious, and forget these rules quickly. But for fuck sake, there are only three of them. And yes, I can confirm that they work. Quite well, in fact.

Follow these rules and your sex life may reach blissful new heights. These rules are the foundation for opening up your woman sexually and taking her places she's never been (and can't take herself). They are the foundation for building the emotional trust a woman needs to let go and allow herself to be filled with your presence.

**RULE ONE: Approach your partner as if she is the most sexually adventurous, open-minded woman on the planet.**

Assume your partner will like everything you do *to* her and *with* her. The average man violates this rule in two significant ways. The first is by approaching his woman passively. The second is by waiting for his woman to initiate sex so he can feel wanted.

Women are not biologically wired to initiate sex; they are wired to be receptive. Again, the Masculine does and the Feminine is done to. Women are designed to be penetrated.

"If a woman doesn't like sex, it usually means one of two things," explains Dr. Glover. "Either she's been sexually abused or violated at some point in her life – it's terribly sad how many women have. Or she's with a man who doesn't fuck her well. Our evolutionary forefathers likely didn't sit around waiting for women to initiate sex, they didn't use sex for validation, they didn't buy women drinks. They didn't listen to women talk about their problems and think it was good foreplay. They took their women and they ravished them."

Of course, this is not to suggest you be animalistic or aggressive (unless your woman likes that sort of thing). But you do need to set the tone, take the lead, and be passionate.

"If you want real passion," writes David Deida in *The Way of the Superior Man*, "you need a ravisher and ravishee; otherwise, you just have two buddies who decide to rub genitals in bed."

Be the doer. Women are turned off by needy and insecure Nice Guys. A healthy woman wants to be penetrated by a charming, confident man; not manipulated by a passive little boy.

"This rule is not about some specific technique," adds Dr. Glover. "It's about you not censoring yourself. It's about letting go of attachment to outcome. It's about not holding back. And it's about her *trusting* you enough to take her beyond her comfort zone. Knowing you would never do anything to hurt her builds trust, which allows her to feel secure. Increased physical and emotional arousal makes her want to trust you even more. It's a beautiful, positive feedback loop."

**RULE TWO: It's her job to tell you 'No.'**

Following Rule Number Two is essential if you follow Rule Number One. If you know that she will tell you when she doesn't want to do something, then you won't feel inclined to hold back in any way. Your woman is an adult. She will tell you 'No' if she isn't comfortable with what you're doing. And of course, you will respect her if she does say 'No.'

Don't assume No, however. Assume Yes.

"Don't do her job for her," suggests Dr. Glover. "Don't try to decide ahead of time what she may or may not like. This will make you tentative and timid. It's a recipe for boring, infrequent sex. You need to boldly set the tone and take the lead until you get a 'No.' But if you follow Rule Number One, you will rarely get a 'No.'"

Incidentally, 'No' often just means 'No, not now.'

A woman might say 'No' to something one night and 'Fuck yes' to it another night. Don't try to make sense of it. Remember: Women are like *the weather*. They can change from moment to moment. Use this information to your advantage.

**RULE THREE: If she tells you 'No,' don't take it personally. (Then, go back to Rule Number One.)**

This may be hard for you to believe – particularly if you're a Nice Guy – but 'No' just means 'No' (or 'No, not right now'). It doesn't mean you did something wrong. It doesn't mean she thinks you're a bad man. It doesn't mean she wants you to stop setting the tone and taking the lead. And it doesn't mean she wants to stop having sex. It just means she doesn't want to engage in a particular sexual act at that moment.

If she says 'No,' don't take it personally. Don't whine and pout and make her rescue you from your Lower Masculine place. Simply do something else that you want. Her 'No' might be momentary. Keep setting the tone and taking the lead with love, and a 'No' can very easily turn into a 'Yes.' Unless of course she says, "If you ever do that again, I'll cut your fucking dick off." That probably means No forever.

***

If you have a partner, consider telling her the Three Rules for Amazing Sex. There's a good chance her eyes will light up when you do. Tell her that you expect her to tell you 'No,' and how you'll respond if she does.

Women tend to be more receptive than men to the Three Rules. Knowing they can say 'No' and that you won't take it personally makes it easier for them to say 'Yes.' The Three Rules are liberating to most women. If you regularly practice the Three Rules, your woman will stay in an almost perpetual state of desire for you. Her trust in you will continue to deepen.

Furthermore, the Three Rules are a powerful way to get to ~~rejection~~ quickly. If you're with a new partner, the Three Rules will help you determine if you're a good sexual match.

"Don't try to arouse an unaroused woman," advises Dr. Glover. "If you set the tone and take the lead, she'll show up wet. Otherwise, you can decide that you aren't a great fit."

The Three Rules for Amazing Sex[109], incidentally, are also rules for an amazing life. Approach the world as if. Don't hold back. If you get a No, don't take it personally. Just go back to Rule Number One.

---

**INTEGRATED ACTION:**
- ✓ What are the Three Rules for Amazing Sex? Try to write them down without referring back to this chapter.
- ✓ Why do you think these rules work? Write your answers in your journal.
- ✓ As soon as you have the chance to practice the Three Rules, do it. Write about your experience in your journal. And share your experience with a safe person (or people).

---

109 For more on the Three Rules for Amazing Sex, see Glover, Robert A. *All The Way In*. "Lesson Eight: Transform Your Sex Life in 24 Hours or Less By Following Three Simple Rules." (TPI University, www.drglover.com) and Glover, Robert A. "Podcast 24: Part 3 of Three-Part Series on Sex." Podcast Audio. www.drglover.com

# INEXPERIENCE

Sex can be a doorway to remarkable growth. Dr. David Schnarch, the author of *Passionate Marriage*, refers to this as the Crucible Approach. Through sex, we can conquer many of our problems as human beings. Sex provides an opportunity to develop personal awareness. It can show us where we need to mature, what we need to learn about ourselves, and how we can challenge ourselves.

But what if you have little to no sexual experience?

Sexual inexperience is more common than you might think, especially amongst Nice Guys. This is often due to things like:

- Sexual shame
- Sexual anxiety
- A lack of social skills
- Religious influences
- Being monogamous to your mother
- Trying to be different from your father
- Trying to be "nice" to women
- General anxiety around women
- Porn addiction

But just as sex can be a vehicle for personal growth, so can your sexual desire. You can use your sexual desire as a reason to step outside your comfort zone, much like I did in my late 20s and early 30s. You can use your sexual desire to work out your shame, your anxiety, and your insecurities.

---

**HARSH TRUTH**

Nobody is having as much sex as you think they are. Young men especially tend to talk a big game. But most people are likely sexually frustrated. Why do you think porn drives the internet?

---

If you have little to no sexual experience,[110] there are plenty of things you can do to start becoming a more sexual and sexually comfortable man. Consider the following recommendations from Dr. Glover:

- **Stop watching porn**. Porn creates all kinds of problems for men. Practice healthy masturbation.

- **Get an education**. Read quality books and watch informative videos on sex (not porn).

- **Talk to a professional**. Work on letting go of your sexual shame. Get comfortable talking about sex and being a sexual being.

- **Quit comparing yourself to others**. It serves no purpose. And it's just your mind's way of fucking with you.

- **Quit feeling sorry for yourself and hating on other people**. These are not attractive characteristics.

- **Improve your social skills**. It's hard to get laid without good social skills. There's no substitute for this. Get out of the house and talk to everyone you meet.

- **Do something different**. If you keep doing what you've always done, you'll keep getting what you've always got. Add new tools to your toolbox.

- **Stop thinking that your lack of experience is a liability**. Be playful about it.

---

110 For more insight into what you can do if you are sexually inexperienced, see Glover, Robert A. "Podcasts 114-115: Parts 1 & 2 of a Two-Part Series on How to Get Laid When You Have Little or No Sexual Experience." Podcast Audio. www. drglover.com

- **Don't make so many assumptions about women**. Specifically, don't make assumptions about their experience level or their skill level.
- **Use Mojo Mantras**. As a reminder, some examples of mojo mantras are:
  - *I love to fuck, and women love to be fucked by me.*
  - *Everywhere I go, women want me.*
  - *I'll take a woman places she's never been before.*
  - *My cock is a weapon of mass destruction.*

Dr. Glover often shares that his first two wives were also his first two sexual partners. So, after his second divorce, Dr. Glover felt like he had some catching up to do. He became an Integrated Man Whore. He consciously said 'Yes' to almost every sexual opportunity that presented itself. He admits to sleeping with older women, younger women, hot women, plain women, and even a few lesbians.

"If you are sexually inexperienced, I encourage you to walk through every door of opportunity," proclaims Dr. Glover. "Be willing to fuck a few women who wouldn't necessarily appear in your fantasies. I know that may sound disrespectful; it's not meant to be. But a lot of men remain sexually inexperienced because they're obsessed with sleeping with only the hottest women. They only want the so-called 10s. But all this does is perpetuate their sexual frustration as well as their negativity towards women. It's immature and misguided. It's like saying: If I can't drive a Bentley, I'm not going to drive at all."

If you want to drive a Bentley, you might first have to drive a perfectly nice Honda Civic, just as Dr. Glover did.

"Get your feet wet," he advises. "Actually, get your dick wet. And work your way up. You'll probably discover, as I did, that the women you might typically consider more average-looking - the so-called 5s and 6s - are actually some of the coolest women and the most fun in bed. The 10s don't really have to try."

Ultimately, everyone bumbles and stumbles their way through sex, especially early on. Everyone had to start their sexual journey somewhere, usually by doing things that made them uncomfortable. So, if you want to gain more sexual experience and become more sexually confident, you must get out of your comfort zone.

Be willing to take risks, look foolish, and crash and fucking burn. Before anything, though, *get out of the house, expand your route, linger in public, talk to people everywhere you go, test for interest, and walk through the open doors.* It's the only way. And it's totally worth it.

---

**INTEGRATED ACTION:**
  ✓ Get out of the house, expand your route, linger in public, talk to people everywhere you go, test for interest, and walk through the open doors.

---

# PORN

If you're a living, breathing human male, then you've almost certainly watched porn. While this may sound presumptuous, research shows that **98 percent** of men have indeed watched porn at least once. It's less clear how many actually have an addiction to porn, but recent studies suggest that nearly 20 percent of men believe that they are addicted or that they might be addicted.

It's no surprise that so many men watch porn. Porn is easy. When you watch porn, you don't have to deal with real, live, unpredictable women. You don't have to leave the house and try to get a date. You don't have to deal with anxiety, rejection, and drama.

But watching porn can easily become a serious issue. Porn can completely disrupt and even destroy the lives of men. According to the science, porn is considered a "supranormal" stimulus, which means that it activates the normal reward mechanisms in the brain but does so at such a high level that we perceive it to be far more pleasurable than the average stimulus. Research also suggests that porn addiction leads to structural changes in the brain and shares basic mechanisms with drug and alcohol addiction.

Porn[111] can lead to anxiety, low-self-esteem, and feelings of isolation in men. If you are in a relationship, it can produce the same negative effects in your partner. Porn can lead to sexual problems and sexual dysfunction in a relationship. Not to mention that it can cause a deterioration of trust and safety. Additionally:

- Porn creates unrealistic expectations around beauty and sex.
- Porn can easily become a substitute for a real sexual relationship
- Porn compounds shame because it is usually watched in secret.
- Porn is a big fucking waste of time.

And the list goes on.

There are some amazing resources out there to help you break a porn addiction, if you think you have one. But here are some of Dr. Glover's more practical suggestions:

- **Make the decision to stop**. Don't stop because of shame or personal judgment. Shame can actually drive you back to porn. Stop because it's not healthy and it negatively affects your life.
- **Observe the impulse**. Be the observer of your thoughts without judgment. Notice when your brain tells you to watch porn. If you can observe it without judgment, you'll gain insight into what's going on.
- **Block porn sites from your devices**. Temptation can be difficult to resist using sheer willpower. Take the time to create an environment that sets you up for success.
- **Temporarily stop masturbating altogether.** This is key for a lot of men who are trying to break a porn addiction. It's a powerful way to reset, recharge, and gain perspective.
- **Don't beat yourself up**. If you relapse, it's okay. Don't judge yourself. You are going to have moments of weakness. You're human.

---

111 For more information on porn and porn addiction, see Glover, Robert A. "Podcast 164: Breaking the Porn and Fantasy Habit, Part 1" and "Podcast 165: Breaking the Porn and Fantasy Habit, Part 2." Podcast Audio. www.drglover.com

Again, there are some amazing resources out there to help you break a porn addiction. And it's crucial that you reveal yourself to a safe person or safe people. Talk to a therapist or coach, attend a 12-step group, or find an online community. Use them for ongoing support and accountability.

Perhaps you've already found out that porn will give you far more problems than it will pleasure. Don't let porn disrupt your life any further. Start your recovery journey today.

---

**INTEGRATED ACTION:**
- ✓ Do you have an addiction to porn? Be honest with yourself. Write about your addiction in your journal.
- ✓ Talk to a safe person about your porn habit.
- ✓ Take one step towards breaking your addiction.

---

# DICK PROBLEMS

After becoming single and learning to consciously date in his mid-40s, Dr. Glover frequently – and happily – found himself in the bedroom with new sexual partners. While this would be exciting for almost any man of any age, it did present Dr. Glover with a bit of a dilemma. At some point, he would have to deal with his anxiety around getting and keeping an erection.

"I'm a recovering Nice Guy," shares Dr. Glover. "And remember, Nice Guy Syndrome is primarily an anxiety-based disorder. This anxiety seems to be a serious issue in relationships and sex. It definitely was for me. I tried ED drugs but ultimately decided that I didn't want to be dependent on a pill to enjoy sex. So, I learned to soothe my anxiety and let go of old baggage."

In discussions around sex, we often use the term *performance anxiety,* which is a problem in and of itself. Sex is not a performance, and thinking about it as such only perpetuates our difficulties. Men often try so hard to please a woman that it ratchets up their nerves, their perfectionism, and their fear of abandonment, all of which compound to significantly increase anxiety. Perhaps it goes without saying that erections and anxiety aren't very good friends.

Sex is a way you can experience pleasure, connection, and deep, personal growth with another person. But thinking of sex as a performance limits your ability to experience any of these things. Sex is much more than sticking your penis in a vagina. And it is certainly much more than jack-hammering a woman as portrayed in so much porn. As Dr. Glover likes to say, "Sex is anything and everything that you wouldn't do with your sister."

He adds, "Sex involves so many things. It's how we interact with a person, how we connect, how we touch, how we engage. It's immature to think that sex is strictly about putting your penis in a vagina. Well, okay. *Sometimes* it's just about putting your penis in a vagina."

# ERECTILE DYSFUNCTION

There are two primary causes of Erectile Dysfunction (ED), which is essentially *the inability to get and keep an erection firm enough for sex.*

The first is physical.

To rule this out, go to your doctor and get a physical exam. Ask your doctor to check for any issues that could cause ED. Antidepressants and other medications are often the culprit.

Additionally, you can do some self-tests:

- Do you get erections at all? Ever?
- Do you get morning wood?
- How about when you watch porn?

If you can get an erection, then the cause of your ED likely isn't physical. In this case, something like Viagra won't help.

"Viagra doesn't treat the cause of the problem if it isn't physical," explains Dr. Glover. "Also, it's very easy to become dependent on these kinds of pills. You fear that if you don't have Viagra, you're fucked. It really can become a full-blown emotional dependency. Besides, the very act of taking the pills puts you in performance mode and it's based on the belief that you need a rock-hard erection to satisfy a woman, as if your penis is your only sex organ. That's a hell of a lot of pressure to put on your penis."

If the cause of your ED isn't physical, then it must be psychological.

Do a self-evaluation.

What is this about?

There are a number of psychological factors that can cause ED, some of which include:

- General feelings of inadequacy around sex
- Body issues
- A need for validation and approval
- Finding women intimidating
- Past sexual failures
- Sexual abuse in childhood
- Religious guilt or shame
- Fear of getting a woman pregnant
- Fear of getting an STD
- Addiction to porn and masturbation
- The state of your current relationship

"Of course, sometimes it's just the fear of failure," says Dr. Glover. "Occasional failures are very normal. But the fear of failure can get in your head. And once the fear of failure gets into your big head, it will control your little head. Once you start thinking about failure, you're toast. Thinking and sex don't go well together."

Overcoming ED requires you to break the psychological loop:

- Depersonalize it and do a self-inventory. What is the history of your ED? What are the potential causes?
- Remember that you can satisfy a woman in many ways.
- Let go of attachment to outcome when you approach sex. When your mind starts thinking of failure, recall times of success. Focus solely on the experience of being sexual with a person, not your erection (or lack thereof). Get to know your partner's body and allow her to get to know your body. Allow yourself to experience pleasure.
- Practice opening condom packages and putting on a condom.
- Have the Sex Talk.
- Tell your partner the Three Rules for Amazing Sex.

- Breathe. Take slow, deep breaths. If you can, match your partner's breathing.

- If you have a long-time partner, ask yourself what issues there might be. Are you keeping secrets? Is there built-up resentment? Are you no longer attracted to her? Deal with any issues head-on.

Dr. Glover acknowledges that he frequently experienced erectile dysfunction, particularly with new sexual partners.

"I tried everything under the sun looking for answers," he shares. "I finally decided to just relax and come clean. I'd have the Sex Talk with every new partner and matter-of-factly share my issues with getting or keeping an erection. Then, I would propose that we just get naked, roll around together, and explore each other's bodies. Women eagerly embraced this because it took the pressure off them, too. It took the performance out of it. Once the need to perform was gone - once I let go of attachment to outcome - my plumbing worked just fine."

As you work to break your own psychological loop, don't forget to take care of yourself. What's good for your heart and your brain is also good for your penis. Eat healthy, stop smoking, and avoid heavy drinking. Exercise. Cut back on porn, fantasy, and masturbation unless you're sharing these things with your partner. As Dr. Glover often says: *Live a phallic life*.

"How you do life says a lot about how you do sex," asserts Dr. Glover. "Create your Great Cake. Do things with men. Pursue your passions. Lean into challenge. Bring this energy into the bedroom. Penetrate your partner with more than just your cock. Let go of attachment and have an adventure."

## PREMATURE EJACULATION

Famed research team Masters and Johnson defined Premature Ejaculation (PE) as *the condition in which a man ejaculates before his sex partner achieves orgasm in more than 50 percent of their sexual encounters*. Perhaps the most common definition is ejaculating within two minutes of penetration. These definitions imply that PE is a rare condition. But renowned sexologist Alfred Kinsey demonstrated that a whopping 75 percent of men do indeed ejaculate within two minutes of penetration in at least 50 percent of their sexual encounters. On the one hand, this might make you feel better about your own sexual misfortunes. On the other hand, it sounds like a sad state of affairs.

But as Dr. Glover asserts, there's a problem with these kinds of definitions and statistical norms, if there even are *norms*.

"If you think about it, there really is no such thing as PE unless you ejaculate before actually putting your penis in a vagina," he explains. "PE is just a term that we've created. If you can get in, ejaculate, and get out, you've served mother nature's purpose. A few hundred thousand years ago, if you were a young man, going slow probably wouldn't have been a good idea because the leader of the tribe would come home. I'd bet that our forefathers never had conversations about ejaculating too quickly."

If you've diagnosed yourself with PE, it might just be that you're young, inexperienced, and excited about doing Mother Nature's bidding. Or maybe you have an overwhelming desire to satisfy. While that's wonderfully sweet of you, trying desperately to satisfy a woman will fuck with your head…and your cock, and lead to boring, routine, uninteresting sex.

Nevertheless, I don't think it's presumptuous to say that most of us men would like to last a little (or a lot) longer in bed. And most women would appreciate it if we did. So, allow me to tease you with some common causes of PE before bringing this to climax with some potential solutions.

Common causes of PE include:

- **General unawareness.** If you're not aware of what's going on in your body because you're thinking too much, orgasm can creep up on you.
- **Conditioning from masturbation**. If you've always masturbated in secret or with shame, you've likely conditioned yourself to ejaculate quickly.

- **Pleasing behavior**. Seeing sex as a performance increases your anxiety and your attachment to outcome.
- **Depression.**
- **Stress.**
- **Relationship problems.**
- **Sexual Anxiety**. Most sexual problems are caused by anxiety. If you have a problem once and then let it create a negative feedback loop in your mind, the problem will persist and affect your future sexual experiences. Sexual issues usually aren't issues until you start worrying about them. The mind is your biggest sex organ.

With most sexual issues, your penis is trying to tell you something. Listen to it. When it comes to PE specifically, Dr. Glover offers the following remedies:

- **Stop labeling**. Don't even use the term Premature Ejaculation. "Often, when you identify yourself with a term or a diagnosis, it is more difficult to move forward," says Dr. Glover. "You *become* the label."
- **Let go of judgment**. Your judgment around an issue will only magnify it.
- **Let go of attachment to outcome**. When you are attached to a specific outcome – like lasting longer or pleasing a woman – you'll experience significantly more anxiety. "If you are conscious, if you can just be in the moment, you can use sex as a very powerful way to work at letting go of attachment to outcome," says Dr. Glover. "Just let sex be an adventure. Without a goal."
- **Retrain your nervous system**. Ejaculating too quickly is very often the result of a neurological habit. Stop using porn. Stop masturbating with a goal. Stop fantasizing. Stop obsessing over sex.
- **Learn to soothe your anxiety**. Anxiety causes shallow breathing, which makes you orgasm more quickly. Breathe slowly and deeply. Match your partner's breathing and maintain eye contact to keep you connected.

- **Talk about your anxieties with your partner(s).**
- **Hug until relaxed**. This comes from Dr. David Schnarch, the previously mentioned author of *Passionate Marriage*. Stand with your partner and hold each other until completely relaxed.
- **Don't think about other things while you're having sex to slow your response down**. This just takes you out of the moment. Be present with your partner.
- **Get rid of any goals (i.e. orgasm)**. Just roll around naked with your partner and see what happens.
- **Find other effective ways to pleasure your partner.**
- **Wait, get hard, fuck again.**

# DELAYED EJACULATION

While delayed ejaculation may not be as common as premature ejaculation, it isn't terribly unusual. Antidepressants can often cause delayed ejaculation. In fact, some doctors even prescribe antidepressants to those who suffer from premature ejaculation. So, if you suffer from delayed ejaculation, first check to see if your medication might be the cause.

If you experience delayed ejaculation with a woman but not during masturbation, it's likely that you've conditioned yourself to do this. You've become neurologically programmed to respond to certain stimuli. If your woman can't exactly match said stimuli, you have trouble ejaculating.

As with premature ejaculation, anxiety can play a role in delayed ejaculation. So can alcohol, fatigue, and simply being attached to a specific outcome. Or perhaps you don't find your partner all that attractive or arousing.

Again, listen to what your penis is telling you. And stop masturbating; not out of shame or guilt, but because it's negatively affecting your sex life. Let your nervous system reset itself. While having sex, relax and enjoy the experience. Only have sex when and with whom you want.

It's also worth repeating that you should *live a phallic life*. Remember, how you do life says a lot about how you do sex. Live with passion and penetrate the world.[112]

---

**INTEGRATED ACTION:**

&check; If you have dick problems, where do you think they come from? Are they physical or psychological in nature? Write your answers in your journal.

&check; How would it feel to take the performance aspect out of sex and simply enjoy being sexual with another person? Write your answer in your journal.

&check; If you have a partner, are there any resentments or secrets between you? Write your answer in your journal.

&check; Are you living a phallic life? Be honest with yourself and write your answer in your journal. Talk to your safe person (or people).

&check; Do you think you conditioned yourself to ejaculate quickly? How so? Write your answers in your journal.

&check; Confront any issues between you and your partner (if you have one) head on.

&check; If you think your dick problems are physical in nature, go see a doctor. In fact, go see a doctor, anyway, just to make sure you don't have any vitamin deficiencies or other issues.

&check; Stop labeling yourself and your issues. And stop judging.

&check; Let the next time you have sex be an adventure, without a goal.

---

112 Glover, Robert A. "Podcast 166: Dick Problems." Podcast Audio. www.drglover. com

# HEALTHY MASTURBATION

Consider this logic: Until you can be sexual with *yourself* without shame, you won't be able to be sexual with someone else without shame. Until you are comfortable giving pleasure to *yourself*, you won't be comfortable letting someone else give you pleasure. And until you can be sexual with *yourself* without needing porn or fantasy as distractions, you won't be able to be sexual with someone else without needing similar distractions.

You can begin to change the relationship you have with your sexuality by practicing what Dr. Glover calls ***Healthy Masturbation***.[113] Healthy Masturbation is probably quite different from the way you currently masturbate. It is simply about letting sexual energy unfold.

There is no goal.

You are not trying to ejaculate.

It doesn't require porn or other outside stimuli.

---

113 Dr. Glover frequently discusses the concept of healthy masturbation in his work. For more information on healthy masturbation, See Glover, Robert A. No More Mr. Nice Guy (Running Press, 2003) pp.167-172 and Glover, Robert A. "Podcast 167: Healthy Masturbation: Pt 1, What Is it?" "Podcast 168: Healthy Masturbation: Pt 2, Questions About Fantasy," "Podcast 169: Healthy Masturbation: Pt 3, What to Think About and Wet Dreams," "Podcast 170: Healthy Mastubation: Pt 4, Erections and NoFap," and "Podcast 171: Healthy Masturbation: Pt 5, Guided Meditation." Podcast Audio. www.drglover.com

Healthy Masturbation is about getting to know your body and paying attention to what feels good.

"Too many men struggle with compulsive masturbation and porn addiction," says Dr. Glover. "When you learn to pleasure yourself without using porn or fantasy, it is unlikely that your behavior will become compulsive. This is just one benefit of Healthy Masturbation – you won't spend all that much time doing it."

Healthy Masturbation can help you let go of the shame you have around everything sexual. It puts you in charge of your own sexual needs and pleasure. It removes dependency on porn or fantasy. And it can greatly enhance the experience of having sex with another person.

---

**HOW TO PRACTICE HEALTHY MASTURBATION**

✓ Choose a comfortable place that is free of distraction.

✓ Look at yourself and pleasure yourself without using porn and without fantasizing.

✓ Pay attention to how it feels to experience your sexuality, without an agenda, without attachment to outcome, and without the goal of having an orgasm.

✓ Observe any tendency you have to distract yourself from what you're experiencing.

---

# SEXUAL TRANSMUTATION

As a man, you have an inherent biological property that makes you more attractive to those around you and allows you to penetrate the world with confidence and charisma. You may not believe you have such power flowing through your veins, especially if you're downtrodden, unmotivated, or failing to live up to your potential. But you do have it. All men do.

It's your sexual energy.

Your sexual energy is part of your life force. And when you learn to properly harness your sexual energy, you can use it to your advantage.

But how do you harness your sexual energy?

The answer lies in a process called *Sexual Transmutation*, which is generally defined as *converting sexual energy into energy of another nature.*

If you are already immersed in the world of men's self-improvement, then perhaps you're familiar with Sexual Transmutation. Perhaps you've heard the term in passing but never paid much attention. Or perhaps you've heard of similar practices like NoFap, Semen Retention, or Tantra.

Call it what you want. (Dr. Glover calls it "just not cumming very often.") But you can put your sexual energy to good use instead of constantly dispersing it into a Kleenex. In fact, if you can channel your drive for sex into other endeavors, there's no telling what you'll achieve.

The concept of Sexual Transmutation may have been first introduced to the public by Napoleon Hill, who wrote about it in his all-time bestselling book, *Think and Grow Rich*. To write the book, Hill studied and interviewed the 500 richest men of his time, including Andrew Carnegie, Henry Ford, and John D. Rockefeller. Hill wanted to find out if there were any common threads between these men.

Since its publication in 1937, tens of millions of readers have used the principles in *Think and Grow Rich* as a guide for increasing motivation, setting goals, and achieving success. If you've read it, then you know that the book is divided into 13 steps, and according to Hill, if you follow these steps, you'll think and become rich. Strangely though, hardly anyone talks about Hill's tenth step toward riches, which is detailed in Chapter 11: *The Mystery of Sex Transmutation*. In this chapter, Hill writes:

*The emotion of sex has back of it the possibility of three constructive potentialities, they are:*

1. *The perpetuation of mankind.*
2. *The maintenance of health, (as a therapeutic agency, it has no equal).*
3. *The transformation of mediocrity into genius through transmutation.*

*Sex transmutation is simple and easily explained. It means the switching of the mind from thoughts of physical expression to thoughts of some other nature. Sex desire is the most powerful of human desires.*

Hill goes on to describe that he analyzed over 25,000 people, and ultimately discovered that men who achieve great success rarely do so before the age of 40. The primary reason for this, he explains, is that younger men have a tendency to disperse their sexual energy through an over-indulgence in the physical expression of sex.

"I think most men – beginning in adolescence – become ejaculation addicts," says Dr. Glover. "We get addicted to ejaculating. That's what drives us around sex. We want to have sex, or we want to masturbate just so we can ejaculate. And I think that robs us. I think it completely robs men of their energy."

You can easily find the names of successful men who've practiced Sexual Transmutation, from William Shakespeare and Abraham Lincoln to Beethoven and Jim Carrey. Should you decide to retain your semen and practice Sexual Transmutation, make no mistake: It can be challenging, particularly if you do have an addiction to ejaculating. Sexual Transmutation isn't just a change in habit; it's also a change in lifestyle. Practice it with diligence, however, and you'll likely begin to see a host of benefits including:

- **Increased Confidence**: Countless studies have shown that frequent porn use and excessive masturbation lead to a variety of problems, including sexual dysfunction, relationship discord, isolation and depression, and decreased confidence. Excessive masturbation wreaks havoc on your dopamine receptors, and low dopamine levels diminish motivation and self-confidence.

- **More Testosterone**: This is perhaps the most scientifically validated result to practicing sexual transmutation. In 2003, for example, Chinese researchers conducted a study that measured the influence of ejaculation frequency on testosterone levels. The researchers found that men who abstained from masturbation for seven days experienced a 145.7% increase in testosterone. Increased testosterone might also explain a number of ancillary benefits to practicing sexual transmutation, including a deeper voice, more strength, and more courage, as well as appearing more attractive to women.

- **Increased Energy and Focus**: Remember, your semen is your life force energy. Each time you ejaculate, you are ridding your body of this energy. When you abstain from ejaculating, you allow this energy to build up. You can then redirect this new-found energy into other endeavors, like tackling that unfinished project in the garage or starting that business you've always dreamt of. Ask any man who practices sexual transmutation about its benefits, and he'll likely report clearer thinking, a greater sense of purpose, and a much stronger drive to achieve his goals.

- **Better Mood**: Rarely does a man vigorously masturbate to porn and think, *Boy, I'm really glad I did that!* Excessive masturbation creates a negative feedback loop in the brain, often defined by feelings of shame, guilt, remorse, and sadness. Furthermore, it can negatively affect your relationships, your sex drive, your social aptitude, and many other parts of your life. Because practicing sexual transmutation can lead to increased energy and higher testosterone levels, you'll naturally feel happier. In fact, optimal testosterone levels are associated with mental health and well-being.

- **Improved Physical Health**: Your semen has over 200 different vitamins, minerals, proteins, and amino acids. It's chock full of nutrients that contribute to your mental and physical health. Frequent ejaculation only depletes your body of these nutrients. When practicing sex transmutation, you'll absorb these nutrients back into your system, ultimately supporting your mind and body.

- **Increased Sexual Stamina**: You'll learn to control your orgasm, allowing you to have sex for longer periods of time.

- **Improved Self-control and Body Awareness**: You'll learn to orgasm without ejaculation.

- **A Stronger, More Radiant Life Force Energy**: There's an inherent spiritual component to Sexual Transmutation. Try it and pay attention to the way others pick up on your energy.

## YES, YOU CAN HAVE SEX

When men first learn of Sexual Transmutation, they often jump to the immediate conclusion that they won't be able to have sex. But this isn't the case. If you're single, there are certainly some amazing benefits to taking a moratorium from sex, dating, and relationships, and learning to practice transmutation on your own. But, if you're in a relationship or you have a regular sex partner, having sex is highly encouraged.

Sexual Transmutation requires one to refrain from having an orgasm, not from having sex. Sex actually provides an amazing way to tap into your creative energy. If you're familiar with Tantric Sex, then you know that the goal is not to orgasm, but to enjoy the experience and the sensations in your body.

Much like Sexual Transmutation, Tantric Sex aims to redirect sexual energy. Explore Sexual Transmutation and Tantra with your partner. Practice together. Let go of expectations. You'll increase the intimacy between you while creating a mind-body connection that can actually lead to multiple, full-body, non-ejaculatory orgasms.

Here are some techniques to try during sex:

- **Vinyasa Flow Breath**: Vinyasa is a common style of yoga practiced in the West. The Vinyasa Flow Breath is an elongated form of breathing. Inhalation expands the belly and ribs, and exhalation contracts the abdomen and torso. During sex, elongate and slow your breath, particularly if you're approaching orgasm. Count to four as you inhale and again to four as you exhale. This type of breathing helps redistribute sexual energy back through your body.

- **Flex your PC Muscles**: Your PC muscles – also known as your pelvic floor muscles – support your bladder and rectum and help control your urine flow. When you pee, practice starting and stopping the flow of urine by squeezing your PC muscles. Squeeze these same muscles when you think you're about to ejaculate.

- **Edging**: This is the practice of getting right to the edge of orgasm, stopping stimulation, waiting, and then starting again. Practice slowing down during masturbation or sex so you can become more aware of how it feels right before you ejaculate. A good rule of thumb is to stop stimulation just as you're about to ejaculate and wait 30 seconds before you start stimulation again. The Vinyasa Flow Breath can help with this process. Once you master edging, you might find that you can have the experience of an orgasm without ejaculating.

# HOW TO PRACTICE SEXUAL TRANSMUTATION

There are a variety of resources on sexual transmutation and a variety of ways to implement it into your life. Generally, though, you can begin to transmute your sexual energy in a few simple steps.

1. **Embrace your sexuality**. If you have any shame or insecurity around sex, you'll want to tackle this first. Sexual Transmutation is not for those who are ashamed of their sexuality. Remember, humans are sexual beings. Sex is natural. Men want it. Women want it. Embrace your sexuality and develop a healthy relationship with sex. Work with a therapist or coach if you feel you need to. If you're in a relationship or otherwise sexually active, talk to your partner (or partners) about your issues around sex.

2. **Become attuned to your sexual energy**. Before you can transmute your sexual energy, you need to be able to recognize when it's building up inside you. For many men, this comes easy. (Raging boners are a pretty clear sign). But for others, particularly those who have sexual shame, becoming aroused can be a bit more challenging. Don't reject your sexual energy. If you're struggling with this, revisit the first step. Do you have sexual shame? Any past traumas? False beliefs around sex? Again, it's vital that you get comfortable with your sexuality.

3. **Define your goals**. The point of Sexual Transmutation is to channel your sex drive into your professional or creative endeavors. As such, you'll want to get clear on your goals. What do you hope to accomplish? Are there projects you've been putting off? Do you have big dreams, like writing a book or starting a business? Write down your goals and keep them handy.

4. **Use a visualization exercise**. A short visualization exercise will help you move your sexual energy into your work.

---

### SIMPLE VISUALIZATION EXERCISE:

**Change your state.** Find a quiet place, sit comfortably with your eyes closed, and relax. Bring your focus inward.

**Slow your breath.** Try the Vinyasa Flow Breath. Inhale to a count of four and exhale to a count of four. Do this several times. This will help you redistribute your sexual energy throughout your body.

**Squeeze your PC muscles.** Clench and release. Keep clenching and releasing. You should feel a pleasant tingling in your genitals.

**Visualize your work.** With your eyes closed, visualize the project you're working on. Imagine that your genital area is filled with powerful energy and light. Imagine shooting this energy directly into your work.

**Repeat.** Is there another project you're working on? Another goal you want to accomplish? Repeat the visualization exercise with this as your focus.

---

In addition to its myriad of other benefits, sexual transmutation - or "just not cumming very often" - is a powerful way to get comfortable with your sexuality.

"I'm a big fan of it," shares Dr. Glover. "And so is my wife. My wife went and told all her girlfriends that they should tell their husbands not to cum. I started experimenting with it when I turned 60, and she saw what it was doing to me. It made me more comfortable, more energized, more aroused, more ready, more creative, more in the moment. Personally, my mantra around not cumming is simply 'not today.' I don't put a lot of pressure on myself. I don't try to go three weeks or two months or whatever. It's just...not today."

**INTEGRATED ACTION:**
- ✓ Try practicing Sexual Transmutation (or just not ejaculating) for at least one week. Pay attention to how it feels. How do you feel at the end of the week? Write about the experience in your journal.
- ✓ If you can practice Sexual Transmutation for a week, you can do it longer. Try it for 30 days. Keep a journal during this time. And regularly check in with your safe person (or people).

# ABSTINENCE

In *No More Mr. Nice Guy*, Dr. Glover tells the story of Aaron. Aaron was frustrated - primarily because his wife, Hannah, never wanted to have sex with him. As Dr. Glover describes, "it was obvious that Aaron believed his wife held the key to his sexual happiness and that he was angry over her willful refusal to use that key."

After weeks of listening to Aaron lament over his practically non-existent sex life, Dr. Glover tasked Aaron with a somewhat puzzling assignment. He told Aaron to go on a sexual moratorium and abstain from having sex with Hannah for at least six months. Dr. Glover then suggested that during these six months, Aaron focus on re-discovering the things he gave up when he got married to Hannah. He also suggested that Aaron share - openly and honestly - whatever he was feeling with Hannah.

"I told Aaron that going on a sexual moratorium would make it easier for him to do the other parts of the assignment because he wouldn't be so concerned with maintaining the possibility of Hannah's sexual availability," explains Dr. Glover. "If they weren't having sex, he wouldn't have to constantly worry about doing something that might make her angry and subsequently withhold sex. Of course, Aaron was confused by how all of this would lead to more sex with Hannah. But the goal was not more sex. The goal was for Aaron to reclaim his key and stop feeling like a victim."

Though hesitant, Aaron agreed to the assignment.

Over the next six months, Aaron reported doing a variety of things that previously would have caused him a great deal of anxiety. He went out with his guy friends. He spent more time on his hobbies. He also began revealing himself to Hannah, even when that meant telling her that he was angry or that he didn't feel like listening to her talk about her problems.

Interestingly enough, Aaron also reported that Hannah had been making regular sexual advances towards him. Because Aaron was no longer relentlessly pursuing Hannah, Hannah felt freer to pursue Aaron. Hannah enjoyed the exchange of sexual energy without the overwhelming pressure to have sex.

At the end of his six-month moratorium, Aaron divulged that he felt much less resentful and much closer to Hannah. He learned that he could express himself in a healthier and more direct way, instead of through sex. When he and Hannah did start having sex again, they were noticeably more connected. And of course, the sex was a hell of a lot better.

While it may seem counterintuitive, Aaron's story demonstrates the power of going on a sexual moratorium. No matter what your relationship status is, a sexual moratorium can be transformative, particularly for Nice Guys.

Going on a sexual moratorium can:

- Help break cycles of dysfunction
- Eliminate pursuing and distancing in relationships
- Eliminate negativity and resentment
- Help you realize you can live without sex
- Help you see how you settle for bad sex
- Help you realize that you hold the key to your own sexual happiness
- Break patterns of addiction to porn, masturbation, and other compulsive sexual behaviors

Should you choose to embark on a sexual moratorium, be sure to set a time frame. Dr. Glover suggests three to six months. If you are in a relationship, discuss the moratorium with your partner. Decide on the parameters.

Then, pay attention to your slips and sabotaging behaviors as well as those of your partner.

"Remember," advises Dr. Glover, "it's all a learning experience. You don't have to do it perfectly."

## TAKE IT FURTHER WITH A FEMININE CLEANSE

Undoubtedly, going on a sexual moratorium can be life-changing. But you can actually take it a step further. In addition to abstaining purely from sex, you can consciously abstain from the Feminine in general. John Wineland, a spiritual teacher and intimacy coach, and the author of *From the Core*, calls this a "Feminine cleanse." (Note: Women can also benefit from a "Masculine cleanse.")

As Wineland describes, "A cleanse from the Feminine allows you to start paying attention to all the ways in which you try to get a 'hit' from the Feminine - through seeking attention, approval, love, validation, etc. - and begin to let those go. You cleanse from sex, dating, flirting, romance, intimacy, eye-gazing, intrigue, and any other ways you get this 'hit.' Every interaction that is not *absolutely platonic* becomes transactional. For example, to a barista, you would simply say, "Thank you for the coffee" and then move on, without lingering in their gaze, flashing a flirty smile, etc. Keep it light and polite."

Should you choose to do a Feminine cleanse, Dr. Glover recommends also cleansing your life of what he calls the "pseudo Feminine." This includes anything you might use to distract yourself, or turn to for a quick emotional or physical release or dopamine hit (i.e. porn, social media, video games, Netflix). For many men, giving up these things feels even more frightening and more painful than giving up contact with actual women. This is exactly why Dr. Glover recommends cleansing your life of them.

Just as you would for a sexual moratorium, you should prepare for a Feminine cleanse. Discuss the parameters - not just with your partner (if you

THE BIG STICK

have one), but with all the women in your life. Lovingly tell them that you are going to be distant for a predetermined amount of time. This should be at least six months.

"You don't find the real shit until after about 90 days," affirms Wineland.

Additionally, you'll want safe people - a coach or a men's group - to provide support, encouragement, and accountability during your cleanse. This allows you a space in which you can bring up your pain, your fears, your impulses, and your discoveries. You'll also want to block out as much time as possible to be with yourself. Wineland recommends at least two or three hours per day.

If doing a Feminine cleanse sounds intimidating - if not ridiculous - to you, consider how frequently sex infiltrates your psyche and dictates your life, perhaps without you even knowing it. Think about all the ways you constantly seek validation from the Feminine - a wink from the waitress, a smirk from the sales rep, a nod from the girl next door. How has your ceaseless need for another "hit" shaped your identity and impacted the way you navigate the world?

Doing a Feminine cleanse allows you to explore the depths of your soul. You get to unearth who you truly are, without distraction.

"Here's what you'll find that will change everything," proclaims Wineland. "If you do this practice long enough, you will get to a place in which you do not *need* women. You will still desire - to give, receive, ravish, nourish, love - but it will no longer come from a place of *need*. It's a death-facing practice. A warrior's practice."[114]

---

114 Wineland, John; "What is a Feminine Cleanse?" www.johnwineland.com

**INTEGRATED ACTION:**

- ✓ If you're in a relationship, consider going on a sexual moratorium. See what unfolds. Write about the experience in your journal. Discuss it with a safe person (or people)
- ✓ Write down all the ways you try to get a "hit" from the Feminine.
- ✓ Consider doing a Feminine cleanse.

# PART VI: RELATIONSHIPS

*We tell ourselves that intimacy (and marriage) takes two people who are willing to work at it-but unfortunately, we rarely have the slightest inkling of our "job" assignments in this project.*
**- David Schnarch, Ph.D**

There's a certain amount of irony in the fact that Dr. Glover is a marriage and family therapist who's been married three times. But Dr. Glover has never been one to sugar-coat relationships as blissful, fairy tale-like experiences. He acknowledges them for what they really are - frequently grueling endeavors that require work and sacrifice, and that seldom lead to happily ever after.

Dr. Glover will be the first to tell you that – just like everyone else - he has bumbled his way through his intimate relationships. He'll also point out the reason that most relationships dissolve: Lifelong pair-bonding is not in our DNA. It is a relatively new idea that ignores our evolutionary history as a tribal species. Knowing this may disappoint you, but it can also set you free. Personally, it has set me free. It has liberated me from a great deal of psychological suffering. I am much happier having accepted a universal truth about humans and relationships: We suck at them.

Relationships by their very nature are complicated and messy. But they can also be valuable learning experiences or what Dr. Glover calls, "powerful personal growth machines." And you don't necessarily have to suck at them. Relationships rarely flourish because of sheer, dumb luck. They flourish when men step up, become conscious, set the tone, take the lead, and learn how to act with genuine love and integrity toward their partner.

In his popular online class, *All the Way In*, Dr. Glover teaches men how to be more present in their intimate relationships. He calls on men to be good "ascertainers," to be more honest and transparent, and to set healthy boundaries. He shows men how to lead with love and how to unleash the sexual potential in their relationships. He also commands men to be good enders.

"Too many men are frustrated because they can't seem to create the kind of passionate and fulfilling relationships they crave," says Dr. Glover. "Whether it's due to fear or self-limiting beliefs or a lack of understanding, men often trudge along, doing the same old shit that doesn't work while expecting different results. If you want the kind of relationship you crave, then you have to commit fully and wholeheartedly. Half-assing a relationship is a recipe for disaster. I know this from decades of experience as both a man and a marriage therapist. You must get all the way in. And if getting all the way in doesn't work, you should probably get all the way out."

In this section, we'll dive into relationships. No matter what your current relationship looks like, you'll learn how you can step up and give it the chance to be all that it can be. You'll learn why you might have certain relationship patterns. You'll learn how to use your relationship as a powerful personal growth machine. You'll learn how to get all the way in. You'll also learn how to get all the way out, if necessary.

So, as Dr. Glover often asks: *Are you ready to blow up your relationship?*

# WHY WE PICK WHO WE PICK

By now, you've likely come to understand that almost everything you do in your intimate relationships – including who you pick as a partner – is rooted in what your first loves taught you. Your first loves, of course, are your mother and father.

You internalized beliefs about relationships based on your perception of how your parents interacted with you during the first few months and years of your life. This is probably when you learned the most about relationships and intimacy. Scary, huh? And now that you are an adult, you are probably unaware of the impact these early learning experiences had on you. You probably don't even remember these experiences. As such, becoming skilled at navigating intimate relationships often requires more *un*learning than learning.

Dr. Glover asserts that two primary factors tend to have the most significant influence on how we navigate relationships. The first is consistency (or lack of it). How often did your parents interact with you and meet your needs? Were they attentive? Did they meet your needs in a timely way? If so, you likely internalized the beliefs that you are lovable, your needs are important, and the world is a safe and abundant place.

Unfortunately, there are no perfect or perfectly attentive parents. There are no perfect families. And there are no perfect people. So, very few of us form wholly positive beliefs about ourselves and about the world.

The second factor that influences how we navigate relationships is that we were all totally helpless as children. Your brain was radically underdeveloped when you first started learning about relationships, but the things you learned were stored in your amygdala. (As a reminder, the amygdala is a primitive, fingernail-sized part of your brain that controls your fight/flight/ freeze mechanism and stores emotional memory). These memories do not have words or images associated with them, just emotions. Your amygdala influences most of your emotional responses, not to mention the types of people you find attractive and how you relate to these people.

As adults, the people to whom we're attracted typically help us recreate our early experiences with our parents. We unconsciously pick partners who can mirror the relationship dynamic we had with mom and dad. Or as Dr. Glover affirms in *No More Mr. Nice Guy*, we tend to be attracted to people who have some of the worst traits of both our parents.

"It makes perfect sense when you think about it," says Dr. Glover. "What value would it be for you to get involved with people who don't require you to use your most developed relationship skills, dysfunctional though they may be? In order for you to do what you do best, you need to hook up with people who are a good mirror of mom and dad – or at least how you experienced them when you were young. For example, if you learned to be a fixer in childhood, it makes sense for you to co-create a relationship with someone who needs fixing."

Dr. Glover frequently acknowledges that he is overwhelmingly attracted to women who are unhappily married or who have a history of painful relationships with men. These types of women activate his inherent desire to fix and rescue. This isn't surprising when you consider that Dr. Glover's first love - his mother - was an unhappily married woman.

As a child, Dr. Glover developed the tools necessary to uplift his mother. He became a good listener. He made himself available. He learned to be different from the men who had made his mother so miserable. He then carried these tools from childhood into adolescence and adulthood. In order to make use of his toolbox, he needed to find women with whom his tools would be most effective.

> **HARSH TRUTH**
>
> While we often unconsciously search for people who can make up for the ways our parents couldn't love us or meet our needs, we tend to pick people who are actually the least capable of doing this.

"Because of the unconscious dynamics at play," explains Dr. Glover, "we often feel the most attracted to those who, on one hand, are the absolute worst for us; but who, on the other hand, offer us the most potential to deal with old relationship baggage. This results in a kind of unconscious balancing act that relationship partners often play out – though, they don't usually realize it's happening. Suffice to say, when you come to understand and accept why most of us pick who we pick, you'll be much better equipped to co-create the kind of relationship you really want."[115]

**INTEGRATED ACTION:**
- ✓ What beliefs did you internalize as a child based on the relationship you had with your parents? Write about them in your journal.
- ✓ How do these beliefs manifest in your adult relationships? Write your answer in your journal.
- ✓ Talk to your safe person (or people) about the beliefs you internalized around intimacy and relationships.

---

115 Glover, Robert A. *All The Way In* "Lesson Two: Why You and Your Partner Worked Together to Create the Relationship You Have." (TPI University. www.drglover. com)

# FUSION & DIFFERENTIATION

I f you've never heard the terms *fusion* and *differentiation*, it's probably because hardly anybody talks about them. But learning and understanding these concepts has had a profound impact on my life and my relationships.

Dr. Glover was first introduced to fusion and differentiation during graduate school, in a lecture given by Dr. Murray Bowen, an American psychiatrist and professor of psychiatry, and a noted pioneer in family therapy. Dr. Bowen died in 1990, but his work lives on. (You can learn more about Bowen Theory from the Bowen Center for the Study of the Family.)

Until recently, perhaps the only other notable psychologist to discuss fusion and differentiation at length was Dr. David Schnarch, the previously mentioned author of *Passionate Marriage* and numerous other books and articles on intimacy, sexuality, and relationships. Schnarch based large parts of his practice on the theoretical assumptions of Bowen. He died in 2020.

Acknowledging Bowen and Schnarch as influences, Dr. Glover uses the concepts of fusion and differentiation to help men create healthy relationships - with both themselves and their partners. As Dr. Glover often illustrates, an Integrated man is a *differentiated* man. Differentiation is how you become your authentic self. It also provides the foundation for a healthy relationship. But to understand differentiation, you must first understand fusion.

According to Bowen Theory, fusion is where "individual choices are set aside in service of achieving harmony in the system." And where "people form intense relationships with others and their actions depend largely on the condition of the relationships at any given time... Decisions depend on what others think and whether the decision will disturb the fusion of the existing relationships.[116]"

Fusion is an epigenetic trait in all herd and pack animals. Members of the pack contribute to the whole. This is how humans operated for over a million years. We lived in tribes, and everything was shared. Even sex. In the last 10,000 years, however, human life has shifted from a communal model to an ownership model. We settle down with one person. We own stuff. We generally stay in one place.

Pack animals have a key survival mechanism – the transmission of anxiety. If one member of the pack experiences danger, it is instantly communicated to all members of the pack. Perhaps you've noticed this while looking at, say, birds on a wire. When one bird gets spooked and flies away, they all fly away.

While we no longer need to live in packs or tribes for survival (most of us spend at least some amount of time living alone), anxiety is still contagious amongst us humans. We have anxiety receptors in our brains. And there are still modern tribal systems – religion, culture, family – that use fusion and the transmission of anxiety to maintain homeostasis, control, and power.

"It's really a top-down manifestation," explains Dr. Glover. "Much of the anxiety you experience in life, you inherited from your parents, your culture, or your religion. It's been used as a way to control you, to keep you small, to keep you afraid, to keep you needy and dependent. And these core ownership messages that you find in fused emotional systems; you also find in many modern relationships."

These core ownership messages basically amount to:

- You are an extension of me.
- You belong to me..

---

116 https://www.thefsi.com.au/definitions-from-bowen-theory/

- My identity is tied up in you.
- My survival is dependent on you.

And therefore, you should:

- Do what I want
- Think like I think
- Be who I want you to be
- Always be there
- Never leave me
- Only be successful in the ways I need you to be successful
- Stay dependent so I never lose you

"Being in a fused system is like always being assimilated into the matrix," describes Dr. Glover. "You have to sacrifice your sense of self to the greater powers that be. Or you have to sacrifice your sense of self for the needs and wants of the person you're in a relationship with. It should go without saying that these kinds of fused systems or fused relationships aren't very healthy – yet this is how most people do intimate relationships."

Fused family systems are especially prevalent in Indian, Asian, and Pakistani cultures. In these cultures, parents tend to hover over their children and push them into extremely narrow passages. Indian men, for example, tend to do exactly what they were told – become a doctor or an engineer. They also have arranged marriages. It's no wonder these cultures have some of the world's highest levels of depression and anxiety.

As Dr. Glover points out, children typically deal with fused systems by becoming either the *I'm So Good Nice Guy* or the *I'm So Bad Nice Guy*. Remember: The *I'm So Good Nice Guy* tries to do everything right, hides his wants and needs, tries to get everyone's approval, and harbors a great deal of guilt and shame. The *I'm So Bad Nice Guy,* on the other hand, is oppositional and defiant, behaves in self-destructive ways, and cuts off his nose to spite his face. He too harbors a great deal of guilt and shame.

But let's turn specifically to relationships.

In fused relationships, it's not all that uncommon for one partner to actually say something like:

- *You are my girlfriend, so you should...*
- *You are my boyfriend, so you need to...*
- *You are my wife, so you must...*
- *You are my husband, so you have to...*

"One can see how we continue to play childhood roles in adult relationships," says Dr. Glover. "We invite the world to keep repeating what feels normal to us. We create familiar systems. We continue to live with guilt and shame, and act in ways that perpetuate this. We bring partners into our lives that guilt us and shame us, that point out our flaws, and ultimately cause us anxiety. And we fuse. We sacrifice major parts of ourselves for another. We lose sight of who we really are and what's really important to us."

So, what's the solution? How do we avoid fusion? The answer is **differentiation**.[117] To break it down as simply as possible, differentiation has three parts:

- Asking yourself: *What do I want? What feels right? What's important to me?*
- Doing it.
- Holding on to yourself in the face of internal pressure (anxiety, guilt) and external pressure (family, spouse).

Dr. Ellyn Bader, co-founder of The Couples Institute, defines differentiation as *the active ongoing process of a person being able to define their thoughts, their feelings, their wishes, and their desires to another and to be able to tolerate the partner doing the same thing.*

---

117 Dr. Glover frequently discusses both fusion and differentiation in both his in-person and virtual Total Personal Integration (TPI) workshops. Additionally, see Glover, Robert A. *All The Way In*. "Lesson Four: The Ascertainer: How to Become the Kind Man of Man You and Your Partner Both Want You to Be." (TPI University. www.drglover.com)

"When people are afraid of differentiating," explains Dr. Bader, "they are afraid if they show their authentic self and the other one doesn't like it or doesn't agree with it, that they're going to end up in a big fight or they're going to end up with the other person leaving. When that's true, they don't show themselves very well to each other."

Adds Bader, "The most stuck relationships are those where each person wants to keep the other unchanging. They remember how they were when they met, and they want that to last forever. Then they don't explore or push each other to grow. They don't take risks or try new things. It becomes a very, very narrow way of living in the world."

The path to differentiation requires you to become conscious of the roles and rules forced on you by fused emotional systems. It requires you to stop hiding. It requires you to clarify and start living by your own personal values. It also requires self-soothing, as you will likely experience some degree of anxiety or guilt.

As Dr. Glover illustrates, a differentiated man:

- Always asks: *What feels right to me? What do I want?* And then follows through
- Has his own values
- Lives with integrity, authenticity, and transparency
- Doesn't give away his freedoms
- Doesn't seek validation and approval
- Doesn't try to fix or save anyone
- Sets good boundaries
- Takes risks
- Is open to love

"Whether you're trying to break away from a fused family system or you're trying to stay differentiated in an intimate relationship, one of the best things a man can do on the path to differentiation is build a tribe of other men for support," offers Dr. Glover. "Remember, a differentiated man is an Integrated Man, and becoming an Integrated Man is work that you shouldn't do alone. Find good guy friends, get a mentor, hire a coach, join a men's group. Tell these people what you want and what feels right to you so they can cheer you on."

---

**INTEGRATED ACTION:**

✓ See Dr. Glover's Fusion Quiz. Answer the questions in your journal.

✓ Where are you on your journey towards becoming a differentiated man? Write your answer in your journal.

✓ Practice asking yourself: *What do I want? What makes me happy? What feels right to me?* Then, do it.

✓ Do you have at least one safe person yet? A coach, a therapist, a trusted friend? If not, get one.

✓ Talk to your safe person (or people) about your desire to become more differentiated. Ask them to hold you accountable.

---

## DR. GLOVER'S FUSION QUIZ

1. Where did you get the most "shoulds" in your life growing up? Where do you get them today? Do you notice you "shoulding" yourself?

2. Growing up, where did you perceive that you needed to hide or sacrifice your needs or that other people's needs were more important than yours?

3. Who was the most anxious person in your family growing up? What roles did family members play to manage their own anxiety by managing the anxiety of this person?

4. How were you influenced by cultural or religious fusion growing up?

5. As a child, did you deal with fusion by "hiding / pleasing," "pushing back, or a hybrid of the two?" Did this change at any point?

6. How and where do you see hiding/pleasing or pushing back showing up in your life today?

7. How have you created or given in to fusion in your adult relationships ("You belong to me, therefore, you should…..")?

8. How have you given up your freedoms in your adult relationships?

9. When you try to differentiate, how does your own neurotic guilt / anxiety get in your way?

10. What is one area of your life today where you are still losing yourself in a fused relationship? Do you hide/please or push back (even subtly)?

11. What is one area of your life today where you can assert yourself more and differentiate?

# LOSING YOURSELF

Have you ever been in a relationship that came to an end and left you feeling like you lost not just the relationship, but like you lost *everything*? Are you currently in a relationship that you're trying desperately to keep intact because the thought of losing it scares the shit out of you? If you immediately nodded 'Yes' to one or both of these questions, it's probably because you do what a lot of men do when getting involved with a woman: You *lose yourself*.[118] Cue Eminem (again).[119]

Dr. Glover likes to use the word *handcuffs* to illustrate how people lose themselves in relationships. He also points out the existential component to this phenomenon.

"Because most of us have existential angst - the fear of nothingness and death - people tend to seek out constants," explains Dr. Glover. "Constants can include status, position, money, a job, an addiction, or another person. We then fuse with the constant because it gives us a sense of security. But this is an illusion. We are all going to die and experience nothingness. None of us

118 Glover, Robert A. "Podcasts 157-158: Parts 1 & 2 of a Two-Part Series on How to Avoid Losing Self in a Relationship." Podcast Audio. www.drglover.com

119 Eminem had a massive hit with "Lose Yourself," which appeared on the soundtrack for *8 Mile*. It was the first hip-hop song to win the Academy Award for Best Original Song. It also won the Grammy Award for Best Rap Song and Best Rap Solo Performance. (It's not about relationships, though)

truly knows what the future holds, or what the reason is for being. Of course, this doesn't keep us from trying to latch onto something that feels secure."

Because many men - especially Nice Guys - come from a fused family system, they often fuse with their romantic partner.

"A Nice Guy will often slap one side of the handcuffs on his own wrist, slap the other side on his partner's wrist, and then hand his partner the key," describes Dr. Glover. "In the process, he gives away all of his wants and desires, and voluntarily gives up his freedom. Because after all, that's what he thinks love is - loving someone enough to give them control over his life."

Of course, this isn't just misguided, it's a perfect recipe for disaster. When a Nice Guy handcuffs himself to his partner, he always ends up pushing back. Or he retreats underground and hides the things he wants to do. Ironically, he then begins to resent the hell out of this partner for taking his freedom away.

---

### ESPOSAS

Dr. Glover, who now lives permanently in Mexico, began learning Spanish in his 50s. While he is still working to become wholly fluent, it didn't take long for him to discover the linguistic irony of the Spanish word *esposas* - plural for *esposa*, which means "wife." Why is this even remotely interesting? Because *esposas* is also Spanish for "handcuffs." When Dr. Glover points this out to native Spanish speakers, they often look surprised, as if they never knew the word has two hilariously related meanings.

---

Indeed, Nice Guys tend to lose themselves in relationships. They make their partner their emotional center. They don't have lives outside the relationship. But when you're in a relationship, it's essential that you have a rich and fulfilling life outside of it - a Great Cake of a Life.

For most men, the key ingredients for a Great Cake of a Life are:

✓ Spending time with other men

✓ Pursuing your passions

✓ Getting regular exercise

✓ Embracing challenge over comfort

Having a Great Cake of a Life will make you more attractive to women. More importantly, it will make your relationships with them significantly healthier. A woman should be the *icing* on your Great Cake, never the whole cake or even a main ingredient.

This raises another question: **Could you be perfectly happy living alone?**

Far too many men neglect their own needs. They have little passion in life. They isolate and engage in solitary behaviors (especially nowadays, given the ubiquity of things like social media, video games, and porn). They are creatures of habit. They're disconnected from other men and from their own masculinity. They are controlled by their anxieties, and they rarely if ever take risks.

"The average man – and definitely the average Nice guy - doesn't seem to have a Great Cake," asserts Dr. Glover. "And if he does, he usually sacrifices parts of it for a relationship. Or he makes the woman his whole cake. A woman can't be your cake. And she doesn't want to be. Even if she pushes you to fuse or give up the things you enjoy, it's not a good idea. You need to hold onto yourself. If you do fuse, you'll end up feeling needy and she'll end up feeling burdened. You won't be the same guy anymore and she'll lose attraction."

---

**Emotional Cannibals** [ə'mōSH(ə)n(ə)l /'kænɪb(ə)ls]

*noun Sociology*

Two people who are in a relationship and feed off each other because neither has a Great Cake of a Life outside the relationship.

---

When I began working with Dr. Glover, I was not in the depths of a long-term relationship. I was, however, emotionally fused with a woman I'd been dating (as I described in this book's introduction). I was head over heels, to say the least. I'd have done anything to make her my partner. I was never quite sure if she felt the same way about me, which only fueled me to try harder. I lost sight of everything else in my life and focused all my attention on her – calling her, texting her, buying her gifts, constantly making myself available. But all of this just turned her off. And that's an understatement.

When she cruelly discarded me from her life, I felt like I had nothing left. Nothing to live for. No reason to get out of bed. I had no semblance of a Great Cake. It was, in a word, *pathetic*.

In two words, it was *pathetic* and *stupid*.

No matter your relationship status, don't make the same mistake I did.

**Always** be working on your Great Cake.

---

### Dr. Glover's
### Daily Consciousness Practice

Every night before you go to bed, ask yourself:

✓ *What did I do today to build my Great Cake?*

✓ *Did I connect with men?*

✓ *Did I pursue my interests?*

✓ *Did I challenge myself?*

✓ *Did I get any exercise, mentally and physically?*

If you failed in any of these areas, don't judge yourself. Just commit to doing better tomorrow.

---

In part, working on your Great Cake means getting out of the nursery and challenging yourself in the world of masculinity. Find ways to do things you enjoy with other men. Test for interest with men in the same way you would test for interest with women. Just like women, men will come and go from your life for various reasons. Make cultivating relationships with men an ongoing practice. Reach out to any male friends with whom you've lost touch.

It bears repeating that many men do not have a Great Cake of a Life. Or they did at one time but ended up sacrificing it for a woman. But a woman will not make you happy. Nor will she make you sure of yourself.

"If you ever get involved with a woman who says you need to make her your number one priority, run like hell," advises Dr. Glover. "You shouldn't have to give up anything important to you for the sake of a relationship. If you feel forced to give up things that are important to you, you are with the wrong woman. A Really Great Woman will support you, encourage you, and lighten your load. She will want you to have a Great Cake of a Life. In fact, she'll bless your life. And, she'll have a Great Cake of her own."[120]

---

**INTEGRATED ACTION:**
- ✓ Do you tend to lose yourself in relationships? Write about these experiences in your journal.
- ✓ Could you be perfectly okay living alone? Why or why not? Write your answers in your journal.
- ✓ Do you have a Great Cake of a Life? Have you sacrificed your Great Cake in past relationships? Write about these experiences in your journal.
- ✓ Do at least one thing this week to work on your Great Cake.
- ✓ Get out of the house, linger in public, talk to people everywhere you go, test for interest, walk through the open doors.

---

120 For more on getting out of the nursery, see Glover, Robert A. "Podcasts 157-158: Parts 1 & 2 of a Two-Part Series on How to Avoid Losing Self in a Relationship." Podcast Audio. www.drglover.com

# SECOND ORDER RELATIONSHIPS

Now is an appropriate time to introduce another name for Nice Guys (or men who have classic Nice Guy tendencies in relationships): *First Order Males*.

Dr. Glover defines a First Order Male[121] as *a man who tries to control the situations and people outside of himself so he can manage the anxiety he feels inside of himself.* First Order Males have an overwhelming need for things to stay constant in their lives. Consequently, they are attached to outcomes and don't deal well with change.

Sound familiar?

It should come as no surprise that First Order Males usually find themselves in First Order Relationships – basically two lizard-brained people trying to manage their anxiety by controlling each other.

"In First Order Relationships, both people waste a ridiculous amount of energy using their childhood defense mechanisms to protect themselves from feeling vulnerable, from getting hurt, from being found out, from being abandoned, and from feeling their toxic shame," explains Dr. Glover. "As couples do this, both people assume without reservation that their partner is the cause of how they feel. They believe that if their partner were different,

---

121 Glover, Robert A. *All the Way In*. "Lesson Three: Turn Your Relationship into a Powerful Personal Growth Machine." (TPI University. www.drglover.com)

everything would be just fine. So, they try to manage their anxiety by managing their partner."

First Order Males try desperately to make their partner happy, thinking this will lead to a smooth, conflict-free relationship. First Order Males are fixers. They see almost every mood, feeling, or behavior exhibited by their partner as a problem that needs to be solved. But navigating relationships this way only keeps men feeling helpless and powerless.

When describing the behavior of First Order Males, Dr. Glover likes to use the phrase "putting the wet stuff on the red stuff," which he borrowed from a longtime friend and (now retired) firefighter. Old-timey firefighters think that simply spraying water - the wet stuff - on flames - the red stuff - is the way to extinguish any fire, no matter what kind of fire it is. But this is ridiculous, as Dr. Glover's friend will tell you, because every fire is unique. Every fire requires an ability to ascertain the best approach for dealing with it.

"First Order Males are like old-timey firefighters," explains Dr. Glover. "They respond to every situation the same way. They use the same problem-solving strategy they've been using their whole lives, even if it doesn't work. Every time their partner is moody or emotional, they put the wet stuff on the red stuff, and it usually just makes matters worse."

First Order Relationships are not healthy relationships.

So, what does a healthy relationship – or a **Second Order Relationship**[122] – look like? To answer this, I first need to reference a declaration often made by Cartman from *South Park*:

"Whatever, I do what I want!"

You probably said this as a kid, particularly when your parents forbade you from doing something you wanted to do. Of course, when you say this as a kid, you're kind of a little shit. But it's pretty important that you say this as an adult. Sadly, a lot of men don't.

---

122 See Glover, Robert A. *All the Way In*. "Lesson Three: Turn Your Relationship into a Powerful Personal Growth Machine." (TPI University. www.drglover.com)

Are you doing what *you* want?

Too many men aren't doing what they want. They're not very mature, either. They seek approval and avoid conflict. They're always looking for permission to do what they want. If they seemingly can't do what they want, they pout and throw fits or withdraw and manipulate.

"A mature male does what feels right to him," explains Dr. Glover. "He takes responsibility for getting his needs met. He is accountable for his actions, feelings, choices, and life circumstances. He recognizes that in all situations he is a volunteer, not a victim."

Furthermore, healthy adults are on a lifelong journey of growth. They look deep within themselves, and they allow their partners to do the same. They are willing to be fully honest and transparent. A healthy relationship is made of two individuals who are - or who aspire to become - healthy adults.

No single relationship can meet all your needs. Healthy, mature people recognize this. Unfortunately, many people dwell on the other side of the spectrum, latching on to one relationship with one partner and expecting that person to meet all their needs (without being asked). Then, they become frustrated and resentful when that person fails to meet their absurd expectations.

# THE RELATIONSHIP
# TEETER-TOTTER

When you challenge yourself to step up in your relationship, you will inevitably create what Dr. Glover calls *the Relationship Teeter-Totter*.[123] This teeter-totter effect can turn your relationships into vehicles for profound personal growth.

---

123 See Glover, Robert A. *All the Way In*. "Lesson Three: Turn Your Relationship into a Powerful Personal Growth Machine." (TPI University. www.drglover. com)

Consider this: If the man in a relationship (Partner A) makes a personal change – like deciding to set the tone and take the lead – it might unsettle the woman (Partner B), even if she likes the change. Partner A has now gone up on the Teeter-Totter and skewed the balance.

If Partner B resists the change, Partner A can either hold onto himself and continue to change, or he can give in and let the Teeter-Totter fall back into balance. If Partner A does hold onto himself and Partner B loves Partner A and values the relationship, Partner B needs to make a choice: Either she can find some way to bring Partner A back down to her level or she can challenge herself to start growing in her own way. If she decides to challenge herself to grow, her side of the Teeter-Totter will go up.

A relationship in which both people continually ride the teeter-totter is, as you may have guessed, a **Second Order Relationship.** And the change created by the teeter-totter is known as *Second Order Change*. Second Order Change occurs when there are real, fundamental shifts.

"Be willing to ride the Relationship Teeter-Totter," advises Dr. Glover. "If you're in a healthy relationship with a mature partner, you'll both keep raising the bar. When two people keep raising the bar for each other by challenging themselves, the opportunity for growth is practically limitless."

**INTEGRATED ACTION:**
- ✓ Are you in a First Order or Second Order Relationship? Write your answer in your journal. Describe what makes your relationship First Order or Second Order.
- ✓ What can you do to go from First Order to Second Order? How can you make Second Order change? Write your answers in your journal.
- ✓ When you challenge yourself to grow, does your partner do the same? Write your answer in your journal.

# SETTING THE TONE & TAKING THE LEAD II

There's an old joke that goes something like: *Relationships are just two people constantly asking each other what they want to eat until one of them dies.* Most jokes, however, are rooted in truth. And the truth is that all of those infuriating and seemingly endless conversations about what's for dinner usually indicate a much bigger problem: The man isn't stepping up, setting the tone, and taking the lead.

Relationships generally suffer when the woman takes the driver's seat and the man sits in the passenger seat, lackadaisically staring out the window. As Dr. Glover illustrates in the first lesson of *All the Way In*, when the woman is forced to set the tone and take the lead, this is usually what happens:

- **The woman becomes controlling and bitter**. Being the CEO of the relationship goes against her nature. The Feminine wants to be led, nurtured, and protected. Remember, women tend to be security-security seeking creatures. A woman doesn't feel secure with a man who doesn't set the tone and take the lead.

- **The man feels inadequate**. When the woman is in the driver's seat, the man thinks she's trying to control him. He feels like a subservient little boy.

- **The man employs Nice Guy strategies to relieve the woman's dissatisfaction**. He placates, he pleases, he uses covert contracts, he withdraws. But none of these things work. So, the man feels like he can never do anything right. He puts his guard up. He becomes defensive and wary, wondering how he can fix his wife's constant bad moods.

- **The woman feels dismissed and lonely**. The man's attempts to solve her problems actually feel uncaring. She begins to feel unloved. She then continues to behave in ways that make the man feel controlled.
- **Their sex life suffers**. The woman doesn't want to be sexual with a weak, emotionally unavailable man. And the man doesn't want to be sexual with a moody, controlling woman.
- **Both the man and the woman feel frustrated, resentful, and misunderstood.**

As a man, it is your responsibility to set the tone and take the lead in your relationship. When you set the tone and take the lead, you give your relationship the greatest opportunity to flourish. Setting the tone and taking the lead requires you to:

✓ Be more conscious.

✓ Promote open communication.

✓ Be honest and transparent.

✓ Deal with conflict head on.

✓ Make decisions.

✓ Bring humor and playfulness to the relationship.

✓ Bring passion to the relationship.

"Remember, setting the tone and taking the lead is not controlling," asserts Dr. Glover. "It is an act of love and integrity. Women are tired of driving the fucking bus. Particularly if they are in their masculine all day long, as a job might demand. They don't want to drive the bus of their relationship. They are tired of being the gatekeepers. They are tired of you asking, 'What do you want for dinner?' They want you to lead."

# GETTING ALL THE WAY IN

Men who are stuck in their relationships usually feel this way because they are not all the way in. Nor are they all the way out. Again, half-assing a relationship is a recipe for disaster. It just doesn't work.

"Men frequently report that they love their partners but aren't sure if they should stay or leave," explains Dr. Glover. "They have one foot in and one foot out. They are confused about what to do. The solution is to get all the way in. This means making a conscious, unwavering commitment to setting the tone and taking the lead, to being honest and transparent, to being present, and to bringing passion into the relationship. When a man gets all the way in, his relationship will either flourish and grow, or it will wither and die. Then he'll know if he should get all the way out."

At this point, you might be thinking:

*Why is it all on me?*

*What about her?*

*What about all the terrible things she has done?*

*What about her shitty behavior?*

Understandable.

Your partner hasn't been perfect, and that's likely an understatement. But you need to find out just how much of her bad behavior is due to your failure to get all the way in, set the tone, and take the lead.

"Often, when a man starts setting the tone and taking the lead with love and integrity, his woman's bad behavior starts to disappear," says Dr. Glover. "By getting all the way in and consciously leading, you get to find out who your woman really is. If she still sucks, then you can get all the way out."[124]

---

124 Glover, Robert A. "Podcast 128: Applying the Principles of Conscious Dating to Long-Term Relationships: Part 4, Setting the Tone and Taking the Lead. Podcast Audio. www.drglover.com. For additional information on setting the tone and taking the lead in relationships, see *All The Way In*. "Lesson One: Why Women and Men Tend to Be Equally Bad at Intimacy, and Why the Health of Your Relationship is in Your Hands"

**INTEGRATED ACTION:**

- ✓ Do you fail to set the tone and take the lead in your relationships? How so? Write about these experiences in your journal.
- ✓ In what ways do you need to get all the way in? What would it look like if you got all the way in? Write your answers in your journal.
- ✓ Has getting all the way *out* crossed your mind? Write about it in your journal.
- ✓ If you're in a relationship, sit down and have an honest conversation with your partner. Let them know that you're going to get all the way in, and that you're going to start setting the tone and taking the lead.

# POSITIVE EMOTIONAL TENSION II

As you've learned, it is important that you create ***Positive Emotional Tension*** (PET)[125] if you want to experience success in dating. But it's just as important to create PET when you're in a long-term relationship. Remember, a woman needs to experience tension to *stay* attracted and attached to a man. Work at creating PET on an ongoing basis.

Like many men, I had trouble wrapping my head around the concept of PET when I first learned of it. Because, like many men, I am always looking for precise, easy-to-follow, step-by-step instructions. But PET is not some kind of magic formula you can use to manipulate or seduce women. There's no "right way" to create PET, and there are no precise, step-by-step instructions. Ultimately, PET is about how you show up in the world and interact with everyone around you. It's an energetic state. You can create the most PET by just being yourself.

Before we dive further into PET, however, you should know that if you're with a woman who is always unavailable or who always treats you badly, you're with the wrong woman. As Dr. Glover says, "Creating PET with a woman is an invitation to dance with you. So, if a woman doesn't want to dance, resists your lead, or repeatedly criticizes how you lead, do both your-

---

125 For more insight into creating *Positive Emotional Tension*, see Glover, Robert A. Positive Emotional Tension (TPI University. www.drglover.com) and Glover, Robert A. "Podcasts 37-41: Parts 1-5 of a Five-Part Series on Creating Positive Emotional Tension with Women." Podcast Audio. www.drglover.com

self and her a favor and cut her loose. You should only be in a long-term relationship with a receptive dance partner – a Really Great Woman."

That said, here are some of Dr. Glover's tried-and-true ways to create PET in your long-term relationship:

**Be you.**

This may not be what you want to hear given that it's a complete and utter cliché; but it's true. Being your authentic self is perhaps the most powerful way to create PET with a woman. Hiding the real you while constantly seeking the approval of others only inhibits your ability to create PET.

If you're always trying to hide your flaws and mistakes, then you probably think you need to be perfect. But what is attractive about perfect? Not only is there no such thing as perfect, but it's your quirks and idiosyncrasies and rough edges that make you interesting. When you accept yourself just as you are, you'll exude a natural confidence that women can't resist. You won't hold back or censor yourself. This is what it means to be an authentic, congruent, and Integrated Man.

**Always be working on your Great Cake.**

How much PET do you think you can create and how attractive do you think your partner will continue to find you if you don't have a life? Always be working on your Great Cake. At the very least, this should include spending time with other men, pursuing your interests and passions, consistently challenging yourself, and getting regular exercise.

**Be bold and take risks.**

You'll never create any tension if you always play it safe. Single men end up in the Friend Zone because they hold back and play it safe. For the same reason, men in relationships often wonder why their partner is never in the mood for sex. Playing it safe kills tension.

**Keep her tea kettle heated up.**

When you are in an intimate relationship with a woman, you should create the kind of tension that keeps her in an almost constant state of sexual arousal and desire. Or as Dr. Glover likes to say, you should "keep her tea kettle heated up." Even little things - like sending her an unexpected naughty text message or whispering a few sweet nothings in her ear - can heat up her tea kettle. There are endless possibilities for keeping your woman endlessly wet.

**Practice The Three Ts.**

In case you need another brief refresher, The Three Ts are: Touch, Tease, and Tell. And they are a powerful way to create Positive Emotional Tension. Single men are too afraid to practice The Three Ts, which is another reason they end up flailing around in the friend zone. Men in relationships don't practice The Three Ts either, which is why they actually have to make a plan to have sex. Touch your woman regularly. Don't hold back. Tease her in playful and loving ways. And tell her what to do. Don't ask

**Practice the Three Rules for Amazing Sex.**

Need another refresher? The Three Rules for Amazing Sex are:

1. Approach your partner as if she is the most sexually adventurous, open-minded woman on the planet.
2. It's her job to tell you 'No.'
3. If she tells you 'No,' don't take it personally. Then, go back to rule number one.

Practice these rules throughout the day, every day, without attachment to outcome.

**Build trust.**

Remember, *trust equals lust*. Be a man of integrity. Tell the truth. Keep your word. Follow through on the things you say you are going to do. Most women have never experienced being deeply penetrated by a man they trust.

**Stop doing The White Guy Shuffle.**

In Salsa dancing, there's a phrase used to describe a guy who doesn't have a plan, doesn't think ahead, and keeps doing the same stupid move, over and over. That phrase is *the White Guy Shuffle*.

"Most white dudes who learn to Salsa dance tend to play it safe," shares Dr. Glover. "I know this because I am a white dude who learned to Salsa dance. They're anxious about trying something new, they fear making a mistake, or they don't want to look foolish. But dance is a metaphor for life. If you do the White Guy Shuffle, women will get bored with you and find someone else to dance with."

Stop doing the White Guy Shuffle. Live with passion. Get out of your comfort zone. Have some fun, for fuck sake.

# EIGHT EVOLUTIONARY PET TRIGGERS

Dr. Glover believes there are eight core, evolutionary PET hacks – or *triggers* - that are most effective for stirring up attraction and arousal in women.

"Together, these eight things explain everything you have never understood about women and how to turn them on," proclaims Dr. Glover. "They are the very foundation of PET. The man who masters the ability to consciously activate and navigate these triggers will not only experience a powerful masculine initiation but he will also give a profound gift to women and the world."

### 1. Attention

If a woman did not get attention during tribal times, she would die. To be seen and attended to meant that she would receive her share of the tribe's resources - food, clothing, shelter, protection, and yes, cock. Today, one of the most common complaints women make about their relationships is that they don't feel seen, heard, or validated.

"This is painful to women," explains Dr. Glover. "It feels like death when those closest to them don't see, hear, or get them. This need for attention - which leads to connection - is wired into the deepest part of a woman's emotional brain."

Men typically make two major mistakes: 1) They fail to notice, understand, or respond to their woman's signals that she desires attention, and 2) they give their woman way too much of what she wants.

"When a man learns to understand a woman's call for attention, he can walk through countless doors of opportunity," explains Dr. Glover. "And when he understands how to build tension by giving a woman some of what she wants - but not all of what she wants, every time she wants it - he can create a pressure cooker of attraction and arousal."

## 2. Security

Remember, women tend to be security-seeking creatures. For a million years, women looked to men to be their security system. Tribal women were provided for and protected by masterful, tribal men.

Ask any modern woman if she feels safe walking alone at night through her own neighborhood. Her response will likely be visceral. Most men will never really know the vulnerability that women experience every single day. Women want to feel safe. But more often than not, they don't feel safe.

"Most of the pseudo-intellectuals in the dating and pickup world are wrong about women's desires," asserts Dr. Glover. "These men try to sound smart by talking about things like hypergamy, but they tend to be off base. Yes, there are certainly some gold-digger type women out there who will gladly take advantage of men's insecurities and stupidity. But it is generally not in the nature of a woman to seek the richest guy or the guy with the most 'alpha' characteristics. It is the nature of a woman to seek a man with whom she can feel safe. A man she can trust. A man she knows she can count on. A man she can open up and submit to. This is security."

## 3. Procreation and Pleasure

Women are evolutionarily wired to be fucked well and fucked often. Women are highly tuned sexual machines. They are the most sexually evolved creatures on the planet. And yet, humans today have bought into the myth that women don't like or don't care about sex. As Dr. Glover illustrates, this is due to:

- A few thousand years of patriarchy during which men have worked exceptionally hard to control and repress female sexuality

- Women's vulnerability to sexual assault, rape, and violence (committed primarily by the men who should be protecting them)
- Rampant slut shaming

"Many women have been conditioned to dislike or avoid sex," explains Dr. Glover. "But beneath their wounds and their armor - and putting aside the ways that culture makes sex costly for them - women are amazing sexual beings who yearn to be ravished by loving, masculine, and masterful men. So, getting comfortable with your sexual self, overcoming your inaccurate beliefs about women and sex, cleaning the porn, fantasy, and masturbation out of your life – all these things factor into learning how to be masterful. This may take work, but it is the most powerful masculine initiation I know of. And it's the most loving gift a man can give a woman."

### 4. Competition and Status

Though tribal life was communal, women still competed for scarce resources. Back then, there was only so much of everything to go around, including sexual access. So, if a woman was first in line, it ensured that she got two things: 1) the most and best sperm, and 2) the greatest amount of pleasure. This created a status-based pecking order amongst tribal women.

Today, the desire for status paints an unflattering picture of women. Female competition can get ugly, and often manifests as gold-digging, envy, gossiping, back-stabbing, slut-shaming, flirting with married men, and a whole host of other disreputable behaviors. This is not meant as an insult to women, but rather as a way to help you understand that their evolutionary traits are still very much present. Just ask a woman how well she trusts other women.

For many women, having a man is a status symbol, particularly if it's a man that other women might desire. And for many men, having a woman makes them more attractive because it creates *social proof.* If you are single, there's a good chance you'll have better luck getting laid if you're wearing a wedding ring. When a woman knows you have other options, she'll see you as more desirable, which triggers her deepest desire to win.

No matter your relationship status, women will tend to want you more when they know you don't need them. You can create powerful tension by being a social animal, by being comfortable in your own skin, and by letting go of the need for a woman's approval.

### 5. Anticipation and Uncertainty

Tribal men used to leave the tribe for long periods of time, usually to hunt, gather, or fight. The women stayed behind, tending to the children and the other dependent tribe members. Subsequently, women experienced constant anticipation and uncertainty. They never knew when, or in what condition, the men would return.

Now, if you were to pick up any modern romance novel, watch pretty much any chick flick, or eavesdrop on two women chatting at a coffee shop, you'll almost certainly notice elements of anticipation and uncertainty. This is the foundation of all female drama and arousal.

"Even the most put-together, liberated, highly-functioning, successful female still loves the feeling of butterflies in her stomach created by the anticipation and uncertainty of seeing a certain man she just can't get out of her head," describes Dr. Glover. "Notice that in chick flicks and romance novels the heroine is almost always a strong, accomplished woman who fights being drawn into the intense uncertainty and vulnerability created by a man, only to finally succumb. Then, she pushes him away once she has him because certainty kills the tension. It's formulaic. But the formula works…because it works."

As a man, you can create PET by being unpredictable, by maintaining a slight air of mystery, by never being too available, and by regularly mixing things up (in other words, by creating anticipation and uncertainty). Unfortunately, when it comes to sex and relationships, most men hate anticipation and uncertainty. They want to lock a woman down and keep it that way. They want things to be predictable. So, they *become* predictable. But predictable is fucking boring, and women hate boring.

### 6. Variety and Novelty

For most of human history, life involved change. Our ancestors were hunters and gatherers who never stayed in one place for too long. They kept moving. Each day brought a new adventure. And each night brought sexual variety.

Again, women hate boring.

"Two-million years of nomadic tribal life created constant variety and novelty for our foremothers," explains Dr. Glover. "Modern women are wired to crave the same today. I don't believe a man is responsible for keeping a woman entertained. But he better not be fucking boring."

### 7. Drama, Intrigue, and Escape

Because tribal men would leave the tribe for lengthy periods, tribal women had to do something to fill the time. So, they huddled together, creating drama and intrigue to stave off boredom until the men returned. Yes, women were each other's competition. But they were also each other's companions.

Notice how women interact with each other today. They crave and create drama and intrigue. Whether it's on social media, at work, on the phone, or at home watching reality television, women bathe in drama. As David Deida, the author of *The Way of the Superior Man*, says, "For women, drama is foreplay."

When you can skillfully navigate Feminine drama, you can create PET. A woman doesn't want you to follow her down her emotional rabbit holes. She wants you to be her North Star. If you can stay grounded and set boundaries, if you can respond rather than react, if you can remain in your higher masculine, your woman's attraction for you will only grow.

### 8. Polarity

As you've learned, men and women used to play very distinct roles and they lived very different lives. Men spent their time with other men doing masculine things. And women spend their time with other women doing feminine things. This created an intense polarity between tribal men and women, which is likely a primary reason they had such active and varied sex lives.

"Today, women can get MBAs and men can be stay-at-home dads," acknowledges Dr. Glover. "Men and women have a lot more choices and gender roles are far more fluid. But most women still tend to crave the magnetic polarity that comes from being with a man who is masterful, who is confident, who is comfortable in his own skin, and who can set the tone and take the lead. Even the strongest woman wants a man who can match her strength and lead with consciousness and power. This allows her to let go and relax into his Masculine presence. This is Feminine bliss."

While it is undoubtedly positive that men and women have more choices and we have all but eliminated stereotypical gender roles, it doesn't change the simple fact that opposites attract. Two poles of a magnet come together because they are not the same. Polarity is important in relationships between men and women. The more men and women become the same, the more it kills the kind of polarity that leads to attraction and arousal.

When you relinquish all leadership to a woman, when you censor yourself and play it safe, when you seek validation, you kill the polarity that turns women on. But when you practice the principles of PET, you will develop what Dr. Glover calls *conscious charisma*. This is the kind of charisma that organically, authentically, and magnetically attracts all things Feminine.

**INTEGRATED ACTION:**
- ✓ Do you create P.E.T. with your partner? Write your answer in your journal.
- ✓ Do you have a tendency to do the White Guy Shuffle? How so? Write about it in your journal.
- ✓ Practice creating PET with the woman (or women) in your life. Write about your experiences in your journal.

# MONOGAMY

Perhaps it bears repeating that lifelong monogamy is not really in our DNA. Human beings are not wired to be sexually exclusive. Our tribal ancestors shared everything, including sexual partners. Everybody had access to everybody.

Now, even with the increasing popularity of open relationships, polyamory, and other "alternative" lifestyles, most people want their relationships to be monogamous. Boiled down, true monogamy requires keeping all your sexual energy within the container of your relationship. But very few people are truly monogamous.

This is not to imply that everyone is cheating. But infidelity can take many forms. And in most relationships, at least one partner has hidden feelings or engages in hidden behaviors.

Many men, for example, have a history of masturbating to porn and fantasy. This may have helped dissipate their sex drive during adolescence. But it works against men as they grow older; it hinders maturation as a sexual person. Men also tend to think that once they get into a relationship, they'll lose the desire to masturbate to or fantasize about other women. But this is rarely the case.

Incidentally, there is no "right way" to do sex and relationships. Whoever tells you there is a "right way" is full of shit. There are plenty of benefits to being in a monogamous relationship. There are plenty of benefits to being in an open or non-monogamous relationship. And there are plenty of benefits to being single and promiscuous. But if you are, in fact, in a monogamous relationship that you want to flourish, you should be bringing all your sexual energy to your partner and keeping it within the container of the relationship.

As Dr. Glover illustrates, sexual energy can leak out of the container in several ways including:

- **Porn**. Because porn is so easily and quickly accessible, and comes in so many different varieties, it can become addictive for many men. Porn allows men to avoid dealing with real women. It can also make real women (and real sex) seem less desirable.

- **Fantasy**. Whether you're fantasizing about an ex-girlfriend or a woman you saw at the supermarket, you've turned her into a one-dimensional object for your gratification. "Checking out women is natural and normal, but you should do it with your partner," recommends Dr. Glover. "Notice, comment, and that's it. Share your fantasies with your partner. Fantasy is meant to move you forward. When you hide your fantasies from your partner, you hide yourself. This prevents you from finding out if you and your partner are even a good sexual match. So, have fantasy but keep within the container of your relationship."

- **Flirting**. When you flirt with other women in a way that conveys you'd like to fuck them – even though you have no intention of doing so – it's disrespectful to your partner. It's also confusing to the women with whom you're flirting.

- **Masturbation**. When you're in a monogamous relationship, masturbation can create bad sexual habits. It can lead to premature ejaculation. It can cause your brain to need a specific kind of stimulus. Or it can condition you to only be able to cum in your own hand with a precise amount of pressure. Masturbation takes the sexual energy away from your partner. So, if you're going to masturbate, do so in a way that strengthens your relationship. Share masturbation with your partner. Dr. Glover often acknowledges that he rarely masturbates (or ejaculates, for that matter) and only does so as a gift to his wife. "If I am traveling and away from my wife for a stretch of time, I might shoot a video of myself jerking off and send it to her," he divulges. "I know it heats up her teapot, so to speak. Actually, it makes it boil over!"

- **Cheating**. Anything that takes your sexual energy away from your partner is cheating. This includes "emotional affairs." Giving your heart, your mind, and your attention to someone other than your partner is just as damaging as giving them your body. As Dr. Glover says, "Cheating is cheating, even without sexual intercourse."

- **Social media**. Need I say more?

"You have to make a conscious decision to be monogamous," says Dr. Glover. "Monogamy is a commitment. If you're in a monogamous relationship, decide to remove everything in your life that prevents you from being open and available to your partner. Be all the way in."[126]

---

126 Glover, Robert A. "Podcast 155: Dealing with Infidelity." Podcast Audio. www. drglover.com

# INFIDELITY

If you've ever cheated on a partner, it probably wasn't everything you hyped it up to be in your mind. Maybe it didn't quite live up to your fantasy. Maybe it was stressful. It probably left you riddled with guilt (unless you're a sociopath).

And if you've ever had a partner cheat on you…well, you certainly know how that feels. The craziness. The suspicion. The lies and betrayal. The feeling of abandonment. The anger. The pain and heartbreak.

Infidelity is a bitch.

Dr. Glover likes to define infidelity as "anything you wouldn't do with your sister." He often adds, "or anything your partner wouldn't like you doing if they were looking over your shoulder." As previously mentioned, this can include things like porn, fantasy, and flirting.

Ultimately, it's up to you and your partner to determine what infidelity means within the context of your relationship. Most couples don't proactively sit down and have a mature discussion around fidelity. But they should. It's an important discussion to have. Again, monogamy isn't natural for us humans. So, we're just not very good at it.

"If you think about it," says Dr. Glover, "the definition of monogamy is basically: Hey my penis belongs to you and your vagina belongs to me. This isn't very evolved. It's based around fear and control. To be truly sexually monogamous to one person, you must be conscious. You must make a conscious decision to keep your sexual energy within the container of your relationship."

But what if you do get cheated on?

How should you deal with it?

And why does infidelity hurt so much when we aren't even wired to be sexually monogamous?

Well, there's nothing quite like infidelity to trigger your toxic shame, especially if you're a Nice Guy. It brings up all your insecurities, self-limiting beliefs, and childhood issues. It makes you think: *If she's choosing someone else, I must not be good enough.*

But that's just your mind fucking with you.

"The real issue is the breach of trust," asserts Dr. Glover. "That and hiding oneself from their partner. When someone is cheating, they essentially have to emotionally kill off their partner to feel anything sexual for another person. Trust really is everything in a conscious relationship. If you trust a person, you can be vulnerable with them. You can get close to them. If you can't trust them, there's absolutely no room for growth."

Nobody is perfect. We all know this. So, could you be with an imperfect woman? Surely you could. But could you be with a woman who you can't trust?

Should you get cheated on, it's completely up to you how to handle it. But Dr. Glover offers a few things to consider:

- If your relationship is new – maybe you've been together a few weeks or months – and she cheats on you, you'd be wise to end it. Move on. Remember, you're trying to discover this woman's nature. Cheating early in a relationship is quite indicative of what her nature is.
- If you've been together for a long time, if you have a history, if there are a lot of great things about the relationship, and for whatever reason your partner cheats, the relationship can still work. As Dr. Glover illustrates, "oftentimes infidelity wakes people up and makes them more conscious."

Again, the primary issue here is trust. As a general rule, don't hang out with people you can't trust. But if you're in an intimate relationship, particularly one with a crumbling foundation, you must establish - or *re*establish - trust. And you can start with an honest conversation about infidelity.[127]

---

**INTEGRATED ACTION:**
- ✓ Have you ever cheated or been cheated on? Write about the experience(s) in your journal.
- ✓ If you're in a relationship, have an honest conversation with your partner about what infidelity means within the context of your relationship.

---

127 Glover, Robert A. "Podcast 155: Dealing with Infidelity." Podcast Audio. www. drglover.com

# BOUNDARIES

For many men, boundaries[128] are a significant issue (or more specifically, a *lack* of boundaries). This is probably due in part to the fact that a lot of men don't actually know what boundaries are. Dr. Glover frequently admits that he'd never even heard of boundaries until he was in his 30s - well after he'd earned his Ph.D. in marriage and family therapy - and found himself in a therapy session, trying to figure out how to navigate his second marriage.

When we were children, adults could do whatever they wanted to us, and we couldn't stop them. We were helpless, even when we were treated badly. And quite often, the people who treated us the worst were the very people who were put on this planet to take care of us.

Most of us grow up having no idea what personal boundaries are, let alone how to set and maintain them. Many of us associate love with being treated badly. Like many Nice Guys, Dr. Glover acknowledges that he always believed he had to put up with shit to get love.

Dr. Glover lays out two primary rules for setting boundaries:

1. Boundaries are not about getting anyone else to be different; they're about getting *you* to be different.

---

128 Glover, Robert A. "Podcast 69: Boundaries and Bad Behavior." Podcast Audio. www.drglover.com. Note: Learning to set boundaries is a crucial part of recovery from the Nice Guy Syndrome. Dr. Glover frequently discusses boundaries in his Total Personal Integration workshops, in his online classes, and in interviews.

2. Your power to set a boundary is determined by your willingness and ability to remove yourself from a bad situation.

As a child, you didn't have the ability to remove yourself from a bad situation. As an adult, you almost always have the ability to remove yourself. It's more likely that you're not willing.

If you're not willing to remove yourself, you have no power.

"A lot of men are afraid to set boundaries because it feels unnatural and because they're afraid someone will react negatively," explains Dr. Glover. "But if you're conscious, if you're in your higher Masculine self, you can set boundaries with love and integrity. And the more conscious you are, the more elegant and inviting your boundaries will be. The most loving boundaries lead others into their own higher consciousness and into deeper connection with you."

When men first learn to set boundaries, they often come on too strong or become what Dr. Glover calls a *kamikaze boundary setter*. But you can avoid this by staying conscious. If you don't take things personally and you're not attached to an outcome, you can set boundaries from a truly loving place.

Boundaries, by the way, actually make it possible for people to get closer to each other.

"Think about it," insists Dr. Glover. "If you don't have boundaries, you basically have two options. You can avoid people altogether. Or you can build walls for protection. Neither one lets people get close to you."

## BOUNDARY EXAMPLES

If you are anything like I was, then you are probably racking your brain over how the hell to set boundaries. And you are probably overthinking it. While setting boundaries may initially make you uncomfortable, it isn't complicated. Different situations may call for different boundaries. But you get to decide when and how to set boundaries, and which boundaries to set.

That said, Dr. Glover offers these examples of boundaries that you can use for reference:

- **Clear, Non-Judgmental Statements:**
  - *Please don't do that, it makes me uncomfortable.*
  - *I'm going to hang up the phone now. Call me back when you're in a better mood.*
  - *If you want to hang out with me, you'll need to…*
- **Playful Distraction:**
  - *Let's wrestle.*
  - *Come here, I need to tell you a secret.*
- **Validating Another's Point of View**
  - *I know you'd like me to stay home with you, but I'm going to hang out with the guys for a few hours. I like knowing you'll miss me.*
  - *I know there's still work to be done, but I'm going home now. When I get back tomorrow, you'll have my undivided attention.*
- **Expressing Vulnerability that Invites Them into Higher Consciousness**
  - *Ouch, that hurts. Did you mean it to?*
  - *When you do that, it does damage to our relationship. Is that what you want?*

When setting boundaries, don't defend yourself. It makes you appear and feel weak. You shouldn't have to convince someone not to treat you like shit. Nor should you have to convince someone that it's okay for you to do something that feels right to you. The beauty of being an adult is that you get to do what you want. Of course, this doesn't mean that you can't have a discussion or agree on a compromise. But decide what feels right to you and hold onto it.

# PROFESSIONAL BOUNDARY INVADERS

Everyone has a shit day. Occasionally, you may need to cut people some slack. But if someone consistently treats you badly, then you might be dealing with what Dr. Glover calls a ***Professional Boundary Invader***.[129]

Professional Boundary Invaders are often people who are closest to you. It is likely a fused relationship from which you don't believe you can remove yourself. You can tell that you're dealing with a Professional Boundary Invader if:

- They argue with every one of your boundaries.
- They justify their invasive and inappropriate behavior.
- They seem confused as to why you even have an issue with their behavior.
- They push through every boundary you set as if you never set it. (They might act as though you never even set a boundary.)
- They are oblivious to double standards.
- They act like they are being victimized when you don't let them victimize you.

If you believe you're dealing with a Professional Boundary Invader, know that you can remove yourself from the relationship. And you should.

"Get the fuck away from Professional Boundary Invaders," insists Dr. Glover. "Surround yourself with people who love you and who treat you well. Don't hang around people who treat you badly. Life's too damn short."

---

129 Glover, Robert A. "Podcast 69: Boundaries and Bad Behavior." Podcast Audio. www.drglover.com

**INTEGRATED ACTION:**

- ✓ Where in your life do you fail to set boundaries? How has this served you? Write your answers in your journal.
- ✓ Do you have professional boundary invaders in your life? If so, write about them in your journal.
- ✓ Do you spend time with people who treat you badly? If so, write about them in your journal.
- ✓ Start setting necessary boundaries with love and integrity.
- ✓ Talk to your safe person (or people) about your experience setting boundaries. Ask for feedback.

# BOREDOM

While leading a men's seminar in Los Angeles, Dr. Glover and his longtime friend and colleague, Dr. Michael Pariser, decided to open up the floor and take questions from the audience. Dr. Pariser is a therapist and certified No More Mr. Nice Guy Coach, and the author of *No More Mr. Nice Guy: The Hero's Journey*. Dr. Glover and Dr. Pariser make for an entertaining pair, and the energy in the room was palpable.

After a succession of audience members asked questions (and received thought-provoking answers), one man raised his hand, stood up, and began to sullenly describe his relationship with his wife. Presumably in his mid-to-late 30s, the man said that he's been married for ten years and has two young sons, seven and eight years old.

"I think we're in a classic rut," said the man. "My wife and I have hit a point where after we spend the entire day focused on our children, there's nothing left to say to each other. It's boring. There are silences. We don't share many interests. We don't seem to connect on anything, really. I fantasize about being in a different life. I'm stuck with this idea that the adventure is entirely over for me as a man. I can't help but wonder, is this it? Is this it in terms of a male-female relationship?"

The man continued to lament…until Dr. Glover interrupted.

"You're living in a fantasy world," proclaimed Dr. Glover, lovingly. "It's a fantasy world where you paint your wife as the reason you're unhappy and you're not doing what you want. And the more you fantasize, the more un-happy you are. I'm guessing you haven't shared your fantasies with your wife."

The man agreed.

Dr. Glover then turned to Dr. Pariser and asked, "Have you ever seen a boring relationship where everyone involved is being honest with each other?"

"No," answered Dr. Pariser, without pause. "When partners are honest with each other, the relationship either gets exciting or it ends."

Dr. Glover then turned back to the man.

"If you don't want your relationship to be lifeless and dead, you first have to get out of your own story about what's going on," he advised. "You have to start putting things out there, start being honest. Things may not radically change but you probably won't get rejected in the way you think you will."

Again, the man agreed. And just as he was about to sit down, Dr. Pariser stopped him.

"Before you sit down," said Dr. Pariser, "let me ask you something."

"Sure," said the man.

"What exactly are you waiting for?"

"What do you mean?" asked the man, blankly.

"To start living," answered Dr. Pariser. "What are you waiting for to start living? You don't need your partner to start living, to start pursuing your passions. You can do it alone or with your friends or with family. But start living your life. And model that for your kids."

"Yes, you'll be much happier," added Dr. Glover. "And you'll bring that energy back into the marriage, which will either activate your wife or not. If not, then you can decide whether you should leave."

"Thank you," said the man before finally taking his seat. "I know what I need to do."

***

If your relationship is no longer satisfying, perhaps you can take a bit of comfort in knowing that you aren't alone. Most relationships get stale and boring, and it's no wonder. Men and women never used to spend so much time together in such close proximity.

As Dr. Glover points out, "It really hasn't been that long – perhaps less a century or two – that we've decided a man and a woman are going to be each other's best friend, are going to do everything together, are going to see things the same, are always going to want to be around each other, are only going to have sex with each other, and are going to spend damn near every waking moment together. These are crazy ideas that don't work because they aren't meant to work. This doesn't mean we can't have committed, exclusive, long-term relationships. But healthy relationships take a fuckload of consciousness and effort."

Healthy relationships require both people to make their needs a priority and create systems that allow them to get their needs met. Your partner is not in charge of *your* happiness. Nor is your partner to blame for your *un*happiness. Blaming your partner is a death sentence for any relationship.

If there are fundamental issues in your relationship, it's your job as a man to step up and insist that you work on the relationship as a team, even if it necessitates getting outside help in the form of counseling or therapy. This is part of Masculine leadership. Remember, *a woman can't follow where a man doesn't lead.*

"Still, don't think that if you like baseball, for example, and your partner doesn't, you can't go to a baseball game," insists Dr. Glover. "Go to a fucking game if it excites you and fills your bucket. And encourage your partner to do things that excite her and fill her bucket. This is the remedy for boredom. And the foundation for a healthy relationship."

# BREAKING UP

C hances are you've been there.

I've been there.

Most of us have been there.

The end of the road.

The point of no return.

Fuck.

Why is breaking up so hard to do?

One of the core tenets of Dr. Glover's work is that *being a good ender covers a multitude of sins*. When you're a good ender, you'll find it useful in a variety of situations, from letting go of a toxic friendship to quitting a soul-crushing job. But being a good ender is absolutely terrifying for many men, particularly Nice Guys. And it seems to terrify them the most when ending a relationship with a woman.

Many men can't bring themselves to break up with a woman in a confident, timely, and loving way. They're often indirect or deceitful. They might make multiple attempts before one actually sticks. Dr. Glover often jokes that it takes Nice Guys around nine attempts to end a relationship. Funny enough, this isn't far from the truth.

Breaking up with a woman can produce an almost overwhelming amount of anxiety in men. Dr. Glover believes that this is partly due to the aforementioned evolutionary truth that women tend to be security-seeking creatures.

"From an evolutionary perspective, if a man is breaking up with a woman it is a death sentence to her," contends Dr. Glover. "Why? Because during tribal times, women looked to men to be their providers and protectors. Obviously, things have changed since then, and modern women can take care of themselves. But they are still wired to seek security."

Beyond that, a man might be afraid of breaking up for a multitude of other reasons:

- He fears that breaking up could be a mistake and he'll regret it later.
- He fears that he'll be seen as a jerk.
- He fears that he'll receive backlash due to the negative social view of men who break up with women.
- He fears that he has too much to lose, particularly if he is married with children.
- He has deep-rooted religious beliefs around relationships and breaking up.
- He has a general fear of confrontation.

Married men are especially afraid of breaking up. Most can't accept the notion that their wife will get half of everything. But Dr. Glover often points out that this is a bullshit excuse.

"Actually, she'll probably get more like 70%," says Dr. Glover. "Because once women lawyer up, their math skills go to hell. 50/50 takes on really odd proportions. Besides, right now she has access to *100%* of everything you have, and no judge will tell a married woman that she can't spend it all. Technically, getting divorced improves your financial situation."

***

If you are going to dare to love, at some point you will almost certainly have to face your fears around breaking up, especially if you're actively dating. Dating is a numbers game. And throughout the process, you will meet a lot of women who aren't right for you. Be able to end it quickly.

Being a good ender is crucial for limiting the amount of time you spend with wrong women and for opening up new opportunities to meet the right women. Being a good ender is part of your responsibility as an Integrated Man.

But here's a conundrum: Many men who want a loving, intimate relationship become uneasy when they finally get what they want. Often, this is because they have a fear of intimacy. They think they will end up feeling smothered. Or they think they will have to give up what's important to them to fit into the woman's life.

It's important to remember that you should never make a woman your emotional center. A healthy woman will be far more attracted to you and have far more respect for you if you have a life full of passion, interests, hobbies, and good friends. Invite a woman to be the *icing* on your Great Cake. Making her your whole cake is a recipe for disaster.

That said, how do you know if you should break up with a woman or if you just have a fear of intimacy?

- Ask yourself: *Can I see myself with this woman just as she is for the next several years? If this woman were not in my life just as she is for the next several years, would I miss her?*

- Consider the possibility that you might be experiencing emotional fusion. If you spend too much time with someone, they will almost certainly get on your nerves. Things you once liked about them might become uninteresting, unattractive, or downright irritating. *Ask yourself: Am I experiencing emotional fusion? Was I feeling this way yesterday? Do I need space?*

- Dive all the way into your relationship and see how it feels. Make a conscious effort to be fully present. Set healthy boundaries. Be completely honest and transparent. Work on your Great Cake. Embrace your sexuality. After a few months, you should know if the relationship will work for you or if it is time to break up.

# HOW TO BREAK UP

Breaking up may be scary, but it doesn't have to be complicated. Before we discuss the process, however, here's a pro tip: Have what Dr. Glover calls a *Pre-Breakup Discussion*.

When you've started seeing someone and it feels like your relationship might get serious, sit down and talk to your partner about how you'll break up; because, odds are, you will.

> **HARSH TRUTH**
>
> Most relationships don't last.

"Talking about how you'll break up may seem odd, but it actually makes the woman feel more secure," explains Dr. Glover. "It allows both of you to get all the way in and prevents all the unnecessary speculation that might occur down the road."

Don't overthink your Pre-Breakup Discussion. Just say something like: *I want you to know that if there's anything on mind, I'll let you know. If it ever gets to a place where I feel like the relationship isn't working, I'll let you know. We'll sit down and I'll tell you up front. I will always be honest and transparent with you. No surprises.*

If you do get to a place where you feel like the relationship isn't working and it's time to break up, here are some things to consider:

**If you've been together for a few months…**

This is undoubtedly a crucial period. By this point, you've almost certainly had sex. And you're really starting to get to each other. So:

- Sooner is better than later. Break up as soon as you realize that she is not the right partner for you. The longer you wait, the harder it's going to be.
- Break up in person.

- Keep it short and to the point. When in doubt, use what Dr. Glover calls *The Two-Sentence Rule*. Whatever you need to say can be said in two sentences or less.
- Never say, "It's not you, it's me." That's bullshit and everyone knows it.
- Don't try to offer an explanation. You don't need to explain yourself. The fact is you don't feel enough connection and chemistry to continue the relationship. It's really that simple. Again, stick to The Two-Sentence Rule.

**If you've been together for a few years or more...**

You might think that breaking up needs to be a complicated, drawn-out affair. And logistically, it might need to be if you live together, you are married, or you have children. You and your partner will surely have things to sort out.

However, the actual conversation around breaking up doesn't need to be any more complicated than necessary. In fact, it shouldn't be much different than if you've been together just a few months. Be direct and to the point. The reason you are breaking up is because you have lost interest, the relationship isn't working for you anymore, you don't feel the chemistry and connection that you once did, and you feel it's best to move on. This is the only explanation you need to offer because it's the truth.

Sadly, many married men seem to take one of two very stupid approaches to breaking up. Dr. Glover likes to call these approaches *The Greyhound Divorce* and *The Ben Affleck (or Breakup by Stripper)*.

- **The Greyhound Divorce**: The man never speaks his truth and never takes action. His fear around breaking up is so overwhelming that he resorts to being miserable, while hoping that something outside his control will happen. He thinks: *Maybe my wife will get hit by a Greyhound bus. Then, I won't have to end it.*
- **The Ben Affleck**: The man can't muster up the courage to end his relationship, but he behaves so badly for so long – by gambling, cheating, watching porn, frequenting strip clubs, etc. – that the woman even-

tually breaks up with him. Allegedly, this was Ben Affleck's approach when he was married to Jennifer Lopez (the first time). *Allegedly.*

It should go without saying that neither of these approaches is how an Integrated Man breaks up. Breaking up may be hard, but it's actually a loving thing to do. Don't draw things out if you're unhappy or if you've stopped loving your partner. It's not fair to you and it's not fair to her.

> **DECIDING ON DIVORCE:**
>
> Divorce is a life-changing decision that many men struggle to make.
>
> Chuck Chapman, a licensed psychotherapist and certified No More Mr. Nice Guy coach, and the creator of *No More Mr. Nice Guy: The 30-Day Recovery Journal*, often tells the story of a client who said: "If I left my wife, my life would be easier. But it wouldn't be better."
>
> Chapman now uses this as a kind of measuring stick when helping men decide if they should leave a marriage.
>
> If you're trying to make the same decision, consider asking yourself: *If I left my wife, would my life be easier? Or would it be better?*

Dr. Glover frequently discusses his history as a supremely bad ender.

"I was the poster child for bad enders," he admits. "I shouldn't have gone out on more than three dates with either of my first two wives. Instead, I stayed married to each of them for more than a decade.. By the time those marriages ended, things had deteriorated so badly that neither woman wanted to talk to me for years after we got divorced."

After his second divorce, Dr. Glover came to a stark realization: In order to have better relationships, he had to become both a better picker and a better ender. This realization, in fact, was the seed that would eventually grow into *Dating Essentials for Men.*

"As I worked at becoming a better ender, everything in my relationships with women began to change," shares Dr. Glover. "My breakups were more loving and went much more smoothly. The women continued to think well of me. Some remained close friends and some even remained fuck buddies. All because I was a good ender."

As you work to become a good ender, remember that women's reactions often reflect how they are feeling in a specific moment. Not to mention that all women (and all humans) are different. One woman might react in a certain way to you breaking up with her, while another woman might react in a completely different way. The same woman could also react in a variety of ways, depending on how she's feeling that day or in that moment.

No matter how a woman reacts to you breaking up with her, she will ultimately respect you for being a good ender and behaving like an Integrated Man. So, have integrity, let go of attachment to outcome, and stick to the basics. The same applies in almost every area of life. After all, *being a good ender covers a multitude of sins.*[130]

**INTEGRATED ACTION:**
- ✓ Are you a bad ender? How has being a bad ender affected your life and your relationships? Write your answers in your journal.
- ✓ Why do you think you're a bad ender? What are your fears around ending things? Write your answers in your journal.
- ✓ How do you think your life would change if you were a good ender? Write your answer in your journal. Be as detailed as possible.
- ✓ Is there a relationship or a situation that you need to end? Don't drag it out any longer. End it now.
- ✓ Talk to your safe person (or people) about your fears around becoming a good ender.

---

130 Glover, Robert A. "Podcast 98: Breaking Up" Podcast Audio. www.drglover.com. For more information on bad breakup strategies like The Greyhound Divorce and The Ben Affleck, and having a pre-breakup discussion, see Glover, Robert A. Dating Essentials for Men (Robert A. Glover, Ph.D, Inc. 2019) pp. 208-211

# PART VII: HEARTBREAK

*The heart was made to be broken.*

**– Oscar Wilde**

There's a good chance I never would have read *No More Mr. Nice Guy*, developed a relationship with Dr. Glover, or started my own coaching business had it not been for Tracy, the last woman to mercilessly stomp all over my heart. Tracy did a number on me. But I am better, stronger, smarter, happier, and more resilient because of it.

For a lot of men, heartbreak seems to be the shotgun blast that kicks off a frenzied race to find the answers to a host of swirling questions (*What did I do wrong? Aren't I good enough? How can I possibly move on?*). It's a race that often becomes a sinuous journey, as many of these men veer from the beaten path. They wander down countless rabbit holes, across sunken gorges, and through darkened channels, until they discover Dr. Glover's work, in which they don't just find answers, they find light and hope.

Yes, I am one of these men.

And now, I can't overlook the staggering number of similarly crestfallen men who reach out to me because they are trying desperately to navigate their way through heartbreak. Maybe they broke up with a girlfriend or got divorced. Maybe they're on the brink of divorce. Maybe they were cheated on. Or maybe they were stood up for an eagerly anticipated date. No matter the circumstance, these men are in pain, wondering if they'll ever be able to collect and reassemble the pieces of their broken hearts.

Heartbreak is an age-old issue. But given the nature of modern dating, skewed divorce and family laws, and recent cultural shifts, heartbreak seems more prevalent than ever – particularly in males. I have repeatedly tried to develop a formula for quickly and easily overcoming heartbreak. But I don't know that there is – or ever will be – such a formula. As I've learned from Dr. Glover (who is no stranger to loss and heartbreak), and from my own painful experiences, overcoming heartbreak takes time, it takes perspective, and it takes strength.

Nevertheless, heartbreak can be a catalyst for positive change if you choose to see it this way. It can lead to remarkable personal growth. It can have a truly profound effect on your life, in the best possible way. Which is why I've devoted this section to helping you better understand and navigate heartbreak. So, strap in. Because, as Dr. Glover likes to say, *You haven't really lived until you've had your heart broken.*

# UNDERSTANDING HEARTBREAK

Vincent Van Gogh famously said, "The more you love, the more you suffer." This is a particularly grim sentiment – the idea that if you open up your heart it's bound to get broken. Of course, Van Gogh was a bit of a weirdo, confirmed in 1888 when he sliced off part of his ear, wrapped it up all nice, and kindly gave it to a hooker down the street.

The thing is, though, Van Gogh wasn't wrong. Dare to love and you're going to suffer. It's true in *every* relationship of *every* type. Because, as Dr. David Schnarch points out in his book *Passionate Marriage,* **in every relationship someone gets left.**

This may seem like yet another grim sentiment; but think about it: Unless you and your loved one die at exactly the same time, every relationship ends, and someone gets left. Dr. Glover, incidentally, doesn't find this grim. In fact, he finds it liberating. And I have come to understand why.

"People think it's terrible," acknowledges Dr. Glover. "People don't like the idea that in every relationship someone gets left. But it's true. I don't care if it's you and your employer, you and your dog, you and your mom, you and your wife. Someone is going to get left. This is the impermanence of life. It's what the Buddha talked about. And people tend to ignore it. But really, it should force you to get up and love the hell out of the people you love and who love you back…and stop spending time with people who treat you badly."

So, what if you knew that nothing is permanent?

What if you knew that every relationship ends or in every relationship someone gets left?

How might your approach to relationships change?

How might you be better able to deal with heartbreak?

When it comes to relationships, heartbreak usually isn't caused by the loss of a human being. It's caused by the loss of what we think that human being represents. Still, heartbreak is so excruciatingly difficult to overcome because being in a relationship rewires the brain.

"A monogamous, dependent relationship with a single person is a pretty recent development in human evolution," explains Dr. Glover. "We evolved in tribes, with access to many women. So, losing the entire tribe was a death sentence. But now, we don't spend time in a tribe or a clan. So, losing our most intimate relationship feels like a death sentence."

Brain imaging studies have shown that friendships, romantic relationships, love affairs, and even fantasies have a powerful effect on our brains as well as our general health and wellness. Loving, caring relationships truly impact our lives. Connections make us healthier. Even men who get out of toxic marriages often report that they don't necessarily miss their ex-wives, but they greatly miss the idea of being in a relationship and being closely connected to another person.

Studies have also confirmed that when a person experiences the loss of love, the same part of the brain lights up that does so when a person experiences actual physical pain.[131] Additionally, being in love affects the brain in the same way cocaine and other similar drugs do.[132] It's no wonder, then, that

---

131 Fisher HE, Brown LL, Aron A, Strong G, Mashek D. Reward, addiction, and emotion regulation systems associated with rejection in love. J Neurophysiol. 2010 Jul;104(1):51-60. doi: 10.1152/jn.00784.2009. Epub 2010 May 5. PMID: 20445032.

132 Fisher H, Aron A, Brown LL. Romantic love: an fMRI study of a neural mechanism for mate choice. J Comp Neurol. 2005 Dec 5;493(1):58-62. doi: 10.1002/cne.20772. PMID: 16255001

heartbreak makes you feel like you're going through withdrawal. Love is a motherfucking drug.

"Interestingly, *men* seem to have a tougher time with loss and heartbreak," reports Dr. Glover. "You'd think heartbreak would affect women more than men because of the way women are wired. But men appear to have a more difficult go of it. If you think about it, most of the saddest songs, poems, books, and movies about heartbreak were written by men. Men have given such high status to women that we often feel like if we lose a woman, we may never meet another.[133]"

For Nice Guys in particular, heartbreak is likely to hurt even more. This is due to variety of factors, including:

**Social Anxiety**

Because Nice Guys tend to have at least some degree of social anxiety, especially around attractive women, losing a relationship triggers their fear.

"Our male ancestors didn't have to be pickup artists," says Dr. Glover. "They just had to be part of a tribe. Social anxiety probably wasn't even a thing back then. Because we no longer live in a tribe, men today don't really have the connections that our ancestors did. When Nice Guys experience heartbreak, they often can't imagine venturing out into the world, talking to people, and beginning the process of trying to meet a woman all over again."

**Deprivation Thinking**

Because Nice Guys don't see the world as a place of abundance, they hardly take any risks. If they have something even remotely good, they believe they need to hang onto it for dear life. When Nice Guys lose a relationship, they feel an overwhelming sense of loss, even if the relationship was bad. This wouldn't be the case if Nice Guys thought more abundantly.

---

133 Glover, Robert A. "Podcast 151: Part 1 of a Four-Part Series on Understanding and Getting Over Loss and Heartbreak." Podcast Audio. www.drglover.com

**Toxic Shame**

Because Nice Guys don't believe they are good enough just as they are, they hide their perceived flaws. They think women can instantly see how defective they are. So, they frequently settle in relationships. If they lose a relationship, the associated heartbreak triggers feelings of rejection that only reinforces their toxic shame.

Certainly, heartbreak will continue to affect the lives of humans in every corner of the world. And no, Van Gogh wasn't wrong when he said, "the more you love the more you suffer." But dare to love. If you love yourself, you'll never suffer for too long. Going through any kind of heartbreak is a chance for personal evolution.

As C.S. Lewis said, "If you love deeply, you're going to get hurt badly. But it's still worth it."

---

**INTEGRATED ACTION:**

✓ How do you think your relationships would be different if you knew that in every relationship, somebody gets left? How do you think your experience with heartbreak might be different? Write your answers down in your journal.

---

# THE TWO TYPES OF HEARTBREAK

On February 22, 2013, I was sitting in my office cubicle in Omaha, Nebraska, when the receptionist called to inform me that my dad was in the lobby. I walked out to greet him. He was happy, smiling, and donning one of his signature double-breasted suits. He was there because he needed me to sign some tax preparation forms before he handed them over to his accountant. My dad always took care of things like that.

It was a Friday, late morning. We briefly discussed getting lunch but decided not to in the interest of time. I was going to see him over the weekend, anyway. We were planning a trip. A week prior, my dad told me that he wanted to take me to Vegas for my 30th birthday. We had things to discuss, hotel rooms to book, concert tickets to buy.

I signed the tax forms, thanked my dad, and walked back to my cubicle.

The next morning, my dad died.

My dad, by the way, was the picture of health. He didn't smoke, he didn't drink, he ate a balanced diet, and he exercised almost daily. He had meaningful relationships. He treated everyone with grace and respect. Everyone who knew him loved him. His sudden and unexpected passing didn't just shock my family, it shocked our entire community.

If you've experienced anything similar, then I don't need to tell you: This is pain. Indescribable, gut-wrenching, heartbreaking pain. My sister and I had just lost our father; and my mother had just lost her husband of 40 years. In an instant, our lives were forever changed.

Pain.

Not long after losing my dad, Katie, a woman I'd been dating for just six months, dumped me and then promptly discarded me from her life. I felt like I'd been gutted, my insides strewn about on the cold, hard floor. I lost my appetite, my strength, my ambition. I lost the love of my life…or so I thought.

I was infatuated with Katie. She was smart, successful, and stunningly beautiful. She could make me laugh. She appreciated great music, great writing, and great food. She loved sex. A lot. She was also a twice-divorced mother of three. Our relationship seemed to be on her terms. I didn't see her nearly as much as I wanted to. And when I did see her, she wasn't very nice to me.

It took me months to get over Katie. And eventually, I couldn't help but wonder: *Why did getting dumped by a bitchy, unavailable woman feel more painful than suddenly losing my dad?* Well, as I learned from Dr. Glover, there are two types of heartbreak.[134] And the type that is the most painful may surprise you, just like it surprised me.

Dr. Glover hasn't cleverly named these two types of heartbreak, so let's refer to them simply as **Type I** and **Type II**.

The first type of heartbreak – Type I – occurs when a *healthy*, fulfilling relationship ends naturally, either because of a death or because the people involved came to a mature agreement that the relationship was no longer working. Indeed, this type of heartbreak hurts like hell. And there is a break in your brain's neural connections.

"When you experience Type I heartbreak, you miss the person dearly," explains Dr. Glover. "But you never made this person your entire world. So, you still have a full life. And you still have other connections. Yes, it hurts like hell. But you do move on. Sometimes fairly quickly."

134 Glover, Robert A. "Podcast 154: Part 4 of a Four-Part Series on Understanding and Getting Over Loss and Heartbreak." Podcast Audio. www.drglover.com

The second type of heartbreak – Type II – occurs when an *unhealthy* relationship comes to an end. Often these relationships are downright toxic, and can include:

- Trauma-bonded relationships that are filled with drama, chaos, and constant fighting
- Idealized relationships or fantasies that were never going to materialize
- A relationship where she was a priority to you, but you were just an option to her

Believe it or not, **Type II heartbreak** is often the most painful and, subsequently, the most difficult to get over.

"The loss from these kinds of relationships affects you so deeply because of what your mind believes the person *could* do for you," explains Dr. Glover. "Perhaps you were using this person as a substitute for something you didn't get as a child. When you lose an idealized relationship, for example, you lose the object that you feel completes you or somehow compensates for your belief that you aren't good enough or lovable. So, you aren't just losing human connection, you are also losing something that feels crucial to your well-being. It's a fucking double whammy."

While experiencing heartbreak, it can help just to know what type of heartbreak it is that you're experiencing. Listen to what your mind is telling you. As Dr. Glover illustrates, you're probably dealing with **Type II heartbreak** if:

- You believe that you'll never meet another person like her.
- You feel like you want to die.
- *Everything* reminds you of her, no matter how trivial.
- You can only think about what you did wrong, how you can get her back, and how your life will never be the same.
- You remember the good times but not the many horrible times.

Be honest with yourself about what kind of relationship it was. Was it a trauma-bonded relationship in which you had to work to get her to show up and treat you well? Was it a toxic emotional roller-coaster? Was it an idealized relationship that never became a real relationship?

Or was it a relationship that lightened your load? Did you and your partner make a great team? Did you compliment each other? Were you both available to each other? Did you share each other's values? Did you work together through difficult times?

"The kind of pain that hurts the worst is often the result of emotional dependency," affirms Dr. Glover. "Identifying the type of heartbreak you're experiencing can be crucial to the healing process. Once you identify the type of heartbreak, don't judge it and don't resist it. Let it be. Whatever you're thinking and feeling, be the observer of it. Just sit with it."

## MORE ON TRAUMA-BONDED RELATIONSHIPS

When men ask Dr. Glover to further explain **trauma-bonded relationships**, he usually begins with the question: *Have you ever been in a car accident?*[135]

If you've been in a car accident, it's likely that you can remember even the smallest details about the experience. This is because your brain emits powerful chemicals and neurotransmitters during stressful or traumatic events (like a car accident) that ingrain the experience in your memory. This is evolution's way of ensuring that you remember dangerous situations so you can avoid them in the future.

"Being in a trauma-bonded relationship is like being in repeated car accidents," describes Dr. Glover. "The constant chaos and the drama and the ups and downs is like having a traumatic experience, over and over. These experiences then become very deeply implanted in a survival part of the brain."

---

135 Glover, Robert A. "Podcast 151: Part 1 of a Four-Part Series on Understanding and Getting Over Loss and Heartbreak." Podcast Audio. www.drglover.com

# WHAT A TRAUMA-BONDED RELATIONSHIP LOOKS LIKE:

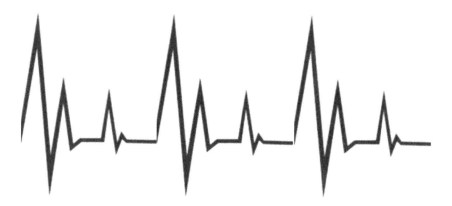

As Dr. Glover illustrates, most trauma-bonded relationships involve one codependent person - often a Nice Guy - who believes he needs to put up with shit to be loved. It feels familiar to him to have to work desperately to get someone to love him and treat him well. Then, there's at least one emotionally unstable or unavailable person - often a Really Wrong Woman. They tend to have Borderline type personalities or mood disorders. They are volatile, vindictive, and dishonest. They usually have a checkered relationship history.

Trauma-bonded relationships generally start with what seems like a blissful honeymoon phase. There's an immediate chemistry. If you're the codependent Nice Guy, you think everything is amazing. You think she is the solution to all your problems, or what Dr. Glover calls your *key-holding goddess.* You think she's perfect, and you can't understand how you got so lucky.

The honeymoon phase is so intensely exciting that you want to fuse quickly, you want to bond, and you soon become addicted to this person. After all, she is beautiful and seductive. She showers you with praise and compliments. She tells you how much she loves and adores you. You're having lots of great and occasionally risky sex. Oh yes, you think you've died and gone to heaven.

Then, something happens.

Suddenly, the relationship starts to cycle downward.

You didn't see it coming.

She breaks up with you. She says she's no longer dating. She becomes rageful. She starts accusing you of things you didn't do.

You question your own reality.

Your mind goes into overdrive.

You panic.

You just want that feeling again, that feeling of bliss you experienced when you met.

You become desperate. Needy. You call her, text her, email her. You tell her you miss her. You just want to talk. She doesn't respond. She blocks you from social media.

You'd do anything to get things back to the way they were. But you decide to pull away. You stop reaching out. It's damn near impossible. You crave her. You want her. You need her. You're fucking miserable. But you know you need to move on. So, you start putting the pieces of your heart back together.

Then…

She shows up again.

You exhale.

You're relieved.

You knew it was meant to be.

You make up.

You have sex.

It's better than ever.

An upward cycle.

Those feelings of bliss and excitement come rushing back. But now… you're anxious. Fearful. You want to fuse even more.

Then…

It happens again.

The downward cycle.

Intensity. Lust.

Love. Hate.

On. Off.

Again and again.

This cycle can repeat itself for years.

It's a fucking rollercoaster, fueled by passion and hope and childhood memories. And the more times you repeat the cycle, the worse off you are.

---

**COMMON CHARACTERISTICS OF
TRAUMA-BONDED RELATIONSHIPS:**

✓ **Constant ups and downs**

✓ **On again, off again cycles**

✓ **Insecurities**

✓ **Accusations and control issues**

✓ **Infidelity**

✓ **Lies and deceit**

✓ **Explosive, intense fights**

✓ **Addictive behaviors**

✓ **Threats**

✓ **Intense make-ups**

✓ **Intense sex**

---

"A trauma-bonded relationship becomes deeply etched in your brain because of two core components," explains Dr. Glover. "These components are intensity and anxiety. You get a potent double dose of hormones and neurotransmitters. Because of the intensity part, you want to keep repeating it, even though it's extremely bad for you. All the hormones kind of get wired together, and it becomes the new normal in your brain. The more the cycle continues, the more bonded you become. Hence the name. You become bonded to someone through trauma – or drama."

Unfortunately, a trauma-bonded relationship is a gift that can keep on giving for years. Long after it's ended, you might keep thinking that you'll never meet another person like your ex. You compare everyone to her. Healthy, stable women even seem boring to you.

If you're dealing with the aftermath of a trauma-bonded relationship, *time* is perhaps the only real, tried-and-true remedy. Be patient with yourself and acknowledge that the relationship is never going to be anything other than it is – a toxic, emotional rollercoaster. Cut off as much contact as possible with your ex. Limit the amount of time you spend talking about her to other people. Make a list of all the terrible things she did to prevent your brain from focusing solely on the good things. Do not respond if she reaches out. Consider working with a coach or therapist to figure out why you think you must put up with shit to be loved. And of course, always be working on your Great Cake of a Life.

**INTEGRATED ACTION:**
- ✓ Think back on your relationships. What kind of relationships were they? What kind of heartbreak did you experience? Write about your experiences in your journal.
- ✓ Have you ever been in an idealized or trauma-bonded relationship? Write about it in your journal.
- ✓ Are you currently experiencing heartbreak? What kind of heartbreak is it? Write your answers in your journal.
- ✓ Talk to your safe person (or people) about your experience with heartbreak.

# ON GETTING AN EX BACK

**M**en in the throes of heartbreak often take to the internet looking for help. Unfortunately, it tends to be the wrong kind of help. Instead of looking for ways to heal their heartbreak and move forward, men frequently look for ways to get an ex back. And there is no shortage of self-proclaimed experts and gurus who claim they know the secret to doing just that.

But why would you want to get your ex back?

"I do not recommend going after an ex," says Dr. Glover. "It's the ultimate in attachment to outcome. And you're trying to recreate a kind of relationship that probably never existed, that was a fantasy in your mind. Coaches and gurus who sell products on getting an ex back are just preying on men with broken hearts and overactive fantasy lives."

No matter the circumstance, your relationship with your ex ended for a reason. People typically don't make deep, fundamental changes all that quickly. If you think your ex has changed, or that things will be different if you get back together, you're living in a fantasy. As Dr. Glover likes to say, *How you found her is how she is. And how she was when the relationship ended is probably how she still is.*

Don't go after an ex. You'll be much better off taking what you learned from the relationship and applying it to future relationships.

"My relationship with my second wife was incredibly toxic," shares Dr. Glover. "I still felt a deep sense of sadness when it ended. But I used the experience to know what to avoid in future relationships. I vowed to become a better dater, a better picker, and a better ender. I also vowed not to let anyone treat me badly. I learned to set boundaries. I started spending time with people who treat me well. I also vowed to create a Great Cake of a Life. I'm grateful for my relationship with my ex. But trying to get her back would have just been stupid."

---

**INTEGRATED ACTION:**
  ✓ Get out of the house, expand your route, linger in public, talk to people everywhere you go, test for interest, and walk through the open doors.

---

# OBSESSION

Have you ever matched with a woman on a dating app – maybe you've even been out on one or two dates – and you think it's going amazingly well…until the woman falls off the planet? Or flakes on you? Or suddenly tells you that she's not in a place to date? And even though you'd like to move on with your life, you can't stop thinking about her? Like she completely consumes your psyche?

I've been there.

Today's dating landscape is littered with booby traps and landmines, and single men are constantly dealing with varying degrees of heartbreak. Single women are, too, of course. But the inherent unpredictability of modern dating seems to be particularly hard on the male brain. Many men fall in love from afar and develop obsessions with women, even women who flake on them or who they don't even know.

These kinds of obsessions result from men pedestalizing attractive women while relying on the various forms of pseudo-communication we now have at our disposal – email, texting, and social media. Because of these things, we don't have the kinds of connections we had when we lived in tribes. So, it's quite easy to feel really connected to someone really quickly, even though your connection isn't real.

Furthermore, as Dr. Glover points out, modern forms of pseudo-communication seriously amp up your brain chemistry. They keep you in a constant state of anxiety and anticipation:

*When will she text me back?*

*Should I text her?*

*Should I wait?*

*I can't double text.*

*Should I call?*

*I know she has her phone on her.*

*She just posted on social media.*

*What the fuck?*

*Why won't she get back to me?*

This combination of anxiety and anticipation is what fuels unhealthy, trauma-bonded type relationships. It's a primary reason men can become obsessed with women they hardly even know, especially if they have a tendency to turn women into their key-holding goddesses. Very often, though, these women don't make even remotely good partners.

When you obsess over a woman, it's just your brain spinning. It's mental masturbation. And it often involves second-guessing:

*Should I have done things differently?*

*Did I send too many texts?*

*Should I have made a move sooner?*

*Did I scare her off?*

"The more time you spend spinning and second-guessing," asserts Dr. Glover, "the more emotionally invested you become, even if you aren't in a relationship with the woman. But you're not actually learning anything. And there's no real way to know what was going on in a woman's head. Trying to figure out why a woman behaves a certain way is a big fucking waste of time."[136]

Should you find yourself obsessing about a woman, catch yourself doing so as quickly as possible. Know that you're obsessing over someone who is

---

136 Glover, Robert A. "Podcast 122: How to Stop Obsessing About a Woman" Podcast Audio. www.drglover.com

either uninterested or unavailable, and be conscious of the fact that you are in your Lower Feminine place. Get out of your head and into your body. Do something Masculine and physical. And keep working on your Great Cake of a Life. If a woman sidetracked you, get back on track.

---

**INTEGRATED ACTION:**

✓ Do you tend to obsess over women, especially unavailable women? Write your answer in your journal.

✓ Do you engage in forms of pseudo-communication? How does it serve you? Write your answer in your journal.

✓ Talk to your safe person (or people) about your tendency to obsess.

---

# CRUSHES

Similar to obsessing over women, men often develop crushes. Just the word "crush" may make you feel like you are back in elementary school. But even in adulthood, many men get crushes that can be seriously debilitating.

We humans can think about someone we barely know – or don't know at all – and get an overwhelmingly intense feeling. This is how powerful the primitive part of the brain can be. It can make snap decisions about people, and these decisions can be enduring and emotional, or completely wrong and misguided. A woman for whom you were head over heels, for example, could turn out to be a total psycho. Or someone you thought was a raging dickhead could eventually become your best friend. (Both of these scenarios have played out in my own life).

As men, our attraction to women - or a specific woman - can be sparked by an almost infinite array of traits and characteristics - body shape, symmetry, genetic diversity, hair color, skin tone, height, leg length, breast size, ass size, dimples, freckles, or something else you might have seen in porn. Sometimes it's personality. Maybe you're turned by cold, angry bitches. Or maybe you love the sweet, caring, innocent type. There are so many factors that it's impossible to break them all down. Not to mention that they are mostly unconscious. Attraction just happens, and we often respond to it without question.

That's all well and good…

Unless it turns into a crush.

The psychological term for a crush is *limerence*.

> **limerence** [li-mer-uhns]
>
> *noun Psychiatry*
>
> the state of being infatuated or obsessed with another person, typically experienced involuntarily, and characterized by a strong desire for reciprocation of one's feelings but not primarily for a sexual relationship.

"Limerence is very common for men," explains Dr. Glover. "Especially Nice Guys. Because instead of acting on their attraction by approaching a woman and testing for interest, Nice Guys typically don't do anything at all - usually due to their fear of rejection, fear of looking foolish, social anxiety, insecurities, and low tolerance for risk."

Dr. Glover has observed that men usually develop two kinds of crushes:

The first kind of crush is **from afar.** This involves a woman you've never met nor spoken to. Yet, you spend an excessive amount of time thinking about her. Maybe you stalk her on social media. But she has no idea that you even exist. It should go without saying that lying around and thinking about a woman who doesn't know you exist is a colossal waste of time.

The second kind of crush is **from the friend zone.** This involves a woman with whom you actually do have a relationship, just not a romantic one. As Dr. Glover would say, you're her "girlfriend with a penis." You listen to her bullshit, you do things together, maybe you even give her dating or relationship advice. But you want her. You'd do anything to have her. Except you don't do anything. You're afraid of ruining the friendship. So, you hope she'll suddenly realize what a catch you are and make the first move.

Never going to happen.

There's a significant amount of neurobiology taking place when you have a crush. Perhaps you're familiar with the phrase *neurons that fire together, wire together*. This is especially applicable to crushes.

"The more time you spend thinking about a woman, the more it creates strong neural pathways in your brain," explains Dr. Glover. "You actually begin to feel *as if* you have a loving, bonded relationship, even when you don't. And crushes can be so intense because of the longing and the anxiety, the constant back and forth. Your brain is flooded with chemicals as it goes through repeated swings of emotions."

Your brain can't effectively distinguish between fantasy and reality. The more you fantasize about a woman, the more your mind believes the connection is real. In many cases, losing a crush can be more painful than losing an actual relationship because a crush is a fantasy that you've built up so perfectly in your mind.

> **HARSH TRUTH:**
>
> Every relationship is better in your head than it is in reality.

Crushes don't reflect reality. Your crush isn't even a real person; it's a one-dimensional object. When you have a crush on a woman, all you see are the parts about her that you think are amazing. Your mind is bullshitting you.

"A crush is often about you and your ego," says Dr. Glover. "You wonder how other people might look at you if your crush was your girlfriend. You think your status would go through the roof. You think women would want you and men would want to be you. In reality, if you ever actually got with your crush, you'd probably act like the quintessential Nice Guy and let her walk all over you. Then you'd be devastated when she left."

Moreover, having a crush is Feminine in nature. Remember, the Masculine *does*. The Masculine takes action. The Masculine penetrates. And the Feminine is *done to*. When you are thinking about a woman but not taking action, you are in your Feminine - more specifically, your Lower Feminine. It's not likely that a woman would be attracted to you when you are in your Lower Feminine state.

If you find yourself crushing hard, consciously address the hope. As Dr. Glover likes to say, *hope keeps all suffering in place.* Hoping a woman will fall for you will only keep you in a place of suffering. You should also focus on the whole of who a woman is. Turn her from an object in your mind into a real person. She almost certainly has flaws, insecurities, and plenty of other issues. (It might help to picture her taking a big, smelly dump.)

Additionally, you should ask yourself: *What will take me in the direction I most want to go?* There's only one way to find out if your crush might feel the same way as you. Take an action that will either lead to a connection or a rejection. Either one is better than the uncertainty that comes with having a crush.[137]

---

**INTEGRATED ACTION:**
- ✓ Have you ever had a crush? Do you currently have a crush? Write about it in your journal. Don't think, just write.
- ✓ How is/was your crush about your ego? Write your answer in your journal.
- ✓ If you have a crush, what action can you take that will either lead to a connection or a rejection? Go do it.
- ✓ Talk to your safe person (or people) about your crush.

---

137 Glover, Robert A. "Podcast 70: Crushes." Podcast Audio. www.drglover.com

# ATTACHMENT THEORY

If you've done any amount of research on dating, relationships, and heartbreak, then you've almost certainly come across **Attachment Theory**. Attachment Theory describes the nature of our emotional attachment to other humans. For me, learning about Attachment Theory helped me understand my behavior in relationships as well as my relationship patterns. It also provided tremendous insight into how I deal with loss and heartbreak.

Your attachment style develops in childhood with your attachment to your parents. The nature of this attachment influences the nature of your attachment to romantic partners in adulthood. Attachment Theory was first introduced in the 1950s, and there is a mountain of research behind it. Perhaps the most comprehensive book on Attachment Theory is *Attached: The New Science of Adult Attachment and How it Can Help You Find – and Keep – Love* by Amir Levine and Rachel Heller.

Psychologists have identified four primary attachment types:

- Secure
- Anxious
- Avoidant
- Anxious-Avoidant

Those with a Secure attachment style are comfortable both displaying affection and being alone. They correctly prioritize their relationships within their lives. They set boundaries. And they generally make the best romantic partners. Secure attachment types can accept rejection and move on despite the pain. Research suggests that around half of all adults are Secure attachment types.

Anxious attachment types need constant reassurance from their partners. They are endlessly stressed about their relationships. They tend to have trouble being alone. They don't trust others. And they often find themselves in unhealthy or toxic relationships. Women are more likely to be Anxious types than men. But having worked with hundreds of Nice Guys, I can confirm that many men can be Anxious types, too.

Avoidant attachment types tend to be uncomfortable with intimacy. They're highly independent, they're afraid of commitment, and they're adept at finding creative ways to extricate themselves from intimate situations. They frequently complain about feeling smothered in relationships. Statistically, men are more likely than women to be Avoidant attachment types.

Looking back on my relationships, I was almost certainly an Anxious-Avoidant, representing the worst of both worlds. Anxious-Avoidants are often referred to as the fearful type. They crave intimacy and connection but fear anyone getting too close. They have intoxicating highs and terrible lows. Anxious-Avoidants seem to either be alone and miserable or in a toxic relationship and miserable.

The four attachment types are quite predictable in the way they configure themselves in relationships. Secure types generally pair up with other secure types. Anxious types and Avoidant types tend to pair up with each other instead of their own types. (After all, Avoidants need someone to run from and Anxious types need someone to chase.) And Anxious-Avoidants...well, they find each other and create shit-shows.

Just as it did for me, learning your attachment style can help you understand your relationship patterns, navigate heartbreak, and cultivate healthier relationships. When you put in the effort, you can change your attachment style over time. As Dr. Levine wrote in *Attached*, "most people are only as needy as their unmet needs."

**INTEGRATED ACTION:**

- ✓ Is this the first you're hearing of attachment theory? If not, where did you first learn about it? Write your answers in your journal.
- ✓ Which attachment style do you think you are? How has this affected your relationships? Write your answers in your journal.
- ✓ What kind of partners do you tend to attract? Write your answers in your journal. Be honest with yourself. And be as detailed as possible.
- ✓ Talk to your safe perosn (or people) about your attachment style.

# CHEMICAL L

D
o you feel lonely?

Join the club.

Loneliness has become something of an epidemic. Many of the men who reach out to me for coaching do so because they're lonely or they're afraid of being lonely. Being lonely, however, is part of the human condition.

"Our ancestors had an inherent drive to connect with other humans," explains Dr. Glover. "The very act of connecting helped ensure they got their needs met. It's likely that primal men who tried to go it alone ended up dying and didn't pass on the gene. Our biological desire to connect is so strong that when we don't connect, it can be painful – emotionally and even physically."

Sadly, we no longer live in tribes like our ancestors did. We used to be communal. We hunted and gathered and fucked and parented together. Now, most of us go it alone. We're individualistic. And generally, we have to work to find connection all by ourselves.

"One of the biggest issues we have today is that we tend to confuse the drive for sex with the drive to connect," adds Dr. Glover. "We wrap them up together and believe that finding 'the one' will solve everything. But this just exacerbates our loneliness. It creates a sense of desperation, and it makes us feel defective. If we have trouble finding a romantic partner, we feel empty and worthless. And often when we do find a partner, we place a great burden on that person to meet all of our needs."

> **HARSH TRUTH:**
>
> One person can't fulfill all your needs. Thinking that one person can fulfill all your needs is what leads to toxic and dysfunctional relationships.

No matter what your relationship status is, you will always have the drive to connect. Men who are in intimate relationships often feel completely alone because they've become disconnected from their male friends. And men who are single often inaccurately compare themselves to those who are in intimate relationships. Additionally, many men lack social skills and suffer from social anxiety, carry around toxic shame, and replace real connection with things like social media, video games, television, and porn.

Worse yet, men often mistake the feeling of loneliness for defectiveness. But feeling lonely does not mean you're defective. Mother Nature simply wired you to feel like shit when you're not connected so you will go out and get connected. Loneliness is just a chemical reaction in your brain. Dr. Glover calls it *Chemical L*.

"Honor the feeling of loneliness," says Dr. Glover. "Don't try to make it go away. And don't mistake it for defectiveness. Shift your mental view of what it means to feel lonely. It doesn't mean people can see right through you. It doesn't mean you're unlovable. It doesn't mean you're a fucking loser. It's just Mother Nature's way of telling you to connect."

## MILKSHAKES & MIRACLES

Dr. Glover frequently tells the story around an 'Aha' moment he experienced after his second divorce. For the first time in his adult life, he was living alone. And he'd made a conscious decision to wait a while before diving into the dating pool.

"After so much heavy lifting in my second marriage, I didn't even want to talk to women," Dr Glover confesses. "But everywhere I looked, I saw couples in love. Couples walking hand in hand, couples laughing and smiling, couples expressing affection. It made me feel really fucking lonely. So, I dove into my work and prepared for my upcoming book tour. I then had an 'Aha' moment while drinking a mocha milkshake at my favorite coffee shop. I realized that even in the depths of sorrow, I could drink one of these damn milkshakes and almost immediately feel better. Contented. Almost…happy. That is until the gut-ache hit."

As Dr. Glover recalls, this is when he truly began to understand the appeal of things like alcohol, drugs, porn, gambling, video games, social media, and dare we say…mocha milkshakes. They all provide a means of escape from Chemical L and the feeling of loneliness it creates (just as it is supposed to).

"Once I discovered that a simple milkshake could dissolve the feeling of loneliness, I realized that I was giving my loneliness all its power. And since I was the one giving it all its power, I could also take its power away. By just feeling it. Because that's all it is. It's just a feeling. So, I began to just sit with my loneliness instead of trying to escape it with a mocha milkshake. And low and behold, that feeling of loneliness would usually disappear pretty quickly on its own."

Dr. Glover's loneliness was not a hint to go looking for a woman or for a sexual escapade. It was just an evolutionary cue - Chemical L - telling him to connect with other humans. It was telling him not to isolate.

Ironically, though, the men who are most afraid of being lonely tend to be the most likely to isolate. But as Dr. Glover likes to profess, *miracles happen around people*. So, you must engage with other human beings.

If you're lonely and have social anxiety, take baby steps. Learn to ask yourself what you want and then act on it. Hold on to yourself when you feel resistance from within you or from outside of you. And remember, you're not the only one who feels lonely. As the actor Viggo Mortensen (playing Tony Lip) professed in the movie *Green Book*, "the world is full of lonely people afraid to make the first move."

"If you want to have a fulfilling life and you don't want to be lonely, you have to take some risks," expounds Dr. Glover. "There's no way around it. So, take the risk of connecting with people. Take the risk of being vulnerable. Take the risk of being found out. Take the risk of getting your heart broken. Don't run away from these things. And know that feeling lonely isn't a reflection of your character or your worth as a human. It's just a reaction in your brain. It's just Chemical L telling you to get out of the goddamn house."[138]

> **INTEGRATED ACTION:**
> ✓ How would you feel if you knew that loneliness was just a chemical reaction in your brain - Mother Nature's way of telling you to connect? Write your answer in your journal.
> ✓ How have you confused the desire for sex with the drive to connect? How has this affected you? Write your answer in your journal.
> ✓ Get out of the house, expand your route, linger in public, talk to people everywhere you go, test for interest, walk through open doors.
> ✓ Connect (or re-connect) with your male friends.

---

138 Glover, Robert A. "Podcast 30: Loneliness, Part 1," and "Podcast 31: Loneliness, Part 2" Podcast Audio. www.drglover.com

# A PRESCRIPTION

Loss and heartbreak do indeed create chemical changes in your brain. The human brain likes to travel the same neural pathways it always does, and it doesn't like to create new ones. We experience withdrawal when old neural pathways are broken. So, heartbreak really does hurt. A whole fucking lot.

"Connection is connection," says Dr. Glover. "Having it makes the brain feel good. Not having it makes the brain feel bad. Emotional pain can hurt every bit as much as physical pain. After my second divorce, I felt a deep sense of loneliness and sadness, even though I didn't really miss my ex-wife. But I did miss the depth of connection, being in a family, the kids, the dog, the house, everything it meant to be in a relationship. It hurt like hell."

If you are dealing with heartbreak, first ask yourself what kind of heartbreak you're dealing with. Is it Type I or Type II? What kind of relationship was it? As previously mentioned, it's crucial to be honest with yourself in this way. When you are completely devastated and feel as though your life will never be the same, you are probably experiencing the loss of an idealized or otherwise unhealthy relationship rather than the loss of a healthy, balanced relationship.

No matter what kind of heartbreak you're dealing with, Dr. Glover offers the following prescription:

✓ **Non-judgment & non-resistance**. If you're feeling bad, don't judge it. And don't resist it. Be with it. Experience it. Just be the observer of it.

✓ **Remind yourself that everything you're experiencing is part of being human**. You've been wired to feel good when you have connection and you've been wired to feel bad when you don't have connection.

✓ **Do not medicate your heartbreak**. Things like alcohol, drugs, and porn will not help. These are the forces that drive addiction. Turn and face whatever you need to face.

✓ **Learn to consciously be alone**. Just be still with yourself. Often, what keeps people in bad relationships is the fear of being alone. Get comfortable being alone. This doesn't mean you should isolate or put up walls. It means that when you happen to be alone – or think you need to get out of a relationship – you know you'll be fine. It's empowering to know that you can comfortably be alone.

✓ **Stay connected**. Be social. Let people be there for you.

✓ **Engage in meaningful activity**. Find things that are important to you and go do them.

✓ **Do not glorify your misery**. And do not play the victim card. Initially, it may get you some attention. But it will quickly wear thin.

✓ **Enjoy the positive memories of the relationships but don't enshrine them**. If it was a bad relationship, don't let your brain dwell on only the good times.

✓ If it was a trauma-bonded relationship, **make a list of all the specific ways your ex treated you badly**. Don't let your mind romanticize the relationship and write a revisionist history.

✓ **Work with a coach or therapist**. This is essentially a form of re-parenting. You're developing a healthy relationship with another human being. Not to mention that you're clearing out old baggage.

✓ **Give it time**.

When all is said and done, remember to practice gratitude and think abundantly. How was your relationship a gift?

"My relationship with my ex-wife was toxic, but it was a gift," shares Dr. Glover. "She got me looking at myself and my Nice Guy tendencies, which caused me to get into recovery. And because of that gift, I wrote *No More Mr. Nice Guy*. I still look back on our relationship as a gift, even though I don't want to be with her. If you've lost someone you still want to be with, look at them as a gift. A gift that was on loan to you. And know that there are many more gifts out there just waiting for you.[139]"

# WHAT A TRIP

In November of 2021, Dr. Glover participated in four Ayahuasca ceremonies at Rythmia Life Enhancement Center in Costa Rica. Having never experimented with drugs of any kind, this was a giant step outside his comfort zone. Nevertheless, Dr. Glover reports that the experience completely transformed his relationship with his wife, Lupita.

"Out of all the insights I had during those four nights," shares Dr. Glover, the one that sticks out as both the simplest and the most profound is this: *We are all here to get our hearts broken.* That's it. That's the meaning of life."

Most of us are terrified of getting hurt – of experiencing a broken heart. We do whatever we can to avoid it. We isolate, we put up walls, we withhold the truth, we avoid risk – all because we don't want to get hurt.

"But here's the thing," proclaims Dr. Glover. "If something has the power to truly break your heart, it must be pretty damn amazing – something you probably wouldn't want to miss. By always walking around with your armor on and your defenses up, how will you ever experience any joy, beauty, adventure, or love in life? Yes, it's true that in every relationship someone is going to get left. Someone is always going to get hurt. *You* are going to get hurt. You are going to have your heart broken. But again, that's life. That's living. Indeed, you haven't really lived until you've had your heart broken."

---

139 Glover, Robert A. "Podcasts 151-154: Parts 1-4 of a Four-Part Series on Understanding and Getting Over Loss and Heartbreak." Podcast Audio. www.drglover.com

# PART VIII: SUCCESS

*Success is not final; failure is not fatal:*
*It is the courage to continue that counts.*
**-Winston Churchill**

In *No More Mr. Nice Guy,* Dr. Glover asks, "If there were no limits on your life, where would you live? What would you be doing with your leisure time? What kind of work would you be engaged in? What would your home and surroundings look like?" He then goes on to point out an ongoing tragedy: The staggering amount of intelligent, industrious, and talented men who are wasting their lives and wallowing in the mire of mediocrity.

Perhaps you are one of these men. Perhaps you aren't even remotely living up to your potential. And when you examine the reality of your life, you become an unfortunate combination of sad, bitter, and angry.

Trust me, I can relate.

After I graduated from the University of Wisconsin, I moved to Chicago to pursue comedy, using what I thought was a brilliantly devised strategy. By day, I'd find inspiration in hip and trendy coffee bistros, or on the L train, gazing out at the quickly passing cityscape. By night, I'd perform at open mics, only to catch the ear of…I don't know…let's say…George Wendt[140], sign a development deal, and be thrust headlong into comedic superstardom. As it turned out, though, telling dick jokes to drunkards on Wednesday nights wasn't going to foot the bill for my 400-square-foot palace without air conditioning. And from what I could tell, George Wendt didn't leave the house much.

To make ends meet, I accepted a position at a billion-dollar advertising firm just gracious enough to pay me $24,000 a year. The company occupied the sixteenth floor of a glossy high-rise on Michigan Avenue, conveniently situated between a Starbucks and another Starbucks. The walls were drab and dull, the desks and chairs were all identical, and the carpet patterns induced a subtle urge to vomit. I muddled through each day, doing work that likely could have been done by a half-trained Capuchin monkey.

I lasted 18 months.

Gripped by depression and angst, I handed in my resignation, abruptly left Chicago, and moved back to Omaha - my hometown - so I could be closer to my family while I tried to "figure things out." But instead of figuring things out, I took yet another job in advertising. Then, another. And then, another. For 15 years, I bounced around from job to job – 11 in total - only to sit dejectedly in a cubicle, building someone else's dream instead of my own.

I tried to convince myself that I had a perfectly nice life, that all of this was just fine, as long as I was making everyone else happy.

But it wasn't just fine.

I was miserable.

Worse yet, I didn't know what to do about it.

I didn't know how to make a change. Or how to ask for help. Or how to ask for what I wanted. I didn't even know *what* I wanted.

---

140 For you youngsters out there, George Wendt is an American actor and comedian best known for playing Norm on the popular sitcom *Cheers*. Wendt was born on the south side of Chicago and still calls Chicago home.

I didn't know how to stop playing small. Or how to stop thinking that the world was against me.

I didn't know if I should or could pursue my passions.

That is, until I got the fuck out of my own way and started believing in myself.

This section covers Dr. Glover's principles for **Success**. While we all have our own definition of success, too many men never experience the kind of success they want. This is primarily due to the ineffective thought processes and behaviors that Dr. Glover details in his popular online class, *Nice Guys Don't Finish Last, They Rot in Middle Management.*

"As a man, you might struggle with success for a number of reasons," says Dr. Glover. "But nine times out of ten, the problem is not related to your talent, your intelligence, or your work ethic. Instead, it is the result of your flawed core beliefs about yourself and your place in the world. Not to mention that when what you are doing isn't working, you probably just try harder and do more of the same thing. You have to try something different."

It's time for you to start living up to your full potential. Whether you're not as successful as you want to be or you're traditionally successful but terribly unfulfilled, the information in this section will help you identify how you prevent yourself from getting what you really want in life. By the end, you'll have new ways of thinking and acting that will propel you towards the kind of success you desire.

---

**INTEGRATED ACTION**
- ✓ Think about your life. Are you happy? Do you enjoy what you do for a living? Are you living up to your potential? Write your answers in your journal.
- ✓ Now, think about your **ideal** life. Describe it in meticulous detail. What does this ideal life look like? Where are you living? What are you doing? How much money are you making? Do you work for yourself or someone else? Don't hold back. Don't let your brain stop you from writing things down.

# SIX DEADLY SINS

In Chapter One of *No More Mr. Nice Guy*, Dr. Glover presents a list of characteristics that define the Nice Guy Syndrome. For many men, these characteristics manifest in every area of their lives. Relative to work and career, however, Dr. Glover has pinpointed what he calls *Six Deadly Sins*. These sins prevent men, especially Nice Guys, from becoming full achievers and living up to their potential. Dr. Glover describes them in *Nice Guys Don't Finish Last, They Rot in Middle Management*. The **Six Deadly Sins** are:

### 1. The Need for Approval

If your behavior is guided by your need for approval, you will always fall prey to what Dr. Glover likes to call your *Committee of Mediocrity*. Your Committee of Mediocrity is composed of all the people whose approval you are seeking. And when you constantly seek their approval, you never act with pure integrity, you never ask for what you want, and you never make your needs and desires a priority. Approval-seeking will never lead to any kind of true success.

### 2. Small Thinking

Do you have a scarcity mindset? Do you settle for scraps? Do you believe there isn't enough to go around? Do you convince yourself that everything is just fine because it's the best you can hope for? This kind of thinking is incredibly damaging, and it prevents you from seeing the abundance of opportunities around you.

### 3. Allowing Fear to Take Over

If you have an ever-present fear of making a mistake, you will always play it safe. This ensures that you keep a glass ceiling of mediocrity over your head.

### 4. Distraction

You fall victim to what Dr. Glover calls *deceptive productivity*. You are easily distracted, and you keep busy by doing things that seem important but aren't.

### 5. Holding on to the Familiar

How long have you been following the same path? How long have you been driving around the same old neighborhood? Maybe you've been doing it for so long – like I did – that you assume it's the only way to live. When you hang on to the familiar, when you keep doing what you've always done, you'll keep getting what you've always got.

### 6. Going it Alone

Many men are terrible at asking for help. They try to do everything themselves. They always go it alone. But if you always go it alone, you will always be busy and only moderately successful. You will never be all that you can be.

---

**INTEGRATED ACTION**

✓ Which of the Six Deadly Sins do you think most affects you in your professional life? How does it manifest? How do you think it has held you back? Write your answers in your journal.

✓ Do you fall victim to "deceptive productivity"? How so? Write some examples in your journal.

✓ Can you make a commitment to doing something different? Write your commitment in your journal.

✓ Talk to your safe person (or people) about which of the Six Deadly Sins affects you the most. Tell them that you are making a commitment to doing something different and ask them to hold you accountable.

---

# PRACTICING INTEGRITY

One of the reasons so many men never experience the kind of success they desire is that everything they do – or don't do – is aimed at gaining the approval of others. As Dr. Glover puts it, "constantly seeking the approval of others is just a really effective way to limit your potential and dilute your talent."

Imagine this scenario, which Dr. Glover offers in *Nice Guys Don't Finish Last, They Rot in Middle Management*:

Your boss calls you into his office and gives you a pressing, last-minute assignment. He needs it by morning. This is an opportunity to maximize your talents and help your company make an important sale. But your Committee of Mediocrity takes over:

*Doesn't he know I'm away from home too much already? The kids are going to be at daycare even longer. What kind of parent does this make me? If I tell the boss 'No,' I may never get a chance like this again. What if I fuck up and it costs the company?*

Sound familiar?

When your Committee of Mediocrity is running your life, you never ask yourself the types of questions that are truly important. These questions might include:

- *How do I feel about this?*
- *What is the best plan of action?*
- *Who do I need to involve to achieve the best results?*

- *What is the most efficient way to get this done?*

"Allowing your Committee of Mediocrity to run the show prevents you from acting with integrity," explains Dr. Glover. "If you're always trying to gain the approval of others, you actually become dishonest. Furthermore, you put a lid on your personal ambitions, you fail to take risks, and you stifle your own creativity."

"Full achievers are directed by a committee of *one*," asserts Dr. Glover. "They don't seek a consensus. They do what feels right, not what's expedient or popular. This is what opens doors to success and accomplishment."

## FOUR TRAITS OF FULL ACHIEVERS

Practicing integrity may not always produce immediate results. It may not even be popular. But practicing integrity isn't about outcomes; it's about doing what's right. In *Nice Guys Don't Finish Last, They Rot in Middle Management*, Dr. Glover lays out four traits of full achievers that illustrate what it means to practice integrity:

**1. Full achievers are open books.**

Harboring a fear of being found out will always affect your integrity. So, do everything in the open. Say what you mean and mean what you say. If you're a classic Nice Guy, this will take practice.

**2. Full achievers embrace their mistakes.**

Actually, there are no mistakes. Just learning experiences. You can't learn from your mistakes if you bury them.

**3. Full achievers are brutally honest.**

Be clear, direct, and transparent. Eliminate covert contracts. If the voice in your head says, *Don't tell them that*, it likely means you need to tell them that. Again, if you're a classic Nice Guy, this will take practice.

**4. Full achievers dare to risk consequences.**

Do what you feel is right. Maybe it's firing a client or telling a customer 'No.' Learn to ask yourself: *If I wasn't afraid of anything or any outcome, how would I handle this situation?* Even if your integrity leads to negative consequences, remind yourself that you handled it, and you'll continue to handle it.

---

**INTEGRATED ACTION:**
- ✓ Tell your safe person (or people) about a recent mistake you made at work. Tell them what you learned from the mistake. Pay attention to how it feels after you do this. We usually experience a tremendous sense of relief after we bring something into the open that we have been hiding.
- ✓ Practice being totally honest with your safe person (or people).
- ✓ Do you think it is possible to be clear, direct, open, and honest in all business situations? Are there situations where it is best to hold back? Write your answers down in your journal
- ✓ Do you know someone who has consistently acted with integrity in the business world, regardless of the consequences? What are your impressions of this person? Write about him or her in your journal.

# EMBRACING ABUNDANCE III

As Dr. Glover often points out, most men can be divided into two categories: 1) Those who don't believe they will ever get good things in life; and 2) Those who hope that one day they will get good things but have no idea how to make it happen. If you fall into one of these categories, you have a deprivation view of the world. And having a deprivation view instead of an abundance view will keep you stuck in the mire of mediocrity.

Deprivation thinking causes you to believe that others get all the opportunities in life. It leads to envy, resentment, and anger. It also makes it damn near impossible for you to live up to your potential. For Nice Guys especially, this is true because:

- Nice Guys don't think their needs are important. They are terrible receivers. They settle for scraps because they believe that's all they deserve.
- Nice Guys have trouble accepting that the world is a place of abundance. They never seem to notice the open doors of opportunity.

"Here's the reality," asserts Dr. Glover. "The very fact that so many people experience wealth, success, and happiness is proof that there is enough to go around. The world really is a place of abundance. Just look. Notice the homes, the cars, the gadgets. Notice the people – they are well-fed and well-dressed, and they are headed off to jobs. You are not dealing with scarcity. You just have a perception of scarcity."

Abundance is not a pursuit. It's a state of mind. It's a matter of awareness and acceptance.

Are you aware of the good things you already have?

Can you see how much you have already been abundantly blessed?

"Abundance is like air," insists Dr. Glover. "You are already experiencing abundance with every breath you take."

---

**ABUNDANCE EXCERISE:**

Think about something good that happened to you during the last week. It could be something grand, it could be something small.

"We are often so consumed with our search for abundance that we don't notice the multitude of blessings flowing continuously throughout our lives," says Dr. Glover.

---

If you want to experience abundance, stop pursuing it. Stop chasing it. Stop searching for it. Instead, work on changing your paradigm – your core beliefs about yourself and about the world. Realize that you don't need to seek abundance because you already have it.[141]

---

141 Glover, Robert A. *Nice Guys Don't Finish Last, They Rot in Middle Management.* "Lesson Four: Embrace Abundance." (TPI University. www.drglover.com)

**INTEGRATED ACTION:**

- ✓ How's your **Gratitude Practice** coming along?
- ✓ Spend some time thinking about all the ways you are blessed. Ideally, you should be alone while you do this. Consider creating a meditative environment, perhaps by lighting a candle and sitting on a comfortable pillow. Make this a regular practice.
- ✓ How do you think simplifying your life would make it easier to be aware of abundance? How do material things get in the way of you experiencing abundance? Write your answers in your journal.
- ✓ Write a paragraph or two arguing for the abundance in the world.
- ✓ How do you feel when you practice gratitude? Do you resist it? Do you embrace it? How do you feel *after* you practice gratitude? Write about your experience in your journal.

# CULTIVATING COURAGE

D r. Glover frequently acknowledges that one of his favorite books is *Feel the Fear…and Do it Anyway* by Dr. Susan Jeffers. He references the book in many of his seminars and workshops, and recommends it to all of his students. He does so for good reason: Too many men let fear dictate their lives.

In the book, Dr. Jeffers explains that there are three levels of fear:

**Level One** fear is surface fear, which includes things that happen to us and things that require action. Examples include aging, losing a loved one, losing a job, public speaking, and ending a relationship.

**Level Two** fear involves the ego and reflects your sense of self. Common Level Two fears include rejection, success, failure, disapproval, and helplessness.

**Level Three** fear underlies both Level One and Level Two fear and reflects your ability to handle things. Level Three fear is simply: *I can't handle it*.

For Nice Guys especially, I can't handle it is a core paradigm:

- *I can't handle losing my job.*
- *I can't handle talking in front of people.*
- *I can't handle failure.*
- *I can't handle the responsibilities of success.*
- *I can't handle people not liking me.*
- *I just can't handle it.*

"Here's the truth about fear," says Dr. Glover. "As long as you continue to grow, your fear will never go away. Active, growing people are always confronted with situations that create fear. Everyone experiences fear when they start something new, or they venture into the unknown, or they experience loss. If you are alive and you get up in the morning and you leave the house, you are probably going to experience some degree of fear."

Unfortunately, many men are paralyzed by fear. Rather than confronting their fear head-on, they look for ways around it. They think that if they avoid uncomfortable or frightening situations, the situations will eventually just go away.

"Successful people don't try to eliminate or avoid fear," adds Dr. Glover. "They know that it is part of life, and they allow it to motivate rather than control them. Changing jobs or getting laid off may be scary, but successful people respond to these challenges with confidence. Successful people don't have an absence of fear. They just know they can handle situations that create fear."

Let's say a man has a great idea for a business or product that could make a lot of money. If he is a fearful Nice Guy, he will think about it endlessly but never do anything about it. If he is an Integrated Man, he will research it, determine if it's a valid idea, and find a way to make it happen.

Or let's say a man makes a mistake at his job. If he is a fearful Nice Guy, he will hide it, make excuses, blame others, get defensive, or some combination of those. If he is an Integrated Man, he will immediately identify the mistake, own up to it, start working on a remedy, and learn what is necessary to ensure that he doesn't make the same mistake again.

So, consider this: If everyone feels fear when confronted with changes in life, yet many people succeed despite that fear, then fear must not be the problem. The problem lies in having the core belief: *I can't handle it*.

But what if you believed that no matter what happens, you could handle it?

What would you possibly have to fear?[142]

Dr. Glover frequently credits *Feel The Fear...and Do it Anyway*, which he initially read in 1987, with not just changing his life, but saving it. At the time, he was in the throes of his first divorce. He was becoming disconnected from his two-year old son. He left his job as a minister to seek employment as a counselor. He was broke, terrified, and filled with shame.

"My life was a mess," remembers Dr. Glover. "After reading Dr. Jeffers' book, I began applying the mantra, 'I'll handle it.' I repeated it to myself, over and over, while trying to fall asleep at night. *I'll handle it. No matter what happens, I'll handle it.* To be honest, I had no fucking clue how I would handle it, but repeating this mantra got me through the night to a new day."

Indeed, Dr. Glover handled it. And soon he began to thrive. Now, some 35 years later, he still uses the mantra 'I'll handle it' to guide his life. As Dr. Glover will tell you, he never quits challenging himself, which means he is always confronting new fears.

"Whether it's been doing television interviews, learning to salsa dance, making big changes in my business, dealing with life-threatening illnesses, or moving to Mexico," shares Dr. Glover, "over the years, I have frequently paused to remind myself that I have handled everything in life that has ever scared me. And I will handle whatever comes that scares me."

If you want to live a big life, reach your potential, and experience success, consider adopting the mantra that has changed countless lives - including Dr. Glover's. Start telling yourself that you'll handle it.

*I'll handle it. No matter what happens, I'll handle it.*

"Even if you have no fucking clue *how* you'll handle it," proclaims Dr. Glover. "the truth is, you've handled every other thing else in your life up to this point. You're still alive and ticking. Assume you'll handle whatever comes your way. Because you will."

---

142 Glover, Robert A. *Nice Guys Don't Finish Last, They Rot in Middle Management.* "Lesson Five: Feel the Fear and Do it Anyway." (TPI University. www.drglover. com)

**INTEGRATED ACTION:**

✓ If you haven't already been saying it to yourself, then starting today your new mantra is "I'll handle it." When you are confronted with frightening or uncomfortable situations, repeat it to yourself. "No matter what happens, I'll handle it."

✓ How does your desire to have a smooth, problem-free life limit your personal power? Write your answer in your journal.

✓ Can you think of a situation in which you initially felt tremendous fear, but ultimately realized that your fears were a product of your mind and not based in reality? Describe the experience in your journal.

✓ What would you do differently if you had no fear? What would you do if you knew you couldn't fail? Write your answers in your journal.

✓ Talk to your safe person (or people) about your fears. Tell them you'd like to start confronting your fears.

# DOING SOMETHING DIFFERENT

If you've been fruitlessly trying to create a smooth, predictable, problem-free life, perhaps it's time for you to face reality. Life is not smooth, predictable, or problem-free. Life is chaotic and ever-changing. But you can handle it.

You are no longer a powerless child. You are an intelligent, capable adult. The roadmap for life that you developed in childhood is outdated and inaccurate. By embracing change and *doing something different*, however, you can develop a new roadmap – one that will take you where you want to go.

Dr. Glover likes to describe life as *an infinite maze lined with countless doors.*

"There are all kinds of good things, bad things, adventures, surprises, and challenges behind every door," he explains. "Successful, Integrated Men spend their lives exploring the maze of life. They notice which doors are open and which are closed. They like to stick their heads through open doors just to see what's on the other side."

Sadly, many men don't explore the maze of life. They pace up and down the same hallways, only opening the doors they've already been through. They are scared shitless to venture down new hallways and open up new doors.

If you were to reflect on the past week, could you think of a positive experience that you had but weren't expecting? Did you bump into a stranger and hit it off? Did you stumble into a new restaurant that you ended up loving? Did you take a wrong turn and find yourself in a vibrant part of town that you'd never previously seen?

"This is how life works on a grand scale," proclaims Dr. Glover. "If life were completely controllable and predictable, nothing interesting would ever happen. If you keep trying to hang on to what feels familiar and comfortable, you will never experience all the amazing things that can come from change."

# STRATEGIES FOR EMBRACING CHANGE

You can't be afraid of change. It bears repeating that *if you keep doing what you've always done, you'll keep getting what you've always got*. In Lesson Seven of *Nice Guys Don't Finish Last, They Rot in Middle Management*, Dr. Glover lays out several strategies for embracing change. These strategies have helped me see the abundance of opportunities in the world and walk through the open doors. They can do the same for you.

1. **If something isn't working, stop doing it**. Stop pounding on closed doors. Just stop. If trying to get your manager's approval isn't working, stop. If trying desperately to make your wife happy isn't working, stop. When you keep repeating the same ineffective behaviors, you keep getting the same results.

2. **Do something new every day**. Doing the same thing over and over again creates cognitive blinders that prevent you from seeing the many choices available to you. But doing something different creates a chain reaction. Eat in a different restaurant, listen to a different radio station, take a different route home from work. The more things you do differently, the more doors open up before you.

3. **Go somewhere you've never been**. And go by yourself. This will help you venture down new hallways and allow you to be more aware of the open doors. When you are by youself in a new place, you are more likely to do things you wouldn't do in old, familiar territory. The more

adventurous you become in life, the more adventurous you will become in your career. So, pick a place you've always wanted to go...and fucking go.

4. **Socialize.** Successful, Integrated Men strike a healthy balance between spending time alone and spending time with people. Talk to people everywhere you go. *Miracles happen around people.*

5. **Learn new skills.** When you step outside your comfort zone and learn something new, it challenges your brain and body to grow. Pick up a musical instrument, take a class, or start studying a new language.

6. **See every closed door as an opportunity.** Did your company decide to downsize and lay you off? How is it an opportunity? Did you get a rejection letter on your passion project? ? How is it an opportunity? Even the most painful or disappointing experiences can lead to wonderful new opportunities.

7. **Practice being a good ender.** Are you someone who stays in shit jobs, shit relationships, and shit situations for way too long? Integrated Men know when it's time to walk away from something bad and make room for something better. As Dr. Glover likes to say, "Don't try and redecorate a pigsty. Get out of the pigsty and find greener pastures."

## FIXING YOUR WINDSHIELD

Because *being a good ender covers a multitude of sins*, it might just be the most powerful success strategy of all. Successful people know when to remove themselves from situations that aren't taking them in the direction they want to go. They know when to cut their losses, learn the appropriate lessons, and move on.

Unfortunately, many of life's situations fall into that frustrating, too-good-to-leave-too-bad-to-stay kind of gray area that leads to what Dr. Glover calls *Cracked Windshield Syndrome.*

Most of us have had the experience of having a small rock fly up and crack our windshield," explains Dr. Glover. "Then, over time, the crack begins to spread. You keep promising yourself you're going to get it fixed. But then you end up living with it for months, even years. You just get used to it, and eventually you hardly even notice it."

We humans have a tendency to constantly put up with things like cracked windshields, missing hubcaps, noisy ceiling fans, barking dogs, poor treatment, and disrespect. We often convince ourselves that something isn't that bad (when it is that bad) or that we'll deal with it later (when we should deal with it now). Then, we do nothing and continue to put up with it.

"What if this is the main cause of us never having everything that we really want in life?" poses Dr. Glover. "Why do we wait until we are selling our car before we get the windshield fixed? Why do we wonder what took us so long when we finally do get up the courage to leave a mediocre job or relationship?"

Dr. Glover has another guiding mantra: **Sometimes you have to give up the things you love to get the things you want.** He frequently uses his second marriage to illustrate this.

"I truly loved my second wife," shares Dr. Glover. "And I did everything I possibly could to make the marriage work. But for 14 years, it was Groundhog Day. Nothing ever actually changed. I finally realized that no matter how much I loved my wife, loved being married, and loved having a family, continuing on was not going to get me what I really wanted in life. It's been over 20 years since I left that cracked windshield of a marriage. I now have a loving, supportive wife, an abundance of male friends, a spectacular home in Mexico, and a prosperous job doing something I'm passionate about. Learning to be a good ender truly is the key to getting what you want in life."

**INTEGRATED ACTION:**

- ✓ Are you ready to admit that you were born to be an explorer? Are you ready to take your foot off the break, step on the gas, and have an adventure? Write your answers in your journal.

- ✓ When you are presented with exciting new opportunities, what goes through your head? How can you start thinking more like a successful, Integrated Man? Write your answers in your journal.

- ✓ If you're a bad ender, how has it caused you unnecessary suffering? Write your answers in your journal.

- ✓ Have you ever walked away from something bad only to find something better? If so, write about the experience in your journal.

- ✓ Each day for the next week, do at least one thing different that stretches you or introduces you to new people or activities. Journal your feelings as you do this. Did you make any unexpected discoveries? Did you have any new experiences? Overall, did you think this exercise was positive or negative?

# FINDING SUPPORT

After several years working with and coaching other men, Dr. Glover began to notice an interesting contradiction: Many men tend to go it alone; and yet, they also tend to get enmeshed in dependent relationships and systems. "Both of these tendencies make life much more difficult than it needs to be," asserts Dr. Glover.

You may find it difficult to wrap your head around the idea that men who go it alone also get enmeshed in dependent systems, but the two actually go hand in hand. Men often spend a great deal of time trying to find a balance between being there for people who "need" them and trying to escape these very same people.

"Many families create a sort of invisible tether that keeps their children connected," explains Dr. Glover. "You might not be aware of this tether because you think it benefits you. As long as you are tethered to a dependent system, you feel safe. This same pattern can manifest in your professional life."

If you want to become a full achiever and realize your full potential, you need to create a different kind of family. You need a tribe. You need a mastermind support group who you can turn to for accountability and encouragement. Additionally, as Dr. Glover recommends:

- Your group should help you learn what your family never taught you about being successful.

- Your group should positively support you as you make changes and try new things.
- Your group should be filled with men who are already doing this work in their own lives, and who can serve as mentors or role models.
- Your group should help you identify your blind spots.
- Your group should consist of safe people to whom you can express yourself.

There is no perfect way to build your mastermind support group. But you need **teachers**, **companions**, and **helpers**. You can start small with just yourself and one trusted person. Teachers can include a therapist, a rabbi or priest, or a good friend who is living up to his potential. Companions can include trusted friends, co-workers, or anyone else who is on a journey of self-improvement. Helpers can include friends, family members, co-workers, or professionals (doctors, accountants, etc.).

**Once you've created your mastermind group:**
- Choose a regular time to talk. Don't let anything get in the way of your meetings.
- Have an agenda.
- Ask everyone in your group to be honest, direct, and supportive.
- Touch base with the people in your group between meetings.
- Ask your group for consistent and constructive feedback.
- Become involved in other groups where you can add value.

**Use your group as a way to practice:**
- Revealing yourself
- Letting people help you
- Delegating
- Setting boundaries
- Dealing with conflict
- Asking for what you want
- Being clear and direct
- Sharing your feelings

- Setting goals
- Taking care of yourself
- Dreaming

"Success takes teamwork," says Dr. Glover. "No one succeeds completely on their own; even the most talented and capable people need help to live up to their full potential. Having a support group that you can ask for help is a powerful way to build self-esteem. Each time you ask for help and they respond positively, it reinforces the message that you are valuable.[143]"

> **INTEGRATED ACTION:**
> ✓ Has taking care of needy, dependent people negatively affected your professional life? Write your answer in your journal.
> ✓ Make a list of teachers, helpers, and companions who could be in your mastermind support group.
> ✓ Start building your mastermind support group. What is your next action required to move this forward? It is perfectly fine to start small with one person and build from there.

143 Glover, Robert A. *Nice Guys Don't Finish Last*, They Rot in Middle Management. "Lesson Eight: Build Your Team." (TPI University. www.drglover.com)

# PROCRASTINATION

Pardon me while I check my email.

What's the weather supposed to be like this weekend?

Shit, I forgot to text my uncle and wish him a happy birthday.

I can't believe only four people liked my Facebook post.

I wonder what my dog is thinking.

Anyway.

Where was I?

Oh, right.

Countless men have an issue with procrastination. It's one of the Nice Guy Syndrome's hideous relatives. And given that the average human now has the attention span of a goldfish[144], it should come as no surprise that procrastination is more pervasive than ever.

Are you a procrastinator?

You are, aren't you?

---

144 In recent years, many news outlets have suggested that humans now have the attention span of a goldfish - which is like 7 seconds. This has actually been debunked. But several studies have shown that the human attention span is in fact decreasing because of the nature of internet scrolling. Then again, we can listen to a 4-hour podcast and binge watch television shows…so, who really knows? Every human is different. We all have different brains, different habits, different routines, different interests, different schedules, different jobs. Anyway, the point is, most of us procrastinate. Like, so many of us. We just waste time on meaningless crap and put off the important stuff. Anyway, like I said, so many of us procrastinate. Stop trying to figure out this footnote and get back to the main text.

You avoid unpleasant tasks. You let things build up. You seek out distractions. You start things and don't finish. You have difficulty staying on track. You spend a great deal of time just…watching the time pass.

And you fool yourself. You fool yourself by saying you'll get to it. Or you do the easiest things on your to-do list to feel productive. That is, if you even have a to-do list.

Procrastination looms over you, doesn't it? It's like a dark cloud. It hangs over you and it causes stress, anxiety, and analysis paralysis. And the longer it looms over you, the more stress it causes.

All of this prevents you from living up to your potential.

Procrastination is one of the biggest reasons people stay stuck. So, why do we do it? Why do we procrastinate, especially if we know that it's hindering our progress? Dr. Glove offers a few explanations:

- **Habit**: Many procrastinators get caught up in the comfort habit. They do what is easy. But this rarely leads to success. "We are the most productive when we are in our stretch zone," says Dr. Glover. "Men in particular are happiest when we are challenged. Our goal is to overcome that challenge so we can get back to calm. But we can get addicted to the calm. And our mind just wants to do what's easiest. When we're in comfort mode, everything seems stressful to us, even things like making a phone call or paying a bill."

- **Adult Attention Deficit Disorder**: Many procrastinating men have A.D.D. They can't focus, can't get started, and can't follow through. These men often feel shame because they know they should be able to follow through, but they can't.

- **Depression**: It's extremely difficult to start and finish things when you're in a depressed state. Procrastination is common for people who live with chronic, low-grade depression.

- **The need for approval**: Many men focus on trying to look busy, pleasing the boss, and taking care of everyone else's needs instead of their own. It's easier for them to put out everyone else's fires than it is to challenge themselves.

- **Perfectionism**: Someone once said that "perfect is the enemy of good." Men often procrastinate because they feel the need to do everything perfectly. But perfectionism is nothing if not hazardous and problematic.

- **Overwhelm**: Often our mind tells us that if we start something – especially a big, new, or complex project - not only will we need to do it perfectly, we will need to finish it *now*. So it makes sense to put it off until later - whenever that is.

- **Fear of success**: Many men, especially Nice Guys, procrastinate because they think success will bring negative consequences.

- **Fear in general**: Some tasks require us to face a fear, get out of our comfort zone, or try something new. Fear - particularly of the unknown - can prevent us from doing what most needs to be done.

So, how do you deal with procrastination? How do you stop wasting time and start living up to your potential? Dr. Glover often advises his procrastinating clients to do the following:

- **Write things down**. If there are things that need to be done, write them down. Make a list and keep it in front of you where you will always see it. "If you don't write things down," explains Dr. Glover, "your brain becomes afraid that you'll forget them, which causes anxiety. You have to close the loops."

- **Prioritize**. Once you make a list, put the items in the order they need to be done.

- **Use reminders**. Keep a calendar. Set alerts.

- **Try the Two-Minute Rule**. If you've been putting off a task, try doing just two minutes of it. If you work on it for two minutes, chances are you'll end up working on it for much longer.

- **Create the proper environment**. While this may require some trial and error, it's important to create an environment that is most conducive to your success. Do you prefer silence or light noise? Do you prefer to be alone or around people? Can you rid your environment of distractions? Find out what kind of working environment helps you stay focused and productive.

- **Turn every "Oh no, I have to" into an "Oh boy, I get to!"**

While these suggestions don't offer a cure-all for procrastination, they can help you get out of your head and into your work. "At the end of the day, you can't think your way out of this," asserts Dr. Glover. "You can only act."

---

**INTEGRATED ACTION:**
- ✓ How has procrastination affected your life and career? How has it prevented you from reaching your full potential? Write your answers in your journal.
- ✓ If there is something you need to get done, write it down. Make this a practice.
- ✓ Start prioritizing.
- ✓ How can you create an environment that will allow you to be more productive? Make it happen.
- ✓ Practice turning every "Oh no, I have to" into an "Oh boy, I get to."

---

# TAKE YOUR JOB AND LOVE IT

Countless polls and studies have shown that, across the globe, over 80 percent of people hate their jobs (Incidentally, attornies lead the list of professionals most dissatisfied with their job while dentists have the highest suicide rate). Surprising? No. Sad? Yes.

Many jobs are boring, exhausting, mind-numbing, and unfulfilling (throw in a terrible boss and some repugnant co-workers and they can be downright stomach-churning). I for one can attest to this. Take a look at my résumé and you'll see that over a 15-year period, I held 11 different jobs. All were respectable, full-time, corporate jobs. Not one brought me any measure of joy.

Most people think they only have three options if they are in a less-than-ideal job: (1) stick it out and be miserable, (2) wait for something to change, or (3) leave. But as Dr. Glover insists, there is actually another option: You can change your attitude and behavior. You can change how you show up.

"It's amazing how many situations can change dramatically when a person decides to do something different," says Dr. Glover. "No matter what kind of job you're presently in – a good job that could be better, a temporary job, or a job you just plain hate – I challenge you to challenge yourself to take your job and love it."

# TEN GAME-CHANGERS

Before you hand in your resignation and tell your boss that he (or she) can take your job and shove it, consider trying Dr. Glover's *Ten Game-Changers to Help You Take Your Job and Love it.*[145] At the very least, they'll help you make a good job even better. Or they'll help you make a shitty job…well…a little less shitty.

1. **Own Your Job**. Treat it like it's your own business. Be an entrepreneur. Don't be passive. "Would you slack off, complain, mail it in, if your job was your company?" asks Dr. Glover. "Make an effort to be the BDE – or Best Damn Employee. Taking ownership of a job is a way for you to be the Best Damn Employee. And you don't need your boss's buy-in to start owning your job. If you're going to get fired, it's better to get fired for owning your job instead of for mailing it in."

2. **Turn Every Oh no, I have to into an Oh boy, I get to**. Do this every time you have a sense of dread or frustration at work. This will help you stop being a victim. Because you're not a victim, you're a volunteer. Nobody is forcing you to do your job, no matter how terrible it is. So, stop complaining. "Complaining is a bad habit – it perpetuates the feeling of helplessness and can make any situation toxic," asserts Dr. Glover. "Also, stop listening to others complain. And stop gathering evidence as to how shitty your boss is."

3. **Don't cheat your employer or yourself**. Put in an honest day's work. No more dicking around. No more Facebook, no more Twitter, no more Wikipedia, no more online gaming, no more staring at the fucking wall. Whatever excuse you have for cheating your boss, drop it. And don't cheat yourself, either. Go home on time. Don't answer emails at night. Don't work on the weekends. Most bosses will respect this as long as you don't cheat them.

---

145 Glover, Robert A. "Take Your Job and Love it! Parts 1 & 2" Podcast Audio. www.drglover.com

4. **Educate your boss**. No matter what kind of boss you have, make it part of your job to educate them. Upper-level management often makes messes and then expects frontline employees to clean up. Communicate, have a voice, be honest. Ask for help. Tell them what you need to succeed. Dr. Glover calls this "managing up."

5. **Say 'NO.'** CEOs say 'NO.' Presidents say 'NO.' Vice Presidents say 'NO.' Every successful person knows how to say 'NO.' This is a powerful key to success.

6. **Ask people for help**. This seems to be one of the hardest things for men to do at work, especially Nice Guys. But trying to be needless and wantless turns you into an overworked, underappreciated victim.

7. **Be social**. While this might seem like a contraction to Game-Changer #3, it isn't. Don't fuck off at work. But spend some time building networks and social connections. "Don't be a lone wolf," advises Dr. Glover. "Even if you're surrounded by turkeys or morons. Too much time alone brings out bad habits. You end up taking on too much, you don't get to be part of a team, you don't contribute, and you spend too much time thinking and ruminating and doing nothing. Being social makes every job easier (and generally more enjoyable). You're more likely to give it your all when you feel connected to a team of co-workers."

8. **Fail forward, fail fast**. Reward is won through risk. Be willing to challenge management. If there's an elephant in the room, bring it up. Fail forward, fail fast, and get to rejection quickly. As Dr. Glover asserts, "Nobody ever got ahead or made a difference by being passive, or by going along to get along," .

9. **Make your passion your job or make your job pay for your passion**. Whether you have a job that *is* your passion or that *pays* for your passion, start doing everything with passion. And remember: *What one man can do; another can do*. If you look around and see people doing what you want to do for a living, you can do it, too.

10. **Be a good ender**. For a lot of men, their job is like a toxic relationship. They unconsciously believe they have to put up with shit. Being a good ender opens the door for something better, even if you don't know what that might be.

Consider practicing these ten game-changers for three to six months. Your job will either become tolerable (or good), or it will become glaringly obvious that you're in the wrong place. If you do realize that you're in the wrong place or that your job is toxic, then leave it. Follow your passions. And remember, you live in an abundant world. There's a better opportunity just waiting for you to come and seize it.

---

**INTEGRATED ACTION:**

✓ Write down at least three things you can do this week to start owning your job. These could be things you're going to stop doing, start doing, or do more of. Talk to your boss about your ideas to improve both your performance and the job itself. Do this without attachment to outcome.

✓ Vow to go one week without complaining.

✓ This week, say 'NO' to at least one thing.

✓ Ask someone to do something for you that you can do yourself. Make this a practice.

✓ If you work in an office, start having lunch with people or going to company functions. This week, do one thing to connect with your co-workers.

✓ Where are you risk averse? Where would you like to assert yourself more? Where would you like to be more challenged? What is an idea you'd like to share with your boss? What is something you can do positively to affect the culture of your workplace? What is something you need to share with management that needs to be changed? Write your answers in your journal. Then, schedule a meeting with your boss.

✓ This week, set aside time every single day to do something you're passionate about.

---

# DISCOVER YOUR PASSION(S)

Perhaps you think your life is meaningless because you haven't been able to find your passion. Perhaps you've been racking your brain for months or even years, trying to discover why you were put on this Earth. And perhaps it's really starting to weigh on you.

Understandable.

Self-help influencers in the manosphere like to perpetuate the idea that a man must have one singular passion.

One purpose.

One quest.

One mission.

Otherwise, you're a big, fat loser.

Well, just so you know, that's bullshit.

***Passion does not need to be singular.***

Telling men (and women) that passion is singular only puts a ridiculous amount of pressure on them to identify the sole reason they exist. Then, when they inevitably fail to come up with the answer, they feel even worse, as if they're somehow failing at life.

So, before you do anything, stop beating yourself because you haven't found the one thing that makes you piss rainbows and that takes precedence over all other things.

Again, passion does not need to be singular.

Of course, you might be saying to yourself: *But I'm not passionate about anything. So, even if passion doesn't have to be singular, how the hell do I figure out what I'm passionate about?*

Fair enough. So, here are some practical tips:

**Start paying attention.**

Before I became a full-time coach and entrepreneur, I worked in advertising for nearly 15 years. I hated almost every second of it. But I had no idea what else I could do. Then, I started paying attention.

I started paying attention in my life.

I quickly realized that I was spending much of my free time reading about psychology, self-improvement, and entrepreneurship. I was fascinated by human behavior and relationships. My bookshelf was full of books about happiness and well-being. My internet browser history pointed mostly to articles and blog posts by people like Tim Ferriss, Mark Manson, and Derek Sivers.

These were all clues – clues that had been there all along.

You are awake for most of the day. You are thinking about *something*. Daydreaming about *something*. Talking about *something*. Reading about *something*. Start paying attention. There's a good chance your passions are staring you right in the face.

**Engage in self-inquiry.**

When was the last time you took some time to do nothing but search the depths of your soul?

"Just take some time to be still," recommends Dr. Glover. "And ask yourself: *If I didn't have to pay the bills, if I didn't have to impress anybody, if I didn't care what anybody thought, if I just did what I wanted in life, what would that look like?* You'll probably find some really good clues when you do this."

You can also ask yourself things like:

- *What do I want to do before I die?*
- *What did I love to do when I was a kid?*
- *Whose careers do I envy?*

**Do everything you do with passion.**

What if you were to wake up each day and live a life of passion, no matter what you're doing?

"Consciously brush your teeth with purpose and passion," says Dr. Glover. "Shave your face with purpose and passion. Drive your car with purpose and passion. Do everything you do with purpose and passion, and you'll start becoming a purposeful, passionate person. Living this way will open doors to things that align with your deepest desires."

**INTEGRATED ACTION:**
- ✓ For the next week, start paying attention in your life. Make note of what you spend your time thinking about, talking about, reading about. What clues did you get? Make note of them in your journal.
- ✓ Make a bucket list, if you haven't already. Write down at least 20 things you want to do before you die.
- ✓ Write down the names of at least five people whose careers you envy. Who do you look at and think *I wanna do what that guy does?*
- ✓ Pretend that you call me a year from now and the first thing you say is "Holy shit, my life is amazing!" Then, you begin to tell me all about it. In your journal, write down how you would describe your amazing life. Be as detailed as possible.
- ✓ Commit to doing everything with passion for one week. Write about the experience in your journal.
- ✓ Tell your safe person (or people) that you want to discover your passion(s). Ask them for feedback, guidance, and support. Ask them what skills you have that you may be overlooking. Ask them if they'll brainstorm ideas with you.

# FEAR OF SUCCESS

We tend to assume that men have an overwhelming fear of ~~rejection~~ and failure. And a good lot of them do. It's why they never ask out that woman, or start that business, or ask for that promotion. Often, though, these men don't just have a fear of failure; they also have a fear of success. And as Dr. Glover often points out, *the fear of success represents a paradoxical truth.*

Let's say, for example, that your relationship history is...less than stellar. Maybe you haven't had many healthy relationships. Maybe you just got divorced from a Really Wrong Woman who made your life a living hell. So, you've decided to learn new dating skills that will help you meet a Really Great Woman. You've taken one of Dr. Glover's classes. You've read a shitload of books on dating and attraction. You even went to one of those pickup bootcamps.

And yet, you haven't applied any of the skills you've learned. You aren't challenging yourself whatsoever. You haven't approached any women. You've barely even left the fucking house.

Ring a bell?

"Some people apply principles and new skills with great success," explains Dr. Glover. "But many never get around to even trying, even if they paid to learn those skills. Why is this? Well, it makes perfect sense when you think about it. People often don't try the skills that lead to success because those skills actually work. And that scares the shit out of them."

Why apply the skills that might lead to another relationship when all of your relationships have been toxic and painful? Why apply the skills that might lead to a promotion if it means that everyone will resent you; or worse, find out how incompetent you really are? Why apply the skills that might lead to fame and fortune if you'll just end up losing it all?

"A fear of success is actually quite logical," explains Dr. Glover. "It makes sense for you not to apply skills that might lead to success if you think the fruits of your success will make your life worse than it is right now."

Humans will usually do more to avoid pain than gain pleasure. And many men associate success with a certain degree of pain. Some of the most common fears around success include:

- Establishing a high bar and feeling pressure to keep performing at that level
- Being in the spotlight and under more scrutiny
- Having one's integrity challenged
- Losing it all (which many believe is worse than not having it to begin with)
- Being taken advantage of.
- Being found out or looking foolish.
- Being the subject of envy or resentment.

So, what are your fears around success? Where do you feel stuck or frustrated? Dating? Fitness? Your career?

The thing is, your fears may seem real. In fact, there is a very real possibility that what you most fear may come to pass. If you get good at attracting women, you may very well attract a psycho bitch from hell. If you get that promotion you covet, you'll almost certainly have more demands placed on you. If you launch your startup and then sell it for a hefty chunk of change, you could lose every dime in an economic downturn.

"In many ways, it makes sense to have some of the fears you have – they really could come true," affirms Dr. Glover. "But as you've probably experienced in the past, when you actually faced a big fear, many of the things your brain conjured up never happened or you handled them if they did. Remember: Whatever comes your way, you'll handle it."

# YOU SHALL OVERCOME

There are two primary reasons you may not be experiencing the success you desire: 1) It doesn't match your image of yourself or the world; and 2) You are certain that all the negative things that could happen will happen.

So, why even face your fear around success? Well, consider the following reasons that Dr. Glover offers:

- **The process of facing your fears will actually change your life more than success will.**
- **Facing your fear of success will bless your life.** It will allow you to open your heart and receive all the good things that the world has to offer.
- **Facing your fear of success can bless the lives of those around you.**
- **Facing your fear of success will make you a role model for others.** You may not think your life is out of the ordinary, but when you face your fears, others will look up to you (especially your children, if you have them).
- **Facing your fear of success will help you make the world a better place, just by how you get up each day and live your life.**
- **Facing your fear of success will help you continue to grow and evolve.**
- **Facing your fear of success will help you live up to your potential.**
- **Facing your fear of success will allow you to lie on your deathbed someday and know that you didn't let fear rule your life.**

Now that you know *why* you should face your fear around success, you might be wondering *how*. The following exercise is a good place to start:

Pick an area of your life where you feel stuck, unfulfilled, or frustrated. Ask yourself: *If I were to achieve success in this area, what are some of the worst possible things that could happen to me?* Write these things down in your journal. Then, repeat the exercise for other areas of your life.

As you do this exercise, you may realize that some of your fears are just bullshit fabrications in your mind. You may also realize that some of your fears are a very real possibility.

What if, for example, you experience success in your sex life? After a long sexual drought, you finally meet a beautiful woman and take her to bed. Or maybe you've learned pickup and you're sleeping with multiple women. How many things could go wrong?

- You might get an STD.
- You might not get an erection.
- You might get an erection and promptly lose it.
- You might cum too quickly or not at all.
- She might tell her girlfriends that you suck in bed.
- You might get into a relationship and feel smothered.
- You might have a messy breakup.
- You might get a woman pregnant, which could lead to, well, you know.

It's true. Any of these things could happen. But if you knew you could stay conscious, if you knew that you could apply sound judgment, if you knew that everything is a learning experience, what would change?

You *can* handle whatever happens. And you will grow and evolve as a result.

Ultimately, overcoming your fear of success[146] requires you to change your view of both yourself and the world. It's also about doing something different. So, here are some suggestions for you to take to heart:

**Practice Gratitude.**

Each morning (or each night), write some things for which you feel grateful. Remember, you are already abundantly blessed, but you must ac-

---

146 For more on overcoming a fear of success, see Glover, Robert A. "Podcasts 49-55: Parts 1-7 of a Seven-Part Series on Overcoming the Fear of Success." Podcast Audio. www.drglover.com

knowledge it. "Be aware of how abundantly blessed you are before you are abundantly blessed," says Dr. Glover. "You'll become more open to good things happening in your life. You'll move out of your lizard brain and begin to see the world in a more accurate way."

**Learn to be a good receiver.**

Start by doing good things for yourself. If you can't receive from yourself, how will you receive from other people? Then, try asking a few people to do something for you that you can't do for yourself. Let people give to you, even if it's just a pat on the back.

**Celebrate your successes.**

Nice Guys especially tend to minimize every success. It's like they have fucking amnesia about everything they accomplish. Make a list of every success or accomplishment you've had since childhood.

**Let go of envy and resentment.**

Many men harbor envy and resentment towards those who are more successful. But when you envy other people, your mind is basically saying that those people shouldn't have what they have. So, your mind will say that you shouldn't have that, either. Remember: What is available to others is available to you. And *what one man can do, another can do.*

**Don't compare yourself to anyone.**

Comparison is a cancer.

**Work on your codependency.**

"Codependency is really about managing your anxiety by trying to control the people around you," asserts Dr. Glover. "You might feel some neurotic guilt about making yourself a priority. But taking care of other people and their problems takes up a lot of time and energy and gets in the way of your own success. It diverts your attention from the things you should be focusing on."

**Learn to say 'No.'**

This is one of the most important parts of becoming an Integrated Man. Successful people say 'No.' So, start saying 'No' to things that don't move you in the direction you'd like to go.

**Be a really, really, *really* good ender.**

In addition to saying 'No,' successful people know when to walk away. Being in a bad relationship will delay you from finding a good one. The same goes for a bad job. You can get out of situations that don't serve you. You're never stuck.

**Stop saying "I can't."**

Because you *can*. Recognize and challenge the bullshit your mind tells you.

---

**INTEGRATED ACTION:**
- ✓ In what area of your life do you feel most stuck? What is the payoff of being stuck in this area? What would change if you were to get unstuck? Who else might be affected? How might they respond? Write your answers in your journal.
- ✓ How's that Gratitude Practice coming along?
- ✓ In your journal, write down examples of how you seem to sabotage yourself. Self-sabotage is the result of unconscious fear.
- ✓ What are your distractions? What things do you get sucked into that don't lead to success? Do you get distracted by other peoples' drama, demands at work, or trivial household chores? Do you constantly engage in junk-food behavior, like video games, watching porn, or binge eating? Write your answers in your journal.
- ✓ Make a vision board. Look at it every day.
- ✓ At least one day this week, have an adventure. Get out of your house, expand your route, linger in public, talk to people everywhere you go, test for interest, and walk through the open doors.
- ✓ Check in with your safe person (or people).

# PART IX: HAPPINESS & WELL-BEING

*Letting go gives us freedom, and freedom*
*is the only condition for happiness. If, in*
*our heart, we still cling to anything – anger,*
*anxiety, or possessions – we cannot be free.*
**– Thich Nhat Hanh**

"Maybe you should stop doing shit that makes you unhappy."

Those were the first words Dr. Glover ever said to me.

According to Dr. Glover's stopwatch, I had just raved and ranted for more than seven minutes – at least a minute longer than the time I was given. It was a swirling tornado of emotional vomit, an out-and-out assault, a rapid-fire stream of complaints and grievances about life and love and heartbreak and misery and women and work and a seemingly wasted existence. It was angry and pitiful and kind of poetic all at the same time. It was also how I introduced myself to the 11 other men at Dr. Glover's summer workshop in Seattle.

"Honestly, I'm fucking exhausted just from listening to you," admitted Dr. Glover. "What about everyone else?"

The other men nodded in agreement.

"I know we're just getting to know each other, Tony. And I'm glad you're here. We're all glad you're here. But I'm going to bring out the big stick right now. You've been playing the victim in every part of your life. But ultimately, you get to choose. You've been doing shit that makes you unhappy for so long, and you get to choose if you want to start doing something different. I can see that you let your constantly spinning mind, and your fear, and your self-limiting beliefs control you. And we'll work on that. But for the love of God, you're not going to be happy until you stop doing shit that makes you *un*happy."

"You're right," I admitted, with a sigh.

"I know," offered a grinning Dr. Glover. "So, welcome to Seattle. It's going to be a great weekend."

Indeed, Dr. Glover was right – about me, and about that weekend. But his words also led me to discover what seems to be a widely ignored and distinctly sad truth about us humans: We spend our lives trying desperately to find happiness and yet, we don't even know what it is. We can't explain, describe, or define it; we just know that we want it because it'll make everything peachy. Time and time again, though, studies have shown that our never-ending quest for happiness is quite often the very thing that fucks us up. Instead of trying to find happiness, it makes far more sense to take stock of your life and get rid of what (or who) is making you miserable.

Of course, if you're anything like me, what makes you the most miserable is right between your ears. Your mind presents you with negative views of yourself and your place in the world. Your mind digs up evidence to support your flawed beliefs. Your mind is your biggest critic when it should be your staunchest ally. Your mind is a lying fucking asshole. And it keeps you from being happy.

While Dr. Glover has helped droves of men abolish their Nice Guy Syndrome, improve their dating skills, and strengthen their relationships, I believe his greatest contribution lies in helping these men get their minds out of the muck, allowing them to finally experience some form of the happiness they've been seeking. For many men, Dr. Glover's work provides much needed relief. His popular online course, *The Ruminating Brain*, in particular, has helped thousands of men find freedom from their psychological angst.

Dr. Glover himself is quite often a light for those trying to plod through darkness. He is almost annoyingly cool and collected. He is bursting with gratitude. He radiates joy. He has a go-with-the-flow, keep-calm-and-carry-on kind of energy – the kind you wish you could somehow bottle and drink and permanently absorb. It's like he's always just gotten up from the world's most glorious nap.

Certainly, Dr. Glover is able to maintain a desirable level of happiness because he practices what he preaches. And what he preaches are practices – simple, easily implementable habits and thought processes that can positively impact the quality of your life. You'll learn these things and more in the pages that follow. So, get comfortable and find your happy place. If you don't have a happy place, chances are you will by the end of this section.

# REPARENTING

Any self-improvement journey, but particularly the journey from Nice Guy to Integrated Man, requires change. Usually, it requires you to reprogram your mind. It also requires you to *reparent* yourself due to the inaccurate beliefs you internalized during childhood.

You can start internalizing new beliefs with **Dr. Glover's Reparenting Visualization**[147] (Download the audio version at www.bigstickbook.com):

Go somewhere quiet, free of distraction. Rest comfortably on a chair, couch, or bed. Get settled.

Breathe in slowly and deeply from your belly, and then slowly exhale.

With each breath, feel the tension slip from your body.

Focus on your breath as it enters and leaves your body.

As you feel yourself beginning to relax, flex and release each muscle group in your body. Start at the top of your body and work down to your feet.

Flex and release your facial muscles.

And then your jaw.

Flex and release your neck muscles.

And then your shoulders.

Move down to your chest and upper back. Flexing, holding, and releasing.

---

147 Glover, Robert A. "Podcast 142: A Reparenting Visualization." Podcast Audio. www.drglover.com

Do the same with your belly muscles.

Now, flex and release your upper arms, biceps, and triceps.

Now, do your lower arms and your hands.

Flex and release your buttocks and your upper legs.

Now, move down to your toes, flexing and releasing.

Allow all the tension to gently flow out of your body.

Out of your fingers and your toes.

Now, listen to the sounds around you. Allow them to become background noise that relaxes you even further.

Continue to observe your breathing. Relaxing even deeper.

For a few moments now, picture yourself resting in a supremely calm and relaxing environment.

It might be a white sandy beach in the Caribbean.

Or next to a crackling fire in a mountain cabin.

Or near a gentle stream in a beautiful meadow.

For a few moments go fully into this special place you've chosen.

Feel the feelings.

Hear the sounds.

Smell the smells.

Observe your surroundings.

Allow yourself to just drift...into pleasant relaxation.

If thoughts enter your mind...just notice them and let them pass.

Bring your attention back to your breathing each time your mind wanders.

Let go of all judgment.

With each breath, let your body sink deeper into relaxation.

As you relax, visualize the following scenario:

*You are a young child, perhaps four or five years old.*

*You are in front of the first house that you remember living in.*

*Walk up the sidewalk to the front door, and walk in.*

*Stand for a moment just inside the front door and notice all the familiar surroundings of your childhood home.*

*As you look around the room, visualize your mother and father sitting next to each other on the couch. They are holding hands and talking. They obviously love each other. They are happy to be together.*

*When your mother and father see you, they smile and invite you to come join them. They both hug you and give you a kiss.*

*You climb onto your father's lap. You feel your father's strength. You see the love in your mother's eyes. You can feel how much both of your parents love you.*

*Your father asks if you'd like to go to the park and have a picnic.*

*You all jump up and get ready.*

*As a family you drive to the park.*

*When you get there, your mother sets down the picnic basket and spreads out the food she has prepared on a blanket.*

*The sun is shining*

*The sky is blue.*

*The air is warm with a gentle cooling breeze.*

*Feel the warmth of the sun on your back.*

*Notice how green the grass is*

*Notice how blue the sky is*

*Notice a few wispy clouds floating by overhead.*

*As you sit on the blanket with your parents....*

*Everyone eats and laughs and has a wonderful time.*

*After lunch, your mother kisses you on the cheek and tells you to go play with your dad.*

*You and your dad play catch with a football, tossing it back and forth between you.*

*Your mother watches, smiling while looking up from a book that she's reading.*

*You throw the ball to your father, and then you try to tackle him by grabbing him by the leg. He playfully drags you along and then tumbles to the ground.*

*You climb on top of your dad and wrestle him, joyfully.*

*After wrestling and laughing for a few minutes, your father picks you up and gives you a piggyback ride back to where your mother is sitting on the blanket.*

*When it's time to leave, you help your mom and dad pack the car.*

*Your parents take you home and help you get ready for bed.*

*They tuck you in and give you a hug and a kiss on the cheek.*

*Then your mom sits on the bed and reads you a short story as you drift off to sleep with a smile on your face.*

*As you fall asleep, your mother closes the book and kisses you on the forehead.*

*You fall asleep, happy and secure.*

*You know you are loved and protected.*

*You know that your needs will always be met.*

*You believe that the world is a place filled with love and abundance.*

*You feel safe and confident.*

*Let these feelings and beliefs sink in.*

*If your mind resists, just smile and observe the resistance.*

Each time you do this visualization, your mind will allow more and more of these good feelings into both your conscious and unconscious mind. You'll slowly begin to see the world as an abundant place. You'll begin to act with more confidence and less fear.

Now, stretch.

And go about your day.

# TOXIC SHAME &
# TOXIC PERFECTIONISM

I t's easy to see why so many men - particularly Nice Guys - rarely experience the happiness they desire. As you've learned, Nice Guys harbor a great deal of toxic shame. They believe they are not okay just as they are. To make matters worse, they think they have to do everything right. This is toxic perfectionism (in perhaps its evilest form).

But even if you don't identify as a classic Nice Guy, you probably still have some degree of both toxic shame and toxic perfectionism. You're human, after all. And you may not always be conscious of your toxic shame or toxic perfectionism. Remember, these things develop early in childhood. Every child develops mechanisms that (1) help him manage the pain caused by whatever he's experienced; and (2) will hopefully prevent similar painful events from happening in the future.

In truth, the best way to mitigate your toxic shame and toxic perfectionism is to **test your assumptions.** If you believe you are undesirable, if you believe you need to be perfect, then start taking proper action to determine whether or not your assumptions are true. Maybe, for example, you don't think a beautiful woman could ever find you attractive. Well, there is only one way to know for sure if your assumption is accurate, or if it's just your mind feeding you a load of bullshit.

No man feels 100 percent confident 100 percent of the time. And no man is completely free of insecurities. We all have insecurities. We all have demons. We all have flaws. Nobody is perfect. And yet, men often think they need to be perfect, particularly when seeking validation from others.

This coupling of toxic shame and toxic perfectionism is a deep, core issue for a lot of men (and women). It creates unnecessary suffering and anxiety. It leads to keeping others at arm's length. And it causes men to refrain from taking action in situations where failure is even a remote possibility.

Many men carry their toxic shame and toxic perfectionism from childhood into adulthood, only to see negative experiences as cold, hard proof that something is wrong with them, that they are defective and unlovable. Consequently, these men typically give up and do nothing. They don't put themselves out there. They don't go after the job they want. They never start that business. They never approach that beautiful woman.

Is it possible to become *completely* free of toxic shame and toxic perfectionism? Probably not. It's likely that your toxic shame and toxic perfectionism will always be with you, lurking in the back of your subconscious. But you can learn to effectively manage these afflictions. You can learn to live with them and do what you want despite them. So, test your assumptions. And make an effort to do the following:

- **Reveal yourself to safe people**. "This cannot be overstated," asserts Dr. Glover. "You cannot do this work alone. The men who stay the most stuck are the ones who keep trying to work on their issues all by themselves. Work with a coach, join a men's group, attend a 12-step program. Then, reveal yourself. And only reveal yourself to people who are non-judgmental and accepting. If it scares you to reveal yourself to safe people, that's all the more reason to do it."

- **Journal**. Write things down about you. This allows you to be completely open and honest with yourself. Write down your fears, your secrets, your desires. Bring them up into consciousness. Then, reveal these things to your safe people. Keep writing, keep revealing. Eventually, your shame will start to diminish.

- **Stop comparing yourself to others, for good or for bad**. Remember, comparison is a cancer. "The most unhappy men I know are those who have a strong tendency to compare themselves to others," shares Dr. Glover. "When you catch yourself comparing, don't judge yourself for it. Just let it go."

- **Show yourself the same compassion you have for your closest friends**. We're usually much harder on ourselves than we are on our friends. Practice asking yourself: *If my best friend behaved the same way, had the same trait, possessed the same characteristics, would I be as hard on them as I am on myself?*

- **Lighten up and laugh**. We all have flaws, we all have judgments, we all have neuroses, and we all make mistakes. "Be playful about your shortcomings," recommends Dr. Glover. "Exaggerate them. Let's not take ourselves too seriously."

- **Put yourself in situations where you will feel vulnerable**. Too many men avoid this altogether. But how are you supposed to grow if you never experience discomfort? Go do things that you can't do perfectly. Take a class. Learn a new skill. Pick up a new hobby. Make this a regular part of your life.

- **Never defend yourself**. Own your beliefs and your values. Own who you are. "Every time you defend yourself, you are trying to take the spotlight off a perceived imperfection in yourself," explains Dr. Glover. "Defending yourself makes you feel powerless. It also causes you to keep your walls up and hide your flaws."

- **Do not hang out with toxic people**. Surround yourself with loving, supportive, positive people. Toxic people feed your shame. Cut them out of your life. Make no exceptions.

- **Ask your friends what they believe are your best qualities**. And ask them what they like about you. When they tell you, let it soak in. Let it wash over you. Observe your brain trying to deny it.

Take these suggestions to heart, and you'll begin to see yourself – and the world – differently. You'll worry less and smile more. You'll notice that your old, flawed beliefs take a backseat to new, healthier beliefs. You'll no longer let toxic shame and toxic perfectionism[148] keep you from living the life that you want.

---

**INTEGRATED ACTION:**

✓ Do you have toxic shame? Do you believe you need to do every-thing right? How does your toxic shame and/or toxic perfec-tionism manifest in your life? Write your answers in your journal.

✓ If you could be totally okay with the fact that not everyone is going to like you, how would your behavior change? Write your answer in your journal.

✓ Write down at least 20 reasons why you're fucking awesome. Keep this list handy and review it often.

✓ Choose two items from the list of practices that can help you manage your toxic shame and toxic perfectionism. Implement them into your life this week.

✓ Hopefully, you have at least one safe person by now. If you don't, it's time to find one. If you're having trouble, Dr. Glover has several certified No More Mr. Nice Guy coaches, many of whom offer free introductory calls. This is a great place to start.

---

148 Toxic Shame and Toxic Perfectionism are core components of the Nice Guy Syndrome, and Dr. Glover discusses them frequently in his work. Toxic Shame is mentioned throughout *No More Mr. Nice Guy* (Running Press, 2013). Additionally, see Glover, Robert A. "Podcasts 42-46: Parts 1-5 of a Five-Part Series on Overcoming Toxic Perfectionism."

# ANXIETY

Feeling a little anxious?

Or *really* anxious?

I know the feeling.

But I also know that it's possible to *soothe* your anxiety.

Too many men live in a constant state of anxiety, always thinking that something is about to go wrong. Many of these men are endlessly searching for the exact right combination of beliefs, behaviors, and thought processes to keep their lives problem-free. But this is what Dr. Glover calls *child-like, magical thinking.*

> **HARSH TRUTH:**
>
> The world is far from problem-free. It is through challenge, chaos, and difficulty that we grow as a species and as individuals.

We must learn to face challenges head on, particularly as men. This is how we evolve. But people with anxiety issues see challenge as something that needs to be avoided, even if they're not conscious of what that challenge might be.

If you suffer from anxiety, your beliefs and behaviors likely grew out of childhood situations in which you did not feel safe. You developed your defense mechanisms to prevent bad things from happening. But now that you're an adult, these defense mechanisms manifest as niceness and perfectionism.

> **ANOTHER HARSH TRUTH:**
>
> Not everyone is going to like you. But believing that everyone should like you keeps you in a state of anxiety. And you will never do everything perfectly. But trying to do everything perfectly also keeps you in a state of anxiety. It's just one big, vicious cycle.

Most men do not like feeling anxious. They'll do anything to avoid the feeling. But as Dr. Glover often points out, anxiety can actually be a good thing.

"Anxiety serves a healthy purpose," says Dr, Glover. "It's like an alarm clock that wakes you up and warns you of a possible danger or threat. But once the alarm clock goes off, you don't need it to keep ringing throughout the day. Unfortunately, this is what anxiety is like for many men, especially Nice Guys. The alarm clock just keeps going off, all fucking day."

Much of the anxiety we experience we create in our heads. We get into seemingly unstoppable mental loops and obsess over threats that usually aren't even real.

"It's emotionally and physically exhausting to stay in the part of your brain that is constantly worrying about things that may or may not happen," adds Dr. Glover. "We have to learn to stop the looping and learn to soothe ourselves instead"

## THE CLOSEST THING TO MAGIC

If there is one practice that has helped me learn to stop the looping in my mind and soothe my anxiety, it is undoubtedly the **Obsess Appointment**, which Dr. Glover describes in *The Ruminating Brain* as "the closest thing to magic."

An Obsess Appointment can help you break a pattern of obsessive thinking, and all it requires is the following:

✓ Find a quiet place where you won't be disturbed. Get comfortable and set a timer for ten minutes.

✓ Close your eyes and *consciously* obsess about the thing you've been *unconsciously* obsessing about. Try doing this for ten minutes. Again, do this *consciously*. "You've probably been unconsciously obsessing about this thing for days, weeks, months, even years," explains Dr. Glover. "And you've been doing it 24/7. But again, you've been doing it unconsciously. An Obsess Appointment requires you to do it consciously. And do it without an agenda."

✓ When your timer goes off, relax, stretch, and then continue your day. If at some point you start obsessing again, remind yourself (and your brain) that you've already had an Obsess Appointment. You can commit to having another Obsess Appointment later in the day if you need to.

An Obsess Appointment forces you to move your obsession from your limbic system to your prefrontal cortex, from your unconscious mind to your conscious mind. When you do this, you will discover that it's actually quite difficult to *consciously* obsess about something for even just ten minutes. You will also notice that answers, solutions, and remedies start coming to you rather quickly.

"When you do an obsess appointment," says Dr. Glover, "you get to become the master of your mind instead of letting your mind master you. Just make sure that if you promise your mind that you'll have another obsess appointment, you'll keep that promise. Your mind won't trust you if you don't keep your word."

## POSITIVELY NEGATIVE

While we can thank Dr. Glover for the Obsess Appointment, there is one other technique that I have found remarkably effective for soothing anxiety and breaking a mental loop. It's called Negative Visualization, and for this we must thank the ancient Stoic philosophers. Are you there, Marcus Aurelius?[149]

Negative Visualization involves actually visualizing negative outcomes and worst-case scenarios. It's a technique that dates back many thousand of years, and it was used by Stoicism's most prominent figures like Aurelius and Seneca. While Negative Visualization may sound like an exercise in fucking torturing yourself, it most decidedly is not. There is great value in visualizing the negative.

Negative Visualization allows you to appreciate what you have. It forces you to be honest with yourself so you can understand possible negative outcomes. And ultimately, it helps you realize that those negative outcomes aren't so bad.

What if you lost your job?

Well, surely you wouldn't die. So, what's the worst that could happen? How would you handle it?

"Use Negative Visualization to ground yourself," suggests Dr. Glover. "Run through the different outcomes you might face. Come to terms with your fears. We often build up our fears to the point that they are larger than life and almost unbearable. Confronting your fears can help you overcome them."

---

**INTEGRATED ACTION:**
- ✓ Do you suffer from anxiety? Do you constantly feel like something will go wrong? Expand on this feeling in your journal. Don't think, just write.
- ✓ How might your behavior change if you saw challenge as an opportunity to grow? Write your answer in your journal.
- ✓ Try doing an obsess appointment.
- ✓ Use Negative Visualization to confront one of your fears.

---

149 If you're unfamiliar with Stoicism, Marcus Aurelius was Roman emperor from 161 to 180 CE and a stoic philosopher. He is the author of the philosophical work *Meditations*.

# GUILT

When I began working with Dr. Glover to abolish my Nice Guy Syndrome – which required me to learn new behaviors and adopt new thought processes - I felt a tremendous amount of guilt, as though I was doing something wrong. I've since noticed that many of my clients have experienced the same feeling. Recovering Nice Guys in particular seem to be ceaselessly plagued by guilt.

Foremost, it helps to know that there are two kinds of guilt:

- **Healthy Guilt** is just that. It's healthy. And it's rational. It's the feeling you get when you know you have done something wrong or when you know you have truly hurt someone. Healthy guilt is important: When you experience healthy guilt, it means you have a conscience. It means you have empathy. It means you're not a fucking sociopath.

- **Unhealthy Guilt**, on the other hand, is what results from telling yourself you've done something wrong when you haven't done anything wrong at all. Unhealthy guilt is also known as *Neurotic* Guilt.

If you feel guilty for making positive changes in your life, you are experiencing Unhealthy – or *Neurotic* – Guilt.

Recovering Nice Guys experience so much Unhealthy Guilt because, well, they're Nice Guys. Becoming Integrated requires them to stop pleasing others all the time and start doing things for themselves. But Nice Guys have been doing their Nice Guy bullshit for so long that once they stop, they think it's hurtful to others.

If someone feels hurt because you're doing what *you* want instead of what *they* want, that's their problem. Not yours. You are not doing anything wrong by becoming Integrated and working to improve your life.

There is no reason to feel guilty for:

- Making your own needs a priority
- Embracing your masculinity
- Healthily expressing your sexuality
- Doing nice things for yourself
- Setting boundaries
- Setting goals and accomplishing them

So, be mindful of the way you are feeling. Guilt can stand in the way of your happiness and well-being. Learn to check your guilt and ask yourself:

✓ *Am I actually doing anything wrong here?*

✓ *Am I acting in accordance with my values?*

✓ *Am I intentionally doing this to harm others?*

Should you come to the conclusion that your guilt is rational, then own up to your behavior. Apologize, make amends, and move on. Odds are, though, your guilt is irrational, unhealthy, and neurotic. If you're simply not sure, talk about your guilt with safe people. They will happily confirm what kind of guilt it is.

# WHEN THE CIRCUS COMES TO TOWN

Dr. Glover likes to borrow a simple line of questioning from spiritual teacher and author, Byron Katie, to help Nice Guys separate out the issues causing their guilt:

*Is this my problem, their problem, or God's problem?*

"There's something about pausing and asking this question that helps you intuitively get to the bottom of whatever kind of guilt you are feeling," affirms Dr. Glover. "If the issue triggering your guilt truly is *your* problem, address it. If it is someone else's problem, let them find their own resolution. If it is God's problem, for God's sake, let it fucking go! As my beautiful, savvy, Mexican wife likes to say: *No es mi circo, no son mis changos* -  which means: Not my circus, not my monkeys."

---

**INTEGRATED ACTION:**

✓ Do you live with constant guilt? Is it healthy guilt or neurotic guilt? Write about your guilt in your journal.

✓ Can you accept that you're not doing anything wrong by working on yourself and learning to become more Integrated? Write your answer in your journal.

✓ Talk to your safe person (or people) about your guilt. Ask for feedback on what kind of guilt you might be experiencing.

---

# YOUR RUMINATING BRAIN

Does your mind beat you up?

Does it make you feel bad about yourself?

Does it degrade you?

Does it constantly remind you of your failures?

Bring up past mistakes?

Recall missed opportunities?

Does it compare you negatively to everyone you see, every single day?

Does it call you a loser?

Does it judge you every time you look in the mirror?

Does it constantly spin, giving you new things to worry about all time?

Does it make you nervous about the future? Tell you that you'll never succeed?

Does it make you angry?

Does it make you feel bad for being angry?

Does it make you feel bad for feeling bad for being angry?

Does it make you feel bad for feeling bad for feeling bad for being angry?

Do you wish you could just tell your mind to shut the fuck up?

Well, congratulations. You've got a ***Ruminating Brain***.

Some call it a Monkey Mind. Or a Wandering Mind. Neuroscientists call it the Default Mode Network (DMN). Dr. Glover, of course, calls it *the Ruminating Brain*. You can call it what you want. But a monkey mind is often an unhappy mind, and a lot of us wish we could just fucking turn it down a smidge.

By now, you should know that your mind is a liar, and that your mind believes everything it tells itself is true. And certainly, *everyone* has a brain that beats them up from time to time. But someone with a Ruminating Brain – a brain that spins 24 fucking 7 – is more likely to suffer from depression, anxiety, loneliness, addiction, procrastination, fear of abandonment, and a whole host of other issues. Nice Guys in particular seem to be the not-so-proud owners of Ruminating Brains.

If you have a Ruminating Brain, I can relate. In fact, Dr. Glover has frequently called me the Poster Boy for Ruminating Brain.

So, with that distinction, I'd like to officially deliver you some good news: You're not defective. You're not unlovable. There's actually nothing wrong with you. You just happen to have a Ruminating Brain, and you believe all the bullshit that it conjures up.

For many men (and women) who have a Ruminating Brain, the remedy is merely **acceptance**. I've seen several men make an impressive turnaround by simply *accepting* that they have a Ruminating Brain, and that having a

Ruminating Brain doesn't mean they're fucked up. It's likely just something they inherited. (Thanks mom and dad!)

Of course, acceptance on its own is hardly a panacea. Most ruminators need additional tools and practices to help them deal with their Ruminating Brains. Perhaps the most effective of these practices is Mindfulness. Learn how to *stop, slow down, breathe, be still, notice your surroundings, and observe your thoughts without judgment.* After all, your thoughts are just thoughts. Learn to be the *observer* of your thoughts, not the *believer* of them.

You also need support systems. By now, you should know how vital it is to have safe people in your life.

"Having those safe people to whom you can reveal yourself is key when you have a Ruminating Brain," explains Dr. Glover. "These people will give you the support you need to realize that even though your brain might have a bit of a programming flaw, you don't. They will help you sort out the noise in your head. They will keep you on track as you develop a new roadmap for living. And they will reveal their own rumination patterns, so you know that you aren't alone."

Ruminators must get out of their heads and into their bodies and lives. Daily rituals - beginning with mindfulness – can help you do this. At least once a day, make it a point to *stop, slow down, breathe, be still, notice your surroundings, and observe your thoughts without judgment.* Beyond that, anything that puts you in a flow state can help put an end to your rumination. Examples include:

- Listening to or playing music
- Journaling
- Dancing
- Singing
- Painting
- Exercising
- Doing yoga
- Spending time in nature

To further understand a Ruminating Brain, take a look at a rumination cycle, as presented by Dr. Glover in *The Ruminating Brain.*

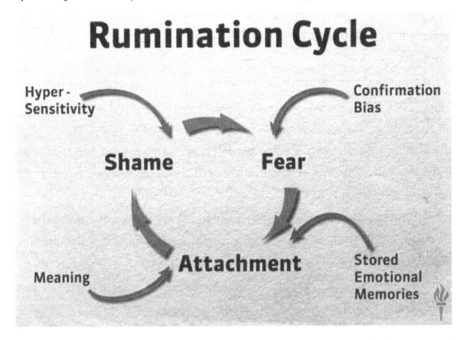

"A rumination cycle is triggered by emotional distress, which is caused by a perceived imminent issue or event, or thoughts about a recent or future issue or event," explains Dr. Glover. "A combination of fear, shame, and/or attachment to outcome can trigger a rumination cycle. And rumination creates the illusion that you're seeking a resolution to the emotional distress caused by the subject of the rumination."

A rumination cycle is generally fueled by stored emotional memories and the meanings we've attached to those memories. Hypersensitivity and confirmation bias also play a role. Furthermore, rumination can significantly amplify the fear, shame, or attachment to outcome that triggered the rumination in the first place. This just causes the subject of the rumination to feel even more threatening. It's yet another vicious cycle.

"Almost anything in life can trigger a rumination cycle," adds Dr. Glover. "Sometimes it's a real event – like getting laid off from a job, or a break-up, or receiving a negative diagnosis from a doctor. But usually it's old emotions, mental habits, or just plain boredom that triggers a rumination cycle. In fact, for a lot of men – particularly Nice Guys – their worst ruminations are triggered when everything is great and they're just waiting for the other shoe to drop."

If you are the unfortunate inheritor of a ruminating brain and you find yourself in a rumination cycle, remember: It's just your mind spinning. That's all. Remember to *stop, slow down, be still, breathe, notice your surroundings, and observe your thoughts*. Remember to get out of your head and into your body and your life. And remember to use the aforementioned mantra, *I'll handle it*.

Behind nearly every rumination is the fear that you won't be able to handle the situation about which you are ruminating. But what if you knew you could handle it? You've handled everything else in your life up to this point, right? So, ask yourself, *What am I really afraid of here?* And then say, *I'll handle it. No matter what happens, I'll handle it.*

Because you will.[150]

---

**INTEGRATED ACTION:**
- ✓ Do you have a Ruminating Brain? Write about it in your journal. Don't think, just write. Write about your rumination patterns. Write about how having a Ruminating Brain has affected your life.
- ✓ How would you feel if you knew that no matter what happens, you could handle it? Write your answer in your journal.
- ✓ Practice combating your Ruminating Brain by observing your thoughts instead of believing them. *Stop, slow down, be still, breathe, notice your surroundings, and observe.* Don't judge, just observe.
- ✓ Choose one ritual to help you get out of your head and into your body. Do it every day this week.

---

150 Glover, Robert A. *The Ruminating Brain* (TPI University. www.drglover.com)

# BEING THE (NON-JUDGMENTAL) OBSERVER OF SELF

At the risk of sounding like a broken record, the biggest obstacle standing between you and happiness is probably your own damn brain. Your brain is what makes you feel bad; and it's what makes you feel bad about yourself. (The same applies to every other human on the planet.)

The language that you use with yourself has great power. So, if you want to experience happiness and emotional well-being, learn to become the **non-judgmental observer of self**. This is a core principle of self-help, and well-recognized as an essential skill for personal growth. What we're really talking about, though, is *consciousness*.

The human brain allows us to be conscious of the fact that we are in fact human. We can observe our feelings, distortions, beliefs, and actions. We can actually observe our subconscious. We can have thoughts…about our thoughts. We can have thoughts about our thoughts about our thoughts. We can even have thoughts about our th…ok, you get the point.

In his wildly bestselling book, *The Power of Now*, spiritual teacher Eckhart Tolle defines consciousness as just being the observer of yourself. But as Dr. Glover points out, it gets much more interesting when you can be the *non-judgmental* observer of yourself.

"This is incredibly powerful," affirms Dr. Glover. "Most of us are highly self-critical, have a deep sense of shame, and spend a shitload of time in our lizard brains, worrying and feeling guilty. Most of us hate seeing the dark side of ourselves. But being the non-judgmental observer of self allows you to simply observe yourself without being critical."

When you're acting as the non-judgmental observer of self, you're just noticing.

If you're worried, you're saying, *Hmm, I'm worried.*

If you're anxious, you're saying, *Hmm, I'm anxious.*

If you're angry, you're saying, *Hmm, I'm angry.*

And you're doing this without judgment.

Again, you're just noticing.

"There's an amusing paradox here," explains Dr. Glover. "When you're being the non-judgmental observer of yourself and you do have judgment, you have to try to not be judgmental of the fact that you're being judgmental."

Dr. Glover frequently shares that he once had a tendency to be highly judgmental of others. He ruthlessly picked apart almost everyone he'd see. But Dr. Glover didn't like this aspect of himself. So, he decided that he was simply going to stop being judgmental. Unsurprisingly, this didn't work.

"I was still judgmental," acknowledges Dr. Glover. "Then I would get angry at myself for being judgmental. I was judgmental of myself for being judgmental. It was a terrible loop. So, I just started observing myself. I started observing myself being judgmental *without* judgment."

When you are the non-judgmental observer of your own mind, you can just smile at yourself. If you're judgmental, you can't really change anything that you're judging, anyway - even if it's about you. This is why so many men are stuck. They repeatedly judge their perceived flaws and imperfections. At the same time, they try to hide them.

"If you want to change," explains Dr. Glover, "you have to learn to be a non-judgmental observer. Being a non-judgmental observer changes both the observer and the observed. In other words, you may hate that you're too fat, or too anxious, or too much in debt. But as long as you *hate* these things, as long as you judge yourself for them, nothing will change. You won't actually be more aware. So, when things like this come up, observe them, and ask yourself if there's something you can do to change.[151]"

The more you can be the non-judgmental observer of yourself, the more you can love yourself. It also expands your ability to love others and let others love you.

## BUT WAIT, THERE'S MORE

In addition to being non-judgmental, you must also be *non-resistant*, which can be just as challenging. *What you resist, persists.* And the things you are resisting (and hating) will probably just keep manifesting. That is, unless you can be non-judgmental and non-resistant.

You must relax and accept what is. This opens you up to new ways of thinking about a problem. When you're confronted with a problem and experience resistance, just breathe and welcome it in. Remind yourself that you've handled similar problems in the past.

As Dr. Glover illustrates, being the non-judgmental, *non-resistant* observer of self allows you to:

- Learn from your mistakes
- Become aware of when you're living in the past or future
- Live more in the moment
- Make more conscious decisions to get of your comfort zone
- Forgive
- Love yourself and accept love from others

Perhaps you are now thinking: *If I don't judge myself – if I accept myself just as I am – why would I work to make changes in my life?*

---

151 Glover, Robert A. "Podcast 156: Becoming the Non-Judgmental Observer of Self." Podcast Audio. www.drglover.com

Well, you can accept yourself as you are and where you are, and still make conscious decisions to progress as a human being. Because you want to. Because you choose to. Because, hopefully, you love growing and evolving.

> **INTEGRATED ACTION:**
> ✓ Practice being the non-judgmental, non-resistant observer of self. Whatever you're feeling, just notice it.
> ✓ Have you been judging yourself? What is it about yourself that you would you like to change? Write your answers in your journal.
> ✓ Talk to your safe person (or people) about your judgments.

# BEING YOUR AUTHENTIC SELF

Going through significant growth and transformation requires you to replace your old paradigms with completely new paradigms. It requires you to shift how you think, how you feel, how you view yourself, how you view others, and how you view the world. This is neither a quick nor easy process.

Even if you have a new roadmap to guide you (like *No More Mr. Nice Guy*, for example), none of it is instinctual. You might have questions, concerns, and doubts. Lots of them. You might struggle to adopt new behaviors or try on new ways of thinking. You might be reluctant to change. And that's okay; it's natural. Your mind prizes the familiar, and it will cling to its old way of operating. Your mind doesn't want to reinvent itself.

Unfortunately, many men make their progress even more difficult because they tend to overthink...***everything.*** Especially Nice Guys. Something as simple and as commonplace as holding the door open for someone can create all sorts of psychological riddles:

*Did I do that out of the goodness of my heart? Or were there strings attached?*

*Was I expecting something in return?*

*Was I seeking approval?*

*I was just being a decent human, wasn't I?*

*What's wrong with being nice?*

*What's wrong with helping people?*

*What's wrong with not being angry all the time?*

*Am I supposed to be a dick?*

*What's wrong with trying to get along with people?*

Making any major philosophical or psychological change will fill you with questions. But recovery from the Nice Guy Syndrome seems to be a distinctly special challenge for those working through the process. Again, Nice Guys tend to overthink *everything*. And they tend to see most things in black and white.

"A lot of men get confused and overwhelmed when trying to overcome the Nice Guy Syndrome or become more Integrated," says Dr. Glover. "This is because healthy, Integrated behaviors can look similar or even identical to toxic, codependent, Nice Guy behaviors. Often, the only difference is the agenda behind them. Holding a door open for someone is great. Holding a door open for someone and then getting angry because you didn't get anything in return…that's not so great."

Ultimately, what men are really trying to figure out when working to become more Integrated is: ***How do I become my authentic self? And how do I know when I'm being my authentic self?*** After all, becoming an Integrated Man means being your authentic self, accepting yourself, loving yourself, and making your needs a priority.

"You have to consider that you've probably been living most of your life based on what you believe others want you to be," asserts Dr. Glover. "As children, we needed external validation to establish a sense of self. This came from our parents meeting our needs in a timely and judicious way. Your parents may have told you they loved you, but that doesn't really do anything. They had to *act* as though they loved you. Now that you're an adult, if you constantly seek love and external validation, it causes you to lose your authentic self."

Learn to observe yourself when you're seeking external validation. Then, you can validate yourself through **Integrated Action**, which might include things like exercising, journaling, paying your bills, meditating, or completing a task you've been putting off. You must also stay *differentiated*, which is a vital part of learning to please yourself instead of others.

Remember, differentiation requires you to ask yourself:

*What do I want?*

*What feels right to me?*

*What would make me happy?*

Then, you must hold on to yourself and do what you want, do what feels right, do what makes you happy, even in the face of internal or external pressure.

Sadly, differentiation isn't appreciated in many cultures. Bear in mind, for example, that around the age of two, children start to gain the ability to think and speak for themselves. One would imagine this to be a universal cause for celebration. Instead, society has deemed this wondrous stage of human growth and development "The Terrible Twos." Yes, when a child begins to come into his own, it's apparently downright fucking terrible.

Some children act out and do the opposite of what their parents want. But some children become complacent and hide. As adults, though, most of us hide. Nice Guys in particular hide almost every part of themselves. They hide their feelings, their thoughts, their needs, their wants, their sexuality. This is why so many men don't know what their passions are. They have spent so long hiding that they don't even look at themselves. And when they do, they very quickly go right back into hiding.

"Part of becoming a mature adult and becoming your authentic self is learning to differentiate," asserts Dr. Glover. "How can you be who you truly are if you can't even ask yourself: *What do I want? What feels right to me? What makes me happy? What is my deepest Yes?* Too many men sacrifice themselves in dating, in relationships, and at work. They're always trying to be what they think others want them to be. This is not the path to happiness. It's why so many men get stuck in unhealthy relationships and rot in middle management."

Waste no more time becoming your true, authentic self. Challenge yourself to be a what-you-see-is-what-you-get kind of person. Stop hiding, stay differentiated, learn to love and enjoy yourself. It is impossible for anyone to love you more than you love yourself. And it is impossible for anyone to trust you if you're not transparent.

From this day forward, commit to being fully you by:

- Taking your censors off
- Saying what comes to mind
- Being honest
- Being clear and direct
- Knowing that you don't have to do everything perfectly
- Saying No
- Letting go of attachment to outcome
- Experimenting
- Taking bold action
- Having more fun
- Pursuing your passions

"If you aren't comfortable in your own skin, work at revealing yourself to your safe people," advises Dr. Glover. "Accept the things about yourself that you cannot change, and work at changing the things you can. Let go of covert contracts. Nothing hidden, nothing half-assed. Do what you want, out in the open, with all of your energy. Wake up every morning and live a self-directed, purposeful life. People will be attracted to your authenticity."[152]

---

152 Glover, Robert A. "Podcast 160: Being Your Authentic Self, Part 1," "Podcast 161: Being Your Authentic Self, Part 2," "Podcast 162: Being Your Authentic self, Part 3," and "Podcast 163: Being Your Authentic self, Part 4." Podcast Audio. www.drglover.com

**INTEGRATED ACTION:**

- ✓ Do you know who you are? Do you like yourself just as you are? Write your answers in your journal. Don't think. Just write.
- ✓ Do you think other people could love you (and like you) just as you are? Write your answer in your journal. Don't think. Just write.
- ✓ Do you think other people could know you - warts and all - and still think you're a good guy? Write your answer in your journal. Don't think. Just write.

# YOUR GREAT CAKE (REPRISE)

If you want to experience happiness and well-being, you should always be working on your *Great Cake of a Life*. Those familiar with Dr. Glover's work have undoubtedly heard him use the words "Great Cake of a Life" time and time again. As you've surely noticed, I've used those words repeatedly throughout this book. Still, a good number of men need clarification on what it means to have a Great Cake of a Life and, more specifically, what ingredients are necessary to make a Great Cake.

> **YOUR GREAT CAKE OF A LIFE**
> **INGREDIENTS:** Other Men, Pursuing Your Passions, Regular Exercise, Embracing Challenge Over Comfort,
> **Contains 2% or less of** Female Drama, Boundary Invaders, Covert Contracts, Masturbating to Porn

Your Great Cake of a Life should, at the very least, contain four key ingredients:

### Ingredient #1: Other Men

Many men don't have healthy male relationships or healthy male role models. This is especially true for Nice Guys. They are disconnected from their own masculinity. Some even feel embarrassed to be a male. Most depend on women for validation and social connection. If they are in a relationship, they tend to be passive and force their partner to set the tone and take the lead.

It's imperative that you get out of the nursery and spend time with other men. This will help you reconnect with your masculinity; it will actually raise your testosterone. It's also the foundation for having healthy relationships with women. Without male friendships, you become too dependent on your partner – or women in general – for connection, and this can create a real problem. Furthermore, you can practice being completely honest and transparent with men because there is no sexual agenda – sex is off the table. The more confident you are being honest and transparent with men, the more you can bring that confidence into your relationships with women.

**Ingredient #2: Pursuing Your Passion(s)**

Too many men lack passion in their lives. For Nice Guys in particular, it's a crisis. It keeps them from taking risks and stepping outside their comfort zone.

Honor your needs and wants. Stop wasting time. Do things because you thoroughly enjoy them. Before you go to bed each night, ask yourself:

- ✓ *Did I live with passion today?*
- ✓ *Did I make an impact in the world?*
- ✓ *Did I have fun?*

And remember, passion doesn't need to be singular.

**Ingredient #3: Regular, Strenuous Exercise**

From combating disease to boosting energy, the countless benefits of exercise are hardly a secret. And yet, most men don't take care of themselves in the way that they should. When you take care of your body, you also take care of your mind and spirit.

Don't overcomplicate this, either. Exercise doesn't have to be grueling. Any activity that forces you to move your body and causes you to break a sweat is sufficient. Join an intramural sports league, take a run along the beach, go for a hike. Do things you enjoy. 20 minutes, three times a week is enough to radically improve your life.

### Ingredient #4: Embracing Challenge Over Comfort

Do you want to die afraid? Or die with regrets? I'm guessing you don't.

Too many men live a life of junk-food comfort. They do what's easiest. Instead of participating in reality, they watch it on TV. Instead of creating actual connection, they text and Tweet. Instead of having sex with real, live women, they whack off to women on a screen. They walk the planet unconscious, bored, and soft – that is, if they get off the fucking couch.

"We men are happiest when we are challenging ourselves," asserts Dr. Glover. "For hundreds of thousands of years, our ancestors had signs on their backs that said 'Eat Me.' We evolved into what we are today because our ancestors were constantly forced to deal with challenge. It was survival of the fittest – eat or be eaten. Now, men just sit around and play World of Warcraft or some other bullshit. It's crucial that you face your fears, and challenge yourself, and keep moving and growing. Don't let fear and anxiety drive your life[153]".

In every one of his in-person workshops, Dr. Glover hands each participant a sheet of paper with nothing on it except the following three words:

# *STRESS*

# *STRETCH*

# *COMFORT*

---

153 Glover, Robert A. "Podcast 148: Part 4 of a Four-Part Series on Personal Recovery from the Nice Guy Syndrome." Podcast Audio. www.drglover.com

Your goal should be to live life in your **Stretch Zone**. In your Stretch Zone, you should feel both scared and excited. In your Stress Zone, you only feel scared. In your Comfort Zone, you don't really feel anything.

Find ways out of your Stress Zone by reframing those stresses into stretches. Find ways out of your Comfort Zone by challenging yourself. Your Stretch Zone is where you'll be happiest.

---

**INTEGRATED ACTION:**
- ✓ Do you have a great cake of a life? Which ingredients do you have? Which ingredients are you missing? What can you do to make your Great Cake the best it can be? Write your answers down in your journal.
- ✓ Where does a woman fit into your Great Cake? Should a woman be a main ingredient? Or the icing?
- ✓ Knowing the key ingredients of a Great Cake, take one action step this week that can help you start building (or re-building) yours.
- ✓ For at least one week, eliminate junk-food behaviors. No video games, no porn, no binge-watching TV. Replace these junk-food behaviors with healthier, more productive behaviors.
- ✓ Before you go to bed, write down at least one way you challenged yourself today and one way you'll challenge yourself tomorrow. In the morning, review what you wrote down. Then, go do it. Make this a daily practice.
- ✓ Check in with your safe person (or people). Let them know what you're doing to build your Great Cake. Ask about their Great Cake. Encourage and support each other.

---

# COOPERATIVE RECIPROCAL RELATIONSHIPS

Remember: No one was put on this planet to meet your needs except you and your parents, and your parents' job is done. As a grown-ass man, you are responsible for getting your needs met. You are responsible for your own happiness and well-being. You are responsible for filling your own bucket.

But you can't do it all by yourself.

It is crucial that you surround yourself with people who can help you get your needs met. And it's just as crucial that you *let them*. Your goal should be to have an overflowing bucket by inviting and allowing others to give to you. When you have an overflowing bucket:

- You feel loved and lovable.
- You won't drive people away with your neediness.
- You'll release toxic shame.
- You'll be attractive to others.
- You'll see the world more abundantly.
- You'll be happier.

To ensure that your bucket is constantly overflowing, you must have what Dr. Glover calls *Cooperative Reciprocal Relationships*. Cooperative Reciprocal Relationships are indeed both cooperative and reciprocal. Everyone involved is getting something of value from the relationship.

Cooperative Reciprocal Relationships are at the core of what makes you feel loved and lovable. Love does not come from outside of you. Love comes from inside of you, as long as you maintain a full and overflowing bucket.

Take a look at the simple graphic. The stick figure in the center represents you and your bucket. The circles represent your Cooperative Reciprocal Relationships.

## AN EXERCISE

Draw the Cooperative Reciprocal Relationships graphic on three separate sheets of paper:

✓ On the first sheet, fill in the circles with Cooperative Reciprocal Relationships that you currently have. This can include your good friends, your employer, your doctor or dentist, and your most trusted family members. It can also include positive daily practices like meditation or yoga.

✓ On the second sheet, fill in the circles with the Cooperative Reciprocal Relationships that you need - or want - to add to your life. Do you need a coach? A men's group? A new financial advisor? A personal trainer? Doing this will help you identify Cooperative Reciprocal Relationships that will make your life better.

✓ On the third sheet, fill in the circles with your Cooperative Reciprocal Relationships that aren't so cooperative or reciprocal. Examples might include a friend who takes and doesn't give, a family member who continually violates your boundaries, or a therapist you've outgrown. Or perhaps you have outdated religious or cultural beliefs that no longer serve you. These are relationships that you either need to renegotiate or completely remove from your life.

*** 

Make this a lifelong practice. Take stock of your Cooperative Reciprocal Relationships at least twice a year. Don't forget, you are responsible for getting your needs met. But you can't do it all by yourself. Practice giving to yourself and practice asking others to give to you. Practice being a good receiver. The more Cooperative Reciprocal Relationships[154] you have, the better your life will be. And the happier you'll feel.

**INTEGRATED ACTION:**
✓ Complete the Cooperative Reciprocal Relationships Exercise.
✓ Start filling your bucket with Cooperative Reciprocal Relationships. If you have any relationships that you need to remove from your life (or renegotiate), step up and do it.
✓ Talk to your safe person (or people). Let them know that you are working to create Cooperative Reciprocal Relationships. Ask them for support.

---

154 Dr. Glover frequently discusses Cooperative Reciprocal Relationships in both his in-person and virtual Total Personal Integration (TPI) workshops

# EMBRACING ABUNDANCE IV

Your emotional well-being is largely dependent on your ability to see the world for what it really is – a place of abundance. You must have an abundance mindset.

The term 'abundance mindset' is thought to have first been coined by Stephen Covey in 1989, in his hugely popular book, *The 7 Habits of Highly Effective People*. According to Covey, having an abundance mindset and believing that there are unlimited resources available for every individual creates a win-win situation for all.

What if you knew that the world was a place of abundance? How would you behave differently?

What if you knew that there was enough to go around?

What if you knew that there were countless opportunities just waiting for you?

Abundance thinking is not woo-woo, airy-fairy horse shit. The world is so big that most of us can't even comprehend it. When you fail (or stubbornly refuse) to see the world for how big and how abundant it is, you are doing yourself a tremendous disservice.

But how do you completely change your way of thinking?

If you have a deprivation view of the world, how do you start embracing abundance? Here are a few simple things you can do:

- **Recognize the power of your thoughts**. Take the time to notice what type of thoughts are circulating in your mind. Be the non-judgmental observer of self. Are your thoughts based in fear and scarcity? Shift your thoughts towards abundance.

- **Practice gratitude.** As Tony Robbins says, "When you are grateful, fear disappears, and abundance appears." How's that gratitude journal coming along?

- **Expand your awareness.** One Harvard study found that when people focus intently on one particular thing, they fail to notice the other possibilities in front of them. Loosen your mind's focus, zoom out, and create an expanded awareness that fosters abundance thinking.

- **Pursue your passions and purpose.** Immerse yourself in the things that you love to do. Learn to share your gifts. Think about how you might provide value to others.

- **Have big goals; take small steps.** When you think abundantly, you can create any kind of life that you want. When you get just one percent better at something each day, you'll be 365 percent better in one year. So, write down a big goal you would like to achieve. Then, make a list of all the small steps you need to take to achieve it. When you focus on small, achievable steps, it won't be long before you successfully reach your goal.

- **Choose your words wisely.** Remember, the language that you use with yourself has great power. It shapes your reality. Are you telling yourself stories of scarcity or stories of abundance? Notice what you are saying about your experience and your beliefs. If you find yourself talking about something you can't have, can't be, or can't do, stop yourself. Then, say something from a place of abundance.

- **Learn something new.** Learning and growth can help stimulate an abundance mindset. Beginners tend to be open and enthusiastic. Commit to taking on something new – a new skill, a new language, a new hobby - so you can place yourself in a state of not knowing.

- **Remember: You'll handle it.** One study from Carnegie Mellon shows that using mantras or affirmations can improve your problem-solving skills, decrease stress, and shift your mentality from scarcity to abundance. Again, one of the most powerful mantras is *I'll handle it*. How would you behave differently if you knew you could handle anything? Do you think you would take more risks? Face your fears more often? Adopt a more abundant view of the world? Write down any fears you have that come from having a deprivation view of the world. Then, write down the opposite of those fears, or what you deeply desire.

---

**INTEGRATED ACTION:**

✓  How would you behave differently if you knew the world was a place of abundance? Write your answer in your journal.

✓  Have you been practicing being the non-judgmental observer of self? If not, start practicing. If so, how is it going? Write about it in your journal.

✓  Start a gratitude practice yet?

✓  Make a commitment to learning something new.

---

# ON GRATITUDE

Research suggests that the human brain has up to 100,000 thoughts a day. This many thoughts could overwhelm the hell out of anyone. Luckily, you get to decide which thoughts you pay attention to and, more importantly, which thoughts you *believe*.

What you think about most is typically the result of mental habits. Practicing gratitude can help you develop new mental habits and new neural pathways.

"Gratitude shifts your focus to a different part of your brain," explains Dr. Glover. "It positively affects your mood and your perspective, and it influences the thoughts your brain will attune itself to in the future."

The fearful part of your brain – the amygdala – is primitive. Remember, the amygdala operates on emotion, and it is highly influenced by past experiences. Most of your fears and negative emotions come from this part of your brain. So, when you are in an unconscious, negative mental state, your amygdala is in control. But when you focus on the things for which you are grateful, a different part of your brain – the part responsible for rational thinking and feeling good – is in control.

Extensive studies have been done on monks who practice daily gratitude and meditation. These monks are naturally calm, optimistic, and caring. The region of their brains responsible for a sense of well-being is physically larger than the same region in the brains of the average population.

Undoubtedly, practicing gratitude may seem hard when you feel like nothing goes your way. But you can start by practicing "Gratitude Lite," a term coined by Dr. Robert Emmons, a professor at UC Davis and one of the world's leading scientific experts on gratitude. In his pioneering experiments, Emmons discovered that a remarkably simple gratitude practice can have a profound impact on one's mental state.

"At the dispositional level," explains Emmons, "grateful people report higher levels of positive emotions, life satisfaction, vitality, and optimism and lower levels of depression and stress."

So, before you go to bed each night, think of at least three things for which you are grateful. Better yet, write them down in a journal specifically for practicing gratitude.

You can be grateful for anything.

Your health.

Your friends.

Your family.

A beautiful sunset.

A great cup of coffee.

A comfortable bed and a roof over your head.

Whatever comes to mind.

During the day, if you notice that you are stressed or anxious, take a few moments to express gratitude. You will likely notice an immediate shift in your mood. Even if it's a small shift, it's better than nothing. As Dr. Emmons once wrote, "Gratitude is, first and foremost, a way of seeing that alters our gaze."

# ATTACHMENT TO OUTCOME

If I could point to one skill that has had the most impact on how I approach nearly every aspect of my life, it is almost certainly **letting go of attachment to outcome**.[155] Yes, it takes practice. It requires mindfulness. And I may never fully master it. But learning to let go of attachment to outcome has reduced my anxiety, improved my relationships, boosted my confidence, and allowed me to experience the kind of happiness and emotional well-being that always seemed well out of reach.

The Buddha famously said, "Life is suffering. Attachment is the source of suffering. The end of attachment will bring the end of suffering." Indeed, the Buddha believed that *attachment* is the cause of all suffering. Dr. Glover often amends this by saying that *attachment is the cause of all suffering and anxiety and non-action.*

So, what exactly does attachment mean? More specifically, what does it mean to be attached to an outcome? And how does it cause suffering?

We are all human, and we all have desires. We want what we want. But when we become attached to those wants and desires, the suffering starts. Why? Because what if those desires don't manifest?

---

155 Letting go of attachment to outcome is a recurring theme throughout Dr. Glover's work. For more on letting go of attachment to outcome, see Glover, Robert A. "Podcast 14: Part 2 of a Two-Part Series on Dealing with Rejection," "Podcast 60: Part 3 of a Three-Part Series on Overcoming the Fear of Rejection," and "Podcasts 134-136: Attachment to Outcome, Parts 1-3." Podcast Audio. www.drglover.com

Consider this: Whenever you're unhappy, anxious, or stressed, or trying to win someone's approval, it is almost always because you are emotionally attached to a specific outcome. This can completely disrupt your well-being, your peace of mind, and your sense of belonging.

Put more simply: You want something to go a specific way. If it doesn't, you feel like shit.

For men, emotionalized attachment to outcome is perhaps most prevalent in dating and relationships. Let's say, for example, that you see a woman you find attractive and think: *I've got to have that woman.* Then, you conjure the balls to approach her, and it doesn't go the way you wanted. How do you feel?

But what if you were to see the very same woman, and you didn't give a fuck what might happen or how she might respond? Even if she responds negatively, how do you feel?

Certainly, the very nature of approaching women has some degree of attachment that comes with it. As does interviewing for a job, or auditioning for a role, or starting a business. Attachment is part of the human condition. This is why we suffer in life.

But you can minimize your suffering.

Right now, think about something you have been struggling to do. Just for a moment, let go of any attachment you have to the outcome you desire. Try to accept that you can influence your life, but you can't control it. Most things are out of your control.

Moving forward, practice asking yourself the following question:

> *Can I be equally okay with whatever outcome transpires in this situation?*

Take inventory of your attachments. Think about everything you are doing – or aren't doing – because you are attached to a specific outcome. What if you could be equally okay with any outcome? Or as Dr. Glover likes to say, what if you could be *outcome agnostic*? How would you feel?

Can you channel your inner Buddha?

---

**INTEGRATED ACTION:**

✓ Where in your life do you get emotionally attached to specific outcomes? How does being attached to an outcome make you feel? Write your answers in your journal.

✓ This week, practice letting go of attachment to outcome. Make a conscious effort to channel your inner Buddha. Write about your experience in your journal.

---

# 30 RULES FOR LIFE

D o you have a set of rules for yourself?

Have you identified your values, and do you live by them?

I've come to believe that everybody needs a set of rules by which they live. At the end of *No More Mr. Nice Guy*, Dr Glover presents his **30 Rules for Life**. Implementing these rules into my life has had a profoundly positive impact on my happiness and well-being.

Certainly, you are free to make your own set of rules (see Rule #13). Until you do, however, it won't hurt to try Dr. Glover's on for size:

**1. If it frightens you, do it.**

**2. Do NOT settle. Every time you settle, you get exactly what you settled for.**

**3. Put yourself first.**

**4. No matter what happens, remember that you'll handle it.**

**5. Whatever you do, do it 100%.**

**6. If you do what you've always done, you'll get what you've always got.**

**7. You are the only person on the planet responsible for your needs and happiness.**

**8. Ask for what you want.**

**9. If what you are doing isn't working, try something different.**

**10. Be clear and direct.**

**11. Learn to say NO.**

12. No excuses.

13. If you're an adult, you can make your own rules.

14. Let people help you.

15. Be honest with yourself.

16. Do not let anyone treat you badly. Ever.

17. Remove yourself from a bad situation instead of waiting for the situation to change.

18. Do NOT tolerate the intolerable. Ever.

19. Stop blaming. Victims never succeed.

20. Live with integrity. Decide what feels right to you, then do it.

21. Accept the consequences of your actions.

22. Be good to yourself.

23. Remember that the world is a place of ABUNDANCE.

24. Face difficult situations and conflict head on.

25. Do not do anything in secret.

26. Do it now.

27. Be willing to let go of what you have so you can get what you want.

28. Have fun. If you aren't having fun, something is wrong.

29. Know that you can fail. There are no mistakes, only learning experiences.

30. Control is an illusion. Let life happen.

---

**INTEGRATED ACTION:**

✓ How might your life be different if you lived by Dr. Glover's rules? Do you have your own set of rules? Are there any rules you would add to this list? Write your answers in your journal.

✓ Make a list of rules for yourself. Or use Dr. Glover's rules. Print them out and keep them in a place where you'll see them regularly.

---

# SURRENDER

In the waning part of 2017, Dr. Glover was almost certain he was about to die. He had rapidly lost more than 30 pounds. He had no semblance of an appetite. He had difficulty going to the bathroom. He could barely work. He had no energy. He took three or four naps a day. He was in constant, searing pain.

And nobody could figure out what was wrong.

"For at least three months, I had no idea what was going on inside my body," describes Dr. Glover. "And neither did anyone else. I was misdiagnosed and mistreated a dozen different ways. In Seattle, a gastroenterologist blamed it on a Mexican bug. In Mexico, I tried every folk remedy you can think of. Was this going to pass? Was it an ulcer? Gastritis? An impacted colon? Was there an amoeba inside me? I just didn't know. I didn't know if I was going to die from this. And that was the hardest part. The unknown."

While lying in bed one night, Dr. Glover was in so much pain, he decided to just breathe into it. He chose to do what he now considers a beautiful and essential skill. He got comfortable with the idea of death. He surrendered.

"The only thing that got me through was surrendering," he shares. "I consciously said to myself, *Ok, I don't know what this is. This might kill me. I don't know how much time I have left. This is what it is.* And that was liberating. I started to become friends with death, and I surrendered."

Though Dr. Glover and death were becoming friends, they weren't exactly strangers. Seven years prior, Dr. Glover lost his father, his sister, and his brother all within 11 months of each other, all unexpectedly. Of course, Dr. Glover did not share the same fate. A doctor in Puerto Vallarta eventually discovered a golf ball-sized tumor blocking Dr. Glover's lower intestine and insisted that he have it immediately removed.

Our existential fears around death cause us a great deal of unhappiness. But we're all going to die. Every single one of us. And because we avoid getting real about death, we avoid getting real about life.

---

### CARTWHEELS THROUGH THE COSMOS

*Why are we here? What's life about? Does anything matter? Why do anything? Who will even remember us?*

These questions plague us humans. And understandably so. We're all going to be dust. How do we deal with that?

"Personally, I like to envision myself doing cartwheels through the cosmos," shares Dr. Glover. "I like to picture myself as like a big balloon, bouncing off the edge of the Universe. I guess that's my way of fucking with the existential. Sure, I question everything, sometimes. But I've learned to welcome the angst, sit with it, embrace it, and dance with it. And I ask it what it wants to teach me."

---

We have a collective inability to surrender to what is.

"Life is uncertain," asserts Dr. Glover. "Get up every day and love the hell out of the people you love. And whatever you're waiting to get around to, maybe go do **it _now_**. Get after your life now. Do what's important now. Stop thinking you'll do it when you get a girlfriend or when you get away from the woman you're with or when you can change jobs or when you get enough money. No. That's bullshit. Do it now.[156]"

---

156 Dr. Glover frequently discusses his experience with surrendering in podcast interviews. See Beaton, Connor, *ManTalks*. "No More Mr. Nice Guy. Connor Beaton & Dr. Robert Glover. June 1, 2020. https://www.youtube.com/watch?v=UB1lvoimc-GY&t=3655s

# ENJOY

As you go about your life, remember that the work you are doing - recovery from the Nice Guy Syndrome, self-improvement, spiritual growth, becoming an Integrated Man – is all a process.

It's a journey.

None of this happens overnight. Or in a week. Or in a month.

Indeed, radical transformation is possible.

More than possible.

It's inevitable…if you do the work.

But men often ask: *When am I going to become Integrated? How long is this going to take? Is there a guide with specific instructions I can follow?*

This book is perhaps the closest thing to a guide. And nobody can know when you're going to become Integrated.

If you're lucky, you will be working on this for the rest of your life.

While others are stagnant, you will be growing and improving. Every day.

You will be living a fulfilling and purposeful life, on your terms.

And you will enjoy the journey. You must.

Life is not a smooth ride. Life is not problem-free. Life is chaotic and messy and unpredictable. There is no way around this.

Surrender to what is.

Accept the things you can't control; change the things you can.

Dare to love.

Take risks.

Life is an adventure. Don't be afraid of it. Embrace it.

Get rid of the belief that you have to do everything right. You can't.

Fuck up.

Break stuff.

Experiment.

Play.

Do what lights you up inside.

Learn to let go.

Laugh. A lot.

Stop taking everything so goddamn seriously.

Enjoy the journey.

Otherwise, what's the point?

# GLOVERISMS

In my coaching business - whether I'm working with a one-on-one client or leading a group - I often find myself directly quoting Dr. Glover. It's not unusual for me to begin a sentence with the phrase, "As Dr. Glover likes to say…"

The man does have a way with words. He also has a distinct ability to take complex ideas and whittle them down into easily digestible nuggets. I like to call these *Gloverisms*. Many of them are now permanently ingrained in my psyche and have positively impacted the way I navigate life.

So, without further ado, I present a lengthy list of Gloverisms:

**ON NICE GUY SYDROME:**
- *Nice Guys do not believe they are okay just as they are, therefore they try to become what they think other people want them to be and try to hide anything that might get a negative reaction.*
- *Nice Guys are notoriously slow learners and amazingly quick forgetters.*
- *Nice Guys are afraid of two kinds of feelings: their own and everyone else's.*
- *Nice Guys tend to be good at being good but not great at being great.*
- *The opposite of crazy is still crazy.\**
- *No good deed goes unpunished.\**

## ON MASCULINITY & FEMININITY:

- *Everything your male brain tells you about the female mind is going to be wrong.*
- *Evolution programmed women to be security-seeking creatures.*
- *A security-seeking creature will tend to trade long-term security for short-term gratification.*
- *A security-seeking creature will always imagine the worst possible outcome.*
- *The Masculine (in both men and women) is the source of love, the Feminine (in both men and women) is the seeker of love.*
- *Husband your own Feminine.*
- *The Feminine (in both men and women) is an empty bucket with a hole in the bottom seeking to be filled.*
- *The Feminine is attracted to a man who is comfortable in his own skin, who knows where he's going, and looks like he's having a good time going there.*
- *The Feminine is repulsed by neediness.*

## ON CONSCIOUS DATING:

- *The way that most people date provides the worst possible foundation upon which to build a healthy long-term relationship.*
- *Go as slowly as possible to find out as quickly as possible what a person's nature is.*
- *How you find them is how they are.*
- *Don't spend more time thinking about a woman than you have actually spent with her.*
- *Women don't put men in the friend zone; men put themselves there.*
- *Rejection doesn't hurt.*
- *Get to rejection quickly.*
- *Being a good ender covers a multitude of sins.*

- *Most people will choose their neurosis and defense mechanisms over love.*
- *Get out of the house, expand your route, linger in public, talk to people everywhere you go, test for interest, and walk through the open doors.*
- *If a woman wants to give you a blowjob in the front seat of your car on a first date – run!*

## ON SEX & SEXUALITY:

- *For women, trust equals lust.*
- *How you do sex tends to be how you do life, and how you do life tends to be how you do sex.*
- *It's called a sex drive because it's supposed to drive you to another person, not your computer screen.*
- *Talk less, fuck more.*
- *Show up with your sexual agenda intact.*
- *Luck favors the man with a condom in his pocket.*

## ON RELATIONSHIPS:

- *Get all the way in to determine if you should get all the way out.*
- *Build a great cake of a life and let a great woman be the icing top.*
- *Nice Guys are constantly monitoring the possibility of a woman's availability.*
- *Don't give the dog a treat for pissing on the carpet.*
- *The more power you give a woman to make you happy, the more power you give her to make you miserable.*
- *A woman's reaction to anything a man does, does not determine the rightness or the wrongness of the thing the man did.*
- *Don't try and get unavailable people to be available, or unapproving people to be approving.*
- *Conscious relationships are powerful personal growth machines.*
- *Self-love is the standard for all love.*

- *Don't expect anyone to love you more than you love yourself.*
- *A woman can't follow where a man doesn't lead.*
- *A woman can handle an uncomfortable truth but she can't handle a lie.*
- *Fill your own bucket so you can give from the overflow.*
- *Make your covert contracts overt.*
- *Humans are drawn to each other's rough edges.*
- *You haven't really lived until you've had your heart broken.*

## ON SUCCESS:

- *Fear is your true north.*
- *The majority of people live the lives of cockroaches; They're born, they breed, they consume, they die. And they think that is a good life.*
- *The fear of success represents a paradoxical truth. .*
- *Nothing hidden, nothing half-assed.*
- *Passion isn't singular.*
- *Stop doing everything you aren't doing with passion and start doing everything you do with passion.*
- *The secret to changing any habit is consistency over time.*
- *Fail forward, fail often, fail fast.\**
- *What one man can do, another man can do.\**
- *Luck favors the prepared mind.\**
- *If you keep doing what you've always done, you'll keep getting what you've always got.\**
- *There are no mistakes, only learning experiences.\**
- *How you do anything is how you do everything.\**

## ON HAPPINESS & WELL-BEING

- *Until you get comfortable receiving, you will never get what you want.*
- *No one was put on this planet to meet your needs except you and your parents, and their job is done.*

- *Take responsibility for your needs and surround yourself with people who want to help you get them met.*
- *Boundaries are not about getting anyone else to be different; they're about getting you to be different.*
- *Your power to set a boundary is predicated upon your willingness and ability to remove yourself from a situation.*
- *Don't let anyone treat you badly. Ever.*
- *Be a what-you-see-is-what-you-get kind of guy.*
- *Put yourself first.*
- *Live a phallic life.*
- *Surrender.*
- *Your mind would rather manage old anxieties than confront new ones.*
- *The Buddha said that attachment is the cause of all suffering. It's also the cause of all anxiety and non-action.*
- *Thinking causes anxiety; acting cures it.*
- *Work at becoming outcome agnostic.*
- *Your mind can cause you great suffering and it can set you free.*
- *Get out of your comfort zone. That's where the goodies are.*
- *Every time you leave your comfort zone, your self-limiting beliefs will start screaming at you.*
- *Miracles happen around people (and unless you've got a living room full of people you won't experience any miracles).*
- *Every time you leave the house, expect a miracle.*
- *Learn to lovingly not give a fuck.*
- *Not my circus, not my monkeys.\**
- *You'll handle it. No matter what happens, you'll handle it.\**
- *Hope keeps all suffering in place.\**

**\*Borrowed from others**

# FURTHER READING

## ON THE NICE GUY SYNDROME

- *No More Mr. Nice Guy* by Dr. Robert Glover
- *No More Mr. Nice Guy: The 30-Day Recovery Journal* by Chuck Chapman
- *No More Mr. Nice Guy*: The Hero's Journey by Dr. Michael Pariser
- *The Integrated Man: A Handbook For the Recovering Nice Guy* by Sidharth Agarwal

## ON MASCULINITY

- *As a Man Thinketh* by James Allen
- *Iron John* by Robert Bly
- *The Way of Superior Man* by David Deida

## ON ATTRACTION

- *Dating Essentials for Men* by Dr. Robert Glover
- *Dating Essentials for Men: Frequently Asked Questions* by Dr. Robert Glover
- *Models* by Mark Manson

## ON CONSCIOUS DATING

- *Dating Essentials for Men* by Dr. Robert Glover
- *Dating Essentials for Men: Frequently Asked Questions* by Dr. Robert Glover

- *The Tactical Guide to Women* by Dr. Shawn T. Smith.
- *Dating Sucks But You Don't* by Connell Barrett

## ON SEX & SEXUALITY
- *The Multi-Orgasmic Man* by Mantak Chia and Douglas Abrams
- *The Multi-Orgasmic Couple* by Mantak Chia, Maneewan Chia, et al.

## ON RELATIONSHIPS
- *Passionate Marriage* by David Scharch, PhD
- *Mating in Captivity* by Esther Perel
- *Attached: The New Science of Adult Attachment Theory* by Amir Levine, Rachel Heller, et al.
- *Codependent No More* by Melody Beattie
- *The Five Love Languages* by Gary Chapman

## ON HEARTBREAK
- *When Things Fall Apart* by Pema Chodron

## ON SUCCESS
- *Feel the Fear...and Do it Anyway* by Susan Jeffers, PhD
- *The Big Leap* by Gay Hendricks
- *The War of Art* by Steven Pressfield

## ON HAPPINESS & WELL-BEING
- *Feeling Good* by David D. Burns, M.D.
- *Loving What Is* by Byron Katie
- *No Mud, No Lotus: The Art of Transforming Suffering* by Thich Naht Hanh, Jacob Pinter, et al.
- *The Power of Now* by Eckhart Tolle
- *The Road Less Traveled* by M. Scott Peck, M.D.

Born in Bellevue, Washington, **Dr. Robert Glover** has almost 40 years of experience as a therapist, coach, educator, and public speaker. He is the world's foremost expert on the Nice Guy Syndrome and the author of *No More Mr. Nice Guy*. Through his books, online classes, workshops, podcasts, blogs, consultation services, and therapy groups, Dr. Glover has helped change the lives of countless men and women around the world. Dr. Glover currently lives in Puerto Vallarta, Mexico. Find out more at www.drglover.com.

Born in Omaha, Nebraska, **Tony Endelman** is an author, humorist, popular self-help blogger, certified transformational life coach, and one of Dr. Glover's certified *No More Mr. Nice Guy* coaches. He is perhaps the world's foremost expert on all things Dr. Glover, excluding Dr. Glover himself. Tony offers both one-on-one and group coaching for men who want to transform their lives. Find out more at www.tonyendelman.com.